Nicholas Patrick Wiseman

Sermons on our Lord Jesus Christ

And on His Blessed Mother

Nicholas Patrick Wiseman

Sermons on our Lord Jesus Christ
And on His Blessed Mother

ISBN/EAN: 9783337258900

Printed in Europe, USA, Canada, Australia, Japan

Cover: Foto ©Lupo / pixelio.de

More available books at **www.hansebooks.com**

SERMONS

ON

OUR LORD JESUS CHRIST,

AND ON

HIS BLESSED MOTHER.

BY HIS EMINENCE,

CARDINAL WISEMAN.

DUBLIN:

JAMES DUFFY, 15, WELLINGTON-QUAY;

AND

22, PATERNOSTER-ROW, LONDON.

1864.

DUBLIN:

Printed by J. M. O'Toole & Son,

GT. BRUNSWICK-STREET.

PREFACE.

A VOLUME of Sermons seems hardly to require any Preface. The form, dimensions, topics, and principles of such compositions as it contains, are known beforehand, and need no explanations. Any thing further runs the risk of becoming personal, and perhaps egotistical.

And yet, the author feels that there are a few preliminary matters, with which he would wish his readers to be acquainted, before they proceed to enter on the volume before them.

The first, is the time, the places, and perhaps, the circumstances, connected with their delivery. The title of this volume may lead to the idea that the sermons contained in it compose a series delivered consecutively, and forming a course. Such, however, is far from being the case. But a brief account of these discourses, and their origin, may throw some light on their present publications.

So far, then, from any unities of time or place, existing in this collection, there is an interval of thirty years, and a space of above a thousand miles, between the delivery of some, and that of other sermons, placed side by side in this volume. And the same will be the case in any others that may follow it. Their relative positions have been regulated solely, by order of matter.

Indeed, the author feels it necessary to warn his readers, that most of what they will read, belongs to a remote date.

It was in the year 1827, that the author received a commission from the holy and zealous Pontiff, Leo. **XII.** to preach in
Rome, on the Sundays from Advent to Easter, the season during which foreigners crowd the Eternal City. So honourable,
but unexpected, a commission, or rather command, could not
be refused, even at the expense of much toil and confusion.
Unskilled, and inexperienced, the author was obliged to feel
his way, and measure his steps, slowly and painfully. For
many successive years, he wrote every discourse ; and having
almost annually the same audience, could scarcely venture on
repetitions.   And so the mass of manuscripts accumulated, and
has remained buried for almost a generation.

By degrees, greater confidence was gained, or greater
facility was attained ; while increased occupations, and higher
duties, made encroachments on the time, which, though
gradually diminishing, had been required for the labour of
composing weekly discourses. When this practice had totally
ceased, it was often thought well to have sermons, especially
if preached for some local purpose, taken down in short-hand,
and either printed soon to disappear from before the public, or
left in manuscript with the preacher.

While, therefore, the greatest number of sermons, which it
has been his duty to deliver, have passed away for ever into
oblivion, with the breath that committed them to the hearing,
and he will hope, sometimes, to the hearts of his audience ;
those which he now presumes to publish, belong to one or other
of these two classes, of those originally put into writing by
himself, and those which others have had the skill and
goodness to preserve.

The particular results of these circumstances, to which he
wishes to call his kind reader's attention are the following.

I. The great bulk of these sermons were preached in Rome. This will be often evident without calling special attention to this fact. Allusions to places and objects in that city will meet the eye in many places. Sometimes, even the whole tenor of the composition will manifest this circumstance. Indeed, a departure to another scene would form the exception ; and, where it influences, in any way, what is said will require explanation.

II. The course of sermons annually prescribed, went over a limited portion of the year, comprising always the same Sundays, the same feasts, and the same ecclesiastical seasons. As has been intimated above, it commenced with Advent and ended with Lent. Hence the same Gospels, those read during a few months only, had to suggest topics for the sermons. Hence the only great Mysteries of Our Lord, which the ecclesiastical Calendar brought under the contemplation of the Faithful, were those of the Infancy and the Passion. His glorious Resurrection, His admirable Ascension, Whitsuntide, Corpus Christi, never could enter into our cycle.

This circumstance must give a mutilated, and incomplete appearance to a volume of discourses on Our Divine Saviour ; otherwise almost inexplicable. Should the author be able to publish the Meditations, which he has prepared, he hopes that this defect will be somewhat remedied.

III. The audience which he had to address, was so peculiar, as to affect, no doubt, the character of his Sermons. It was not merely what is called a mixed one. It was clearly divisable into two most distinct elements. The ecclesiastical comprised all the religious communities, and colleges speaking English, in Rome. Theological students, and even professors ; aged and venerable superiors of monasteries, with their novices and scholastics ; and many other priests resident by choice, or for business, in Rome. And seldom is that city without some Bishop, from either side of the Atlantic, or from some Colonial See. The secular portion of the audience was composed of Catholic sojourners in Rome, and of no small proportion of Protestants, who were pleased to attend.

But there were no poor, none of that crowd, docile and simple-hearted, on whom a preacher loves to look down, with affection, and whom he sees with open looks, and open hearts, receiving his plainest words.

All was educated, learned, somewhat formal and perhaps cold. The preacher could not but feel, that he was addressing an audience containing many persons superior to himself, in the very office which he was fulfilling, and entirely made up of a class which claimed the rights of social position, to judge him by their own standards, and over which he could not exercise the prerogatives of a pastor or a master.

Under these circumstances, he was constrained both in the choice, and in the handling of his topics, to select an almost neutral course, so as not to weary with controversy the erudite Catholic portion of his audience ; nor to enter too deeply into the feeling subjects which none but Catholics could understand or appreciate ; nor finally, to throw himself into that affection-ateness of address which the poor and simple alone among Catholics could have felt and enjoyed.

Perhaps the singularity of this position may be reflected on the following discourses. If so, let this plain and unvarnished statement serve to explain the cause.

IV. It may easily have happened that thoughts and illustra-tions recur, in sermons, now brought together, by similarity of subjects. Without wishing to apologise for what may have arisen, in this respect, from poverty of thought, it is fair to observe, that two sermons, exhibiting such resemblances, or even identities, may have been delivered at an interval of twenty years, one perhaps in Italy, and the other in England. The reader, bearing this in mind, will, no doubt, exercise a lenient judgment, upon making such a discovery.

V. But for another, which he is sure to make, the author can offer no deprecatory excuse. It is impossible to have preserved, throughout, uniformity of style and manner. Our frame, our features, our complexion, our voice, cannot remain the same through thirty years; and no more can that style which forms the physiognomy of our writing. It takes its character from our occupations, our society, our health; it catches its colour and hue from the objects that surround us, the very atmosphere which we breathe, from the authors whom we happen to be chiefly reading, and from a thousand unappreciable influences.

Now, as these discourses are not arranged chronologically, there will be found no gradual transition, no sliding from one style of writing to another, as age advanced; but there may be found sudden plunges from one characteristic manner of composition to another, very different. If so, again, let it be observed, that no attempt at excuse is made. The author knows that, at every period of his literary life, he has tried to write naturally, and unartificially; and, that if anything of a contrary nature appear, he has been unconscious of it at the time; and that he has always been more intent on what he ought to say, than on how he had best say it.

Gradually, however, he observes with regret that his Preface seems to have been growing apologetic. This was, by no means, his purport or design. He feels that he has no right to assume such a tone. The responsibilities of a work do not weigh on the time of its composition, but on that of its publication. Had these sermons slept their Horatian novennium in the writer's desk, to receive periodical revisions, emendations, and finishing touches, the intervening period between composing and publishing might be well pleaded in justification of delay.

But here there is no such excuse. These discourses come forth with all their early faults, their very original sin upon their head. They have gained nothing certainly by their prolonged suppression. Even the most indulgent reader may feel justified in asking: " What has induced you to publish them now?" To this question the author does not find it easy to reply. He may throw before him, as his strongest shield of defence, the long-expressed and frequently-repeated solicitation of friends, who still retain a sufficiently favourable recollection, to express a desire of reading what they have formerly heard.

But this is hardly enough to excuse a presumptuous act. He therefore candidly acknowledges that another, and, he hopes, a better motive has seconded these kind demands upon him. Conscious, as he is, beforehand, of the many defects which will be found in this publication, sensible of many motives which ought to deter him from his design, he yet feels impelled to undertake this work, by a desire of doing something for souls.

All good gifts come from God, who distributes them according to His blessed will. One preacher touches one chord, and another another. Each gives forth the same voice of truth; yet the Almighty distributor employs each as best it pleaseth Him. Is it not possible that things said one way may produce a salutary effect, where even better things, better said, have failed? And should not each of us strive to be useful in his day, according to the small measure of power which his Master has left him? May the writer bury what he has, because he has only a single talent, while so many others have received five or ten?

Let him not, then, be reprehended, if now, after many years, he disinter it, and try to put it out to usury. On the contrary, let the charitable reader pray to God for him, and his work, begging that He will bless them both: the one, that he may not be rejected as a useless servant; the other, that, in spite of His husbandman's unworthiness, being the seed of His own Word, it may produce fruit a hundredfold.

LONDON, PASSION WEEK, 1864.

CONTENTS.

APPENDIX.

PASTORALS ON DEVOTION TO THE SACRED HEART OF JESUS
CHRIST, IN CONNECTION WITH EDUCATION.

SERMON I.

On the Incarnation and Birth of Jesus Christ.

LUKE, iii. 6.

" And all flesh shall see the salvation of God."

Two days more, my brethren, will bring us to that festival—fountain of all Christian joy—for which the Church has prepared us through the season of Advent. In that admirable spirit which has been maintained in her from the beginning, she has announced to us the coming solemnity with the same vivid phrase, as she might have been supposed to use, had the event we are going to commemorate been about actually to happen. Not only have the gospels of this preparatory season presented us with the preaching of the precursor John, but all her prayers and offices have spoken to us of the Son of God as about to be born for our salvation. At the beginning of the time, she called upon us to adore the Lord who is preparing to come; as we approached its term, she changed her invitation to the more cheering notice that the Lord was nigh;* her prayers expressed alternately a hope of His speedy appearance, and a fear lest the sins of his people might delay it; and thus our

* " Regem venturum Dominum,—Prope est jam Dominus, venite adoremus."—*Invitatoria* in Advent.

B

affections have been carried back through eighteen centuries to that truer standard of feelings, which closer
attendance on the mysteries of Christ's incarnation and
birth would have procured us.

This, undoubtedly, is the best and most satisfactory
point from which to view the mysteries, whether joyful
or sorrowful, of our redemption.   Their effects, it is
true, have no limit in time, and their saving influence
upon our souls is as great and as effectual as it could be
upon those that witnessed them.   The blood of Jesus is
able to cleanse our stains, upon which it mystically descends, as much as those of Magdalen, or any others of the
pious attendants on His cross, upon whom it actually
was sprinkled.   Yet who envies them not that pang of
killing sorrow—that heart-bursting contrition—and that
mournful love, which none but they could ever feel?

The love of our infant Saviour was as much displayed
for us as for the happy shepherds of Bethlehem; for us
as well as for them, He bore the cold and destitution of
that His first night, and angels sung peace to men, and
to God glory on our behalf, no less than on theirs that
heard them.   Yet who is not jealous of that prerogative
which they had, of gazing on the god-like smile of that
blessed Infant, and feeling that intensity of purest joy,
which the sight of Him under such circumstances could
alone inspire?   And if the service of God hath a right
to man's heart as much as to his understanding—and if
the affections when given to Him, should be brought as
nigh as possible to the full measure of their object, surely
we shall do well to meditate upon the mysteries now
before us, with as much of that fervent piety and devout

affection, as may be supposed to have inspired those who actually beheld them.

When the Jew was told that he should see the salvation of God, what idea would this phrase naturally suggest to Him? One great act of salvation or redemption, wrought by the hand of Almightiness, he held recorded in his annals; and it conveyed to him the idea of terrible and resistless power. Storms of hail, and darkness sensible to the touch; the fields blighted by devouring locusts, and the houses infested by intolerable reptiles; the rivers running with blood, and the chambers of all the first-born defiled with their corpses: such were the forerunners of the great salvation of God's people. The waters of the Red Sea divided; the chariot-wheels of Pharaoh overthrown; an army with its royal leader swallowed up in the billows: such was its conduct, and such the means whereby it was effected. Or if the same Jew sought for precedents in his history, of how a new law was to be presented to the world, he would find only the terrors of Sinai, its clouds and lightnings, and the voice of God's trumpet proclaiming His commands to an affrighted people.

But now that God is about to come and set free His inheritance, not from one tyrant, but, as the Jew supposed, from His numerous and far mightier oppressors,— now that His kingdom has to be established, not within the narrow limits of Palestine, but from sea to sea, from the river to the uttermost bounds of the earth,—now that His law has to be heard, not by a few thousand, that can lie prostrate round the foot of a single mountain, but by Greeks and barbarians, Romans, Parthians, Elemytes, and Medes, what new series of proportionate wonders and signs can He have in store that will fall short of the total destruction of visible nature! If before, he touched the mountains and they smoked, and the rocks melted away through fear, what will it be when He comes from the south, and the holy one from Mount Pharan, but that, as the prophet Habacuc describes it, nations should be melted, and the ancient mountains crushed to pieces, and the entire deep should put forth its voice and lift up its hands? (cap. iii.)

No, the understanding of man could have formed no estimate of that display of magnificence which consists in abasement, or of that exhibition of might which acts in silence and without sensible effort. Even in the visible world there is as much of power, and more of glorious, because beneficent, exercise thereof, in one drop of dew, that refreshes and helps to form the flower hidden in the grass, than there is in the earthquake, that overthrows the solidest works of man's hand: and yet the one passes unheeded, while the latter fills nations with amazement. And so is there more of marvel, of grandeur, and of glory in that silent descent of the Eternal Word on earth, "as the rain upon the fleece, and as showers falling gently upon the earth," (Ps. lxxi. 6) than there could have been in the utmost extension of His almighty arm.

In fact, my brethren, it is matter of mere human prudence and reasonable calculation, to proportion the means employed to the greatness of the ends proposed. Even in things beyond our reach we can estimate this ratio. When we know that God hath taken an enterprise in hand—when He hath pledged His power to its success, we can be surprised at nothing more. Whether it be the destruction of armies by one night's pestilence, or the overthrow of a city's walls by a trumpet's sound, we cease to be astonished: we are prepared for any results when power unlimited is wielded. But for the suppression of all manifestation of power, when the most astonishing energies of Omnipotence are called forth, we could not, by human reasoning, have been prepared. To have been told that the conception of an infant in the bosom of its mother, should be a more wonderful work than the creation of all other existing beings, and should procure more glory for God, and display all His attributes more, than when suns innumerable, with their systems, burst into light and motion, would have involved at once a disproportion between the end and the apparent means, which would take the work out of the reach of man's understanding, and distinguish it as truly God's. And if we should go on to hear, that in that Infant's birth were to be accomplished the destinies of four thousand years which had preceded it, and prepared the blessing and happiness of as many generations as may follow it ; that whatever had been said or done glorious and great till then was all for its sake ; still more if we should learn that in that Child were united all the attributes of the Godhead in their unlimited perfection, we must needs be overpowered with astonishment, and feel how unable we are to comprehend, or to search into, the miracles of God's power.

All these mysteries are comprised by St. John in these solemn words:—" And the Word was made flesh, and dwelt amongst us, and we saw His glory, the glory as it were of the only-begotten Son of the Father, full of grace and truth." (i. 14.) From this we learn that the Word, that is the second person of the adorable Trinity, who was "in the beginning with God, and was Himself God," took to Himself this our mortal flesh, assuming the nature of man, so as to unite the twofold nature of God and man in one person ; that He was born into the world of the Blessed Virgin Mary ; and growing up to man's estate, conversed among men, till by His death He wrought the salvation of mankind.

There are plants, my brethren, which live for many years without producing a single blossom,—their lot seems to be one of barren growth; generations of leaves bud forth, flourish and wither; new stalks and branches sprout from year to year;—still no indication is seen of those fairer ornaments, which form the crown and glory of the vege-table world,—no flower, no promise of fruit. At length the slow preparation of many years is brought to light; its flower appears: a few hours of transient beauty and honour repay past and tedious cultivation : and with the pro-duction of its long-matured growth, the destinies of the plant are closed,—it withers, to rise no more. Is it won-derful, then, that so many years of preparation should have been deemed necessary, before the earth opened and budded salvation, and " the flower rose from the root of Jesse;" (Is. xi. 1) and that, not to close mankind's exist-ence, but to open to it a brighter and endless era of happiness ? It seemed necessary that the earth should earn the blessing that was to be bestowed. And how ? Even as one that is poor, gains more compassionate relief by the helplessness of his destitution ; even as the sick or wounded wins for himself more tender attention by the grievousness of his distemper, by the hideousness of his sores. And so it seemed proper to give full time for all the evils of a corrupted heart to mature, and all the growing difficulties of indebted nature to accumulate, and all the excesses of audacious passions to run riot to their utmost length : till human remedies should have been pronounced powerless, and the most sanguine hopes declared bankrupt, and all moral curbs and restraints had been either broken or cast loose, and borne away in impetuous course. It was proper, too, to give leisure for all human power and wisdom to try its skill upon the evils that broke down prostrate humanity, to see what the hand of iron rule could do towards checking the violence of lawless aims, and what the milder counsels of aged wisdom could effect in taming the boisterous passions, or in unravelling the perplexities of man's nature, that seemed to have produced them. All had been tried, and all had failed. Every empire that had striven to subdue men by might, had stirred up to higher excitement the worst of human passions, and had deranged still further the moral order ; every new sect of boasted wisdom had confused more fearfully the simple principles of duty, and often darkened rather, when it desired to give light.

Such are the moments when the Almighty loves to step in, so to come between the creature and its despair, and show His power, when it may be undistinguishable from His goodness. He would not deliver Israel from bondage, till intolerable hardships and crushing oppression

had rendered it without hope. (Exod. ii. 23.) When
Ezechias was beyond human cure, and had said, " in the
midst of my days I shall go the gates of hell," (Is.
xxxviii. 5) He added fifteen years to his life. When
the sisters of Lazarus asked Him to cure their sick
brother, He allowed him to die, that His benefit might
be more signal, in raising their dead than in healing their
sick. (Jo. xi. 14.) And so in this more grievous distress
of all mankind, He willed not that men should be able to
say, " our mighty hand, and not the Lord, hath done all
these things;" (Deut. xxxii. 27) and therefore, having
given them ample space to exhaust all their resources,
He relieves us at once, in a manner as simple as it is
wonderful, as mighty as it is divested of splendour. God
had been offended and must be appeased; man had fallen
and must be raised: such were the two objects to be
attained.   The required propitiation was for man; who
but man could be called to perform it ? The infinite
distance between him and the offended Being, and the
added infirmity and worthlessness of his fallen nature,
disqualified him completely for attempting it: who but God
could supply his deficiency ? By this marvellous contrivance of Divine wisdom—by the union of God and man
in one person—by the coalition of the guilty nature with
the infinitely powerful, all was reconciled; the debtor in
person discharged his obligations with the riches communicated by the creditor himself. No sacrifice was made
of one just claim to another—no compromise required
between the harmonious attributes of God ; justice received its due, told in solid value to its utmost tittle;
mercy stretched, unrestricted and unembarrassed, its all-

embracing arms; power exerted its might with unlimited magnificence; and graciousness and love triumphed in a new display of unexampled condescension.

Moreover, see what immense advantages attended this exercise of God's power! God hath appeared to us; we know Him no longer in the abstract, or by con-jecture, but as visible, as like to ourselves,—in the form which we habitually love. He can be our friend, one that hath partaken of our infirmities, that hath been tempted like unto us, that hath suffered sorrow and tasted death. How much lighter, too, must his commands appear, spoken as they were by a human mouth! When God thundered forth His law on Sinai, the people entreated Moses, saying, " speak thou to us, and we will hear : let not the Lord speak to us, lest we die." (Exod. xx. 19.) And so, how mildened must not all the precepts of the New Law appear to us, when proceeding from the lips of one so meek, so gentle, so affectionate in our regard!

Still more consoling is the consideration of the sublime dignity to which we have been raised by the incarnation of the Son of God. If He stooped low, indeed, to accom-plish it, He exalted us proportionably high. Our nature subsists in the Godhead, and sitteth at the right hand of God, elevated above the angelic spirits, whose nature He did not assume. Oh, the immensity of the Divine wisdom and power which are comprehended in this ines-timable mystery ! What should we have been without it ? Poor earth-born creatures, condemned for ever to creep upon the surface of this world, or aspire, with ineffectual efforts, after that higher state from which we had fallen ! Oh, how foolish is the wisdom of this world,

its noblest conceptions, its sublimest meditations, compared with its grandeur!   How inadequate is man's
mind to comprehend it, now that it has been revealed
to him! how much more beyond the reach of his antici-
pations before it came to pass!   A mystery in fact it
is, above the sphere of angels', as much as of men's,
thoughts!

But hitherto we seem to have confined our attention
mainly to the Divine energy that planned and executed
this wonderful mystery: it were time that we turned our
thoughts to Him who is its object; and if in the first
view it has seemed to us a mystery of wisdom and
power, it will henceforth appear to us a still greater
mystery of goodness and love.   Let us, for this purpose,
draw near to the birth-place of this incarnate Word of
God, and meditate upon his first appearance amongst us.
See then how Mary, conducted by Joseph, undertakes a
toilsome winter's journey to Bethlehem, the city of David.
The emperor has commanded all to be enrolled in their
own city or town ; and this blessed couple are obeying
the law.   Perhaps of all that travel towards the royal
city, none are so destitute and helpless as they.   Every
one passes them on the way; and when they reach their
journey's end, every lodging has been occupied, and they
have no resource left them but a miserable stable.   Into
this they retire, and there, in the silence of the night,
Mary gives birth to her first-born, Jesus.

When the heir to a throne is born, proclamation is forthwith made to its subjects of the joyful event, that they
may attest their loyalty.   And accordingly, here the
heralds of Heaven descend, and communicate the glad

tidings to a few shepherds, who seek the spot described to them, and find the Child.

The feelings of the principal actors in the moving scenes of our Saviour's first night, are almost too sacred for us to attempt to analyze them. If a woman, when she hath brought forth, hath joy, as our Lord assures us, (Jo., xvi. 21) what must have been her's, who was the first on earth to look upon the face of God's Christ, not only made man, but become her Son ? Her pleasing duty it was to take Him into her arms and warm His trembling limbs, and swathe them, and then feast her eyes, through the long winter's night, upon His sweet and smiling countenance. Ah! what would gilded roofs or painted palaces have been to her that night, in exchange for the shattered shed through which the piercing blast entered on every side.

No dreams of maternal ambition, no swelling thoughts of what she one day may be, through the glories of her Son, disturb the pure unblended joys of motherhood in her chaste and humble bosom. Every toil and pain of the past journey and its distressing end—all sense of present loneliness, penury, and cold,—every anticipation of a future career, be it of splendour or of wretchedness, is swallowed up in the one unalloyed happiness of possessing at that moment such a son. As yet he hardly belongs to the world: besides her faithful spouse, who adores in silence by her side, not a human being has yet passed the threshold of their humble sanctuary, or ruffled the stillness of the solemn scene. Only Heaven has shared their raptures—on earth He is yet their own exclusively.

Gaze on, maiden mother, while yet thou mayest, in

quiet and joy! Make thy first draught at this fountain of
thy gladness, long and inebriating! For soon shalt thou
be able to say to the daughters of Bethlehem, as did thy
ancestress Noemi, " call me Mara, that is, bitter; for the
Lord hath filled me with bitterness." (Ruth, i. 20.) Soon
shall the sword of Herod be waved against thine Infant's
head; soon shall Simeon's prophetic sword be in thine
own heart, to banish for ever the peaceful visions of
this night.

But hark! faltering, reverential steps approach the
door of the miserable hovel: they are those of men who
hesitate if they may venture in. Is it from shame of
visiting so wretched a tenement? or is it from awe at
what it hath been announced they shall find within?
They whisper and deliberate. The angel's words were
indeed explicit: he had said to them, "Fear not; for
behold I bring you tidings of great joy, which shall be
to all the people. For this day is born to you a Saviour,
who is Christ the Lord, in the city of David." When
they had heard these words, their hearts had fallen within
them : how could they hope to gain admittance to the
cradle of this infant King? Wherefore announce to *them*
such tidings? But what a rush took place in the tide
of their feelings, when they heard the concluding words
of the angelic errand:—" And this shall be a sign unto
you: you shall find the infant wrapt in swaddling clothes,
and laid in a manger!" (Luke, ii. 12.) Eternal God!
and was there ever another child born, of whom no
better description could be given than this—You shall
find him laid in a manger! No; perhaps it is not upon
record that any one, before or since, had his first repose

in such a place. And could it have been believed that angels came down from heaven to direct men to one so meanly lodged? Yet it was even so; and these simple men, so divinely guided, venture into the presence of their infant Lord.

They pause upon the threshold: so calm, so pure, so unlike this earth's is the scene that breaks upon them. That venerable man who courteously and cheerfully invites them to approach; that young, mild virgin-mother, all radiant with humble unaffected joy, whose smile encourages them to draw nigher still; that glorious Babe, beautiful beyond the sons of men, whose eyes already beam with intelligence and benignity: so peerless a group, containing every type of human excellence and perfection, could not but appear even to eyes that just came from gazing on the multitude of the heavenly host, a scene of another world, descended for the blessing of men. How deep and ardent was their first adoration, when, sunk in silence on their knees, they meditated upon the mystery of love that shone visible before them. Perhaps as they became more familiar with it, their first awe melted before the increasing warmth of their feelings into tenderness; and they ventured closer, till with the mother's meek consent, they ventured to take in their arms and lovingly embrace the blessed Child.

And why, we may now perhaps ask, were these men the first to be thus invited to pay their homage, and form a court to the Saviour of the world? Leaving it to the wisdom of God alone to know the true motives of such a choice, we can surely discover a reason, in perfect accord-ance with the conduct pursued by divine Providence in

the entire mystery. Had not the entire earth been put
into commotion, that the Son of God might be born in a
stable? For, a message from an angel might have sent
his parents to Bethlehem, as one sent them into Egypt.
But it was more consonant to the dignity of God, and
their virtue, that the ignominious place of His birth
should not have been matter of command, but result
from the pressure of events. For it would have hardly
been a natural fruit of humility in one who knew she
was to bring into the world its Lord and Maker, to
choose such a place for this purpose; neither can we
imagine it to have been enjoined her by His eternal
Father. But had they been sent to Bethlehem under
ordinary circumstances, or perhaps when any less impelling motive than an imperial decree had crowded to
excess its walls, they would have found a poor but decent
lodging; and that extreme of poverty and abasement
would have been avoided, which forms the most striking,
as the most touching, circumstance in our Saviour's
nativity.

As, then, the Emperor's decree seems to have been
necessary to obtain this purpose, so does the preference
given to the shepherds seem directed to complete it.
Who so poor in the neighbourhood of Bethlehem, that
he had not a roof over his head better than a deserted
stable? What husbandman, what labourer, so destitute
as not to possess at least a hovel for himself and his
family? And if any of these had been brought to adore
at the crib, having learnt who it was that lay in it, must
they not have done gentle violence to the holy family,
and obliged them to share their hearth and board, and

accept of such slender, but better, accommodation as
their poverty could supply?   But out of every class, the
shepherds alone, who spent their nights in the open air,
tending their flocks beside their watch-fires, or at most
beneath the scanty shelter of their moveable tents, could
not second any desire their hearts might feel, to better
the condition of those whom they at once revered and
loved.   They might press upon them some small provision, as an offering of love, but they could not ward
off the wintry chill and the dreariness that surrounded
them.

But why this poverty? why this voluntary abjection?
Ah! the heart that answers not this question readily
and decisively, must be dry and barren.   If the Son of
God became man, it was from love for us; the principle
that suggested the great act directed all its circumstances.
He might have appeared to the world, and have performed all that He did for its redemption, without our
being made acquainted with the circumstances of His
infancy.   The veil which overspreads His subsequent
history, till His manifestation before Israel, might have
been extended over the events of His birth; and we might
have known Jesus, sufficiently for our salvation, as the
Master who instructed us, and the Redeemer who died
for us.   But He had two lessons to give us, which
elsewhere He could not so well have taught us as He
did at Bethlehem.

And, first, we cling to the world with obstinate affection from infancy to death.   We wept and fretted in our
very cradle when we first felt discomfort; and those first
tears were but the first fruits of the solicitudes and

anxieties which our love of perishable goods continues to the end to cause us. We love our riches, our reputation, our ease; we surround ourselves with comforts, and repine if they be taken from us. We would not have affliction come near us, and hate the look of sorrow. We would fain that all the crosses we must bear should be made of cedar, and that the lashes wherewith God scourges us should be of silk. Now, then, look upon that Infant, who lies upon a little bundle of straw, between the ox and the ass, and tell me what you think of gold, and luxury, and worship and honour? Are they to be praised—nay, are they to be spoken of in His presence? Who is it? "The wonderful, the Counsellor, God the mighty, the Father of the world to come." (Is. ix. 6.) And did He will to be laid upon so lowly a bed, and to be attended with such mean state, and to be clothed so poorly, and to be known so little: and shall we, sinners and poor slaves, affect great pomp and service, and lose our peace if all things fall not out with us as we desire? Oh! such thoughts will not brook the vicinity of that humble couch; they fit us not to enter in with the shepherds; they belong to the rich and proud inhabitants of Bethlehem, who refused admittance to the poor, but most blessed, parents of Jesus.

And if, in our dear Lord's nativity, we are taught to despise the vain delights of earth, we are surely attracted by a sweet, but powerful, influence to cleave to Him. When He took upon Himself our flesh, He entered into brotherhood with us—He intended thereby greatly to win our love. Every part of His life presents us some peculiar incentive to affection, but none to the same familiarity of love as this of His humble birth into the world. When we contemplate Him upon Calvary, giving us the marvellous evidence of a love strong as death, there is in our returned affection a painful mingling of sorrow, of a culprit's shame, a penitent's remorse, and withal a bitterness of sympathy which greatly disturbs the purity of simple love. When we behold Him breaking open the bolts of death, and triumphing over the tyranny of hell by His glorious resurrection, there is an admixture of reverence and exceeding awe, which tempers our affection and checks our familiarity. But here, in His poor and rough bed of straw, all His majesty is shrouded, all His dazzling and consuming brightness drawn in. He seems to require our loving care, to invite our caresses, and pure, tender, untempered love is the exclusive feeling wherewith we view Him. There is yet no stain of blood upon His tender flesh, no reproaching gash, no ignominious crown. We can imagine Him as yet unconscious of the pain He will one day suffer for us, and of the ingratitude wherewith we shall requite Him : His present miseries seem independent of our worthlessness, and such as we have a full right to sympathize with.

And where would all this sentiment of sincere and sweet affection have been found, had we been called to meditate on an infant royally laid in a bed of state, reposing upon cushions of down, and watched and nursed by princesses ? No; we should have turned away, awed by it, or at least careless of its smile; it would have wanted nought from us—it would be more able already to give than to receive. But had we only come upon such a scene as that on which we meditate unawares—had we

casually, seeking shelter from a storm, found two resigned
and virtuous parents in such a place at such a season,
nursing an unconscious infant just born, through the
lonely night, far more would our hearts have been moved
to tender emotions, than by the pomp and grandeur of
the happier child. And when it is no stranger that is
thus presented to us, but one of our own blood and line,
and closely related to us,—when it is no thoughtless babe
that stretches forth its hand by instinctive impulse, but
one that knows and loves us, and puts on winning ways to
arouse and allure our affections; cold and frozen beyond
the winter's ice must our hearts be, if in spirit, and with
the arms of our affection, we return not the embrace, and
prove that we should not have been unworthy of admission to early and loving familiarity with our Lord.

Yes, blessed Jesus! thanks, eternal thanks to Thee,
for having thought so well of the human heart, as to put
it to this proof of love! Grievous is its perversity,
crooked are its ways, hard, too often, is its very core; but
lost beyond redemption would it have been, if no sympathy had been left in it for Thine infant charms, Thine
infant sufferings, and Thine infant love! Thou hast
found out the way by these claims to win our affections:
keep them close to Thee, to grow with Thy growth, till
they ripen to full maturity upon Calvary, and follow us
thence into the kingdom of love!

With such feelings, my brethren, we will celebrate the
coming solemnities, with admiration at the magnificence
of God's power and wisdom, manifested in the Incarnation
of the uncreated Word, and in grateful affection for the
love displayed to us in His birth into the world. We

will not allow these days to run away in mere festivity and amusement, but in sober joy we will unite ourselves to the shepherds of Bethlehem, to spend some hours at least in devout and feeling meditation by the humble manger. The year will thus close upon us with sentiments worthy of our Christian vocation, and the next will open with fervent desires and renewed endeavours to walk with Christ in newness of life, to the full participation of those abundant mercies which His incarnation and birth brought into the world.

SERMON II.

On the Epiphany.[*]

MATT. ii. 2.

" Where is He that is born King of the Jews? For we have
seen His star in the East, and are come to adore Him."

THAT many would be found in our time ready to
encounter toil and danger for the promotion of science;
that many a bold traveller would present himself ready to
cross inhospitable deserts, and trace the obscure course
of some river, or to explore the capital of some barbarous tribe; that brave navigators would not hesitate
amid the rocks of the torrid, or the icebergs of the frozen
ocean, to make further researches as to the direction of
currents or the dip of the needle, or to discover some new
and, perhaps, impracticable path from ocean to ocean; or
even that this noble spirit of adventure may be still
further ennobled by a glorious object, such as has been of
late the case in the most splendid effort of generous
philanthropy yet on record, the desire to rescue from
destruction one of those martyrs of science, the experience and observation of every day makes sufficiently
evident.

* Preached, in Rome, during the Octave, which is kept solemnly, as
described in the sermon, by the " Pious Union " for foreign impious.

But if any one should be prepared to encounter similar risks and toil for the advancement of mere moral science,—if any one should be found ready to undertake such dangerous and distant pilgrimages for the acquisition of mere truth, nay, for procuring acquaintance with the greatest of truths, those of religion, it would be a phenomenon, were it as common as it is rare amongst us, which could hardly be explicable on the laws which now rule the world. And yet in other times it has not been so. From that distant day when a queen of the East came to Jerusalem to visit Solomon, not that she might be admonished by his riches and magnificence—for she came with camels laden with gold and spices and precious stones—but, as our Lord tells us, attracted by his wisdom, that she might make experiment of it by putting to him hard questions ; through those remote ages when the Catholic scholar went from every part of Europe, and even from more distant continents, across mountains and seas, to visit the schools of that western island by whose ministers this wisdom of religious truth was so excellently taught ; through those subsequent periods when any eminent teacher and expounder of God's Word or of the laws of the Church, whether at Padua, at Paris, or at Oxford, was sure to collect around him thousands of hearers eager for spiritual truth, there has been in the world, almost until our present time, a series of men of whom the kings of the East that came to visit Jerusalem and Bethlehem at the time of our Saviour's birth, have been justly considered as the type. It is on this account, therefore, that the Church of God has considered them as the first fruits of the Gentiles, even as the shepherds were

we analyze this knowledge which they possess, and note how it became to them of a practical character, we shall see that it is composed of two distinct parts; the first consists of the power of observing the phenomena of nature, of reasoning concerning them, and of coming to accurate conclusions from them. But this would not have been sufficient. We cannot doubt that they also had a higher and nobler source of knowledge ; the very words which they speak when they come to Jerusalem, prove to us that their observation of nature had received a comment from a revelation, which they had carefully studied, or which had been treasured up in the traditions of their tribes. A prophet of Asia had spoken, many ages before, words to which their expressions accurately apply. "Where is He," they ask, "that is born King of the Jews? For we have seen His star in the East, and we are come to adore Him." The appearance of this particular star indicates a birth ; it indicates the birth of a king, not in their neighbourhood, not in the centre of Asia, but in the regions of the West ; a King of Judea must have been born when it arose ; for we find the words of a mysterious prophecy laid up in the faithful memory of the East : "A star shall rise out of Jacob, and a sceptre shall spring up from Israel." (Numb. xxiv. 17.)

This star is the star of Jacob ; a new sceptre, a new prince, who will be greater, higher, and nobler than any who have preceded him, shall spring up in the land of Judea. Uniting these two together, they understand that this beacon is intended to guide their steps on their perilous journey across the desert, to seek Him ; and with noble resolution they at once undertake the task.

If we now pursue the course of conversion further still, we shall see how these two means have been those which Providence has used to bring to the knowledge of Christianity, and to communion with the Church, great multitudes of nations. For this two-fold ray, the natural power of reasoning on phenomena which fall under the dominion of the senses, and the being guided by the testimony of the inspired word, which, united together, form the star that led the wise men from the East, has formed the two means whereby the conversion of mankind has been wrought.

Imagine soon after the appearance of this star, a moral and sincere heathen looking abroad on the world. He sees all that is barbarous in it immersed in darkness, and hideous immorality corrupting the more civilized portion. He sees that wonderful mystery, the inequality between different states,—the virtuous man oppressed, ruined, crushed by the foot of the powerful ; the daring sinner exalted, flourishing, and enjoying to the moment of his death all the happiness of this world. Where, he asks, is the solution of this wonderful, this strange, this dark and afflicting mystery ? He knows not where to find it. He sees man, whom he has studied in himself and others, evidently a creature of noble destiny, and fully endowed with powers necessary to attain it ; but at the same time weakened, broken, ruined in every faculty of his mind, and in every feeling of his heart. There he sees him lie, with the consciousness that he is but the wreck of his noble self, and anxious to raise himself from his degradation, but sinking every moment lower and lower, and unable to accomplish that for which he knows he was

created. Where shall he seek for a sufficient solution of
this wonderful mystery ? where will the means be found
to accomplish that which he sees Nature cannot do ?
This reasoning is the star which will lead him forward.
He will seek on every side where this wonderful problem
may be solved, and that star leads him to the East
and to the West, to India, or to Chaldea, or to Egypt,
or to Greece, or to Rome, and he asks priests and scribes
in all those places, and they tell him nothing ; he
is still in sorrowful darkness, and he knows not where
he shall come to the light.

But at last he learns that it has broken forth. He
has heard with the wise men of the East that there is a
child born,—that in that child is the wonderful mystery
which he sees gradually developed,—a mystery which
presents, as clearly as does the sun, a light that at once
sheds a brilliancy over all that till now has perplexed
and darkened him.   The judgment to come of justice and
retribution, from which the Gentiles shrink, is to him
a lesson of consolation.   There, he is told, will be the
final decision by which virtue and vice will be put in
their proper place and proper light, where reward eternal
and punishment perpetual shall be allotted to each ; and
that child comes as the judge that is to render this
righteous judgment to the entire world.   But how is it
possible that in one child this great, this magnificent and
divine office shall be. lodged ?   And this is not all ; the
child, too, comes on the express understanding of teaching
the doctrine itself which solves the whole of the enigma ;
man has fallen, who was created for greatness and glory :
he fell by his own act, was helpless, and has remained so

until a Redeemer has come—a child, indeed, but one who
will bear on Him the iniquity of the world. But how is
it possible that both these sublime offices of God and
Redeemer should be combined, and that in one infant?
When he hears the whole of the mystery, that that child
is not merely the son of man, but that He is God incarnate, then all is clear, all is simple. In Him is that
power, that might, that wisdom, that love, that immense
goodness and mercy which can alone devise and do a
divine act, which can alone empower its performance;
and in Him also are the claims and the rights of man,
which authorise Him to make use of these great attributes
for what might otherwise appear an unlearned and undeserved purpose. The union of God and man, of God
and the Redeemer—the appearance of this solution in
the world, at once clears off all difficulties. The sincere heathen believes all by simple contact with its performance; it meets the problem at every part, it adapts
itself to every, the smallest and feeblest of doubts, and he
embraces at once Christianity, after he has been fully
instructed—by instruction, every word of which only
further strengthens his convictions.

But the upright Jew, like Simeon or Zachary, has no
need thus to go abroad; his star is in his hands; and
seated whether among the columns of the Temple, or
amidst the balsams of Jericho, or under the waving cedars
of Libanus, or beneath his own fig-tree like Nathaniel,
he unrolls the sacred volume before him, and there, sincere, honest, and virtuous, he endeavours to unravel the
mysteries which it presents. The time is come, and must
now indeed have reached its maturity, when the prophe-

cies of which he has long been reading must be fulfilled.
But he finds still so much of doubt, so much of difficulty,
that he seeks somewhere for the solution. There is the
prophecy which speaks of a magnificent kingdom to be
established over the entire world. A King is to come
as the mighty conqueror of all nations, and at the same
time he finds that He is to be poor and weak, riding on
an ass, that His hands and feet are to be pierced, that He
is to be an outcast of the people, and as a worm trodden
under foot, and to be computed among sinners, though at
the same time He is to be blameless before God. So
the Jew, too, wrings his hands ; he knows not which way
to turn, and see where it is possible to find Him who
shall unite in Himself these attributes of greatness and
littleness.

His star is before him : let him follow it step by step
whither it shall lead him, and his doubts shall be cleared
up. Yes, he in time hears that One born in Bethlehem
has grown up, and is preaching among the people. He
goes forth into the wilderness, and witnesses His actions :
holiness, purity, and the sublimest perfection are manifested in His every word and deed ; a power omnipotent
is exerted in a variety of miracles ; death and the grave
are obedient to His voice ; kindness and mercy, affectionate tenderness and forgivingness, and every attribute
of a truly great and divine mind are manifested in Him.
He follows Him into a cavern at night, and sees Him
in " the prayer of God ;" next sought to be made a king ;
still ever equally humble and unpretending. He goes
with Him to the supper of the rich and to the halls of
the Temple, and finds Him inflexible and stern in re-

proving vice ; in truth, he observes in Him every character of the great man whom he expects to be the
deliverer of his nation. He is of the family of David,
for He was born in Bethlehem, according to prophecy.
He exhausts all those grand characteristics of one destined
to rule his people and lead them whither he wills. The
Jew has found the Messiah—his Lord.

But his perplexity is not over. How can he reconcile
what he has heard concerning " the servant of God,"
described by Isaias, (liii.) and the great and beautiful
things which he sees and hears ? I will be, he says, one
of those silent followers in the footsteps of Jesus. And
he will hear with astonishment that the whole of Israel
is in a ferment of fury, and that He whom he has admired,
and in whom he has seen nothing but the great king
destined to free the people, is a captive and in bonds. He
will hear that He has been treated as a malefactor. His
heart will fail within him. He will hear how the priests
have accused Him; how Pilate has condemned and scourged
Him, and that He is led now to be crucified. He follows
Him to Calvary. He sees Him meek and humble nailed
as a victim to the cross The truth of the two-fold
prophecy rushes on his mind. The King of Israel crowned
with thorns; the Saviour and Ruler of His people enthroned
on the cross; His hands that had to hold the sword to lead
them to victory, pierced with nails; and His head, that had
to be erect with the sovereignty of the world, bowed in
death. He strikes his breast and says, " Truly this is the
Son of God."

It was by this two-fold way that the Gentile and the
Jew were brought to the knowledge of Christianity. The

same course has been followed in one form or another
even until now.   Let us then imagine a person, in our
times, anxious and eager for truth as were those Eastern
kings, as were the sagacious Pagan and the devout Jew;
and let us suppose that he has arrived at this conclusion
more strongly than they could have done—that however
various may be the forms of opinion, truth must certainly
be one.   He has wavered from side to side, and gone
from place to place, as he sought truth under various
forms generally conflicting, and he has at last sat
down to reason, by what means it can be found.   He
takes up the argument where the heathen and the Jew
left it ; they sought, he has found his Saviour; he will
say to himself, if the Son of God came down from
heaven to teach mankind truth, surely the discovery of
it cannot be so difficult or so painful as I have found it.
If He came to establish His kingdom on earth, it must
have great and striking characteristics ; it must be
ruled by a principle which secures unity in belief, for
otherwise there cannot be truth ; it must have such
authority and power as to bring down the sublimest
intellects into the acknowledgment and belief of all that
it teaches ; it must have wisdom which will raise the
intelligence of the lowest and most ignorant to the level
of its sublime doctrines ; it must have the means to
make itself known so clear and obvious, that no one can
fail to find it.

And he, like the Pagan, has undoubtedly discovered
that man wants reparation, that he wants strength, that
he wants the means of attaining his high destiny of a
future and better existence ; and further, he is convinced

that, wherever that truth has been deposited, there are with it the means also of healing these wounds of humanity, of strengthening that weakness, of directing those steps, and of making him whom redemption found prostrate and wounded, able to walk on boldly to the eternal crown that is prepared for him. "This is what I should expect; reason and argument tell me that if the Son of God came and established His religion in such a way as to be useful, efficacious, and profitable, I must naturally expect to find such a body as this."

But he will not stop here ; he will take up the sacred volume which the Jew has dropped, when he has discovered that all that it contains is a type,—when he has seen accomplished on Calvary the mysteries previously revealed, and waiting, expecting a new and more perfect revelation. The Christian in search of truth takes up that volume, and finds added to it a shorter, but at least a more perfect record, of the thoughts and words of God. And there, does he find that all is contradictory of what his natural sense and reasoning have taught him to expect, in looking for that which Christ has established on earth, for the sake of making known His truth ? He finds, on the contrary, that, point by point, the two tally perfectly together.

In the Old Testament are the description and prophecy of a kingdom, where is union of peace and truth : in the New Testament is the constitution of the Church, in which unity is secured by infallible teaching and direction, and in which, at the same time, are all the means of grace, and abundant treasures for the renovation of fallen man. There is baptism to wash away original sin ;

there is the food that strengthens him to eternal life ; there is the forgiveness of sins, by which all transgressions may be cancelled.

Then he, too, has found the star which he must follow. He believes, he expects, he hopes that somewhere or other he may be able to find a system of truth, a system of teaching at least, which will have all these characteristics of truth—one that will offer a plain and easy path on which to walk with comfort towards the goal of existence; and he will hope to find it abundantly furnished with whatever is necessary to enable the poor lost creature—man—to perform deeds of virtue worthy of this end. Let him, then, too, follow his star, and see whither by God's blessing it will lead him.

But the kings of the East start on their journey. They must be struck with the difficulties that present themselves at once before them. In the first place they will, perhaps, be astonished at seeing how few pursue the same course as they do. Four of them at most are recorded to have come to Jerusalem to pay homage to the new-born King. How many thousands had seen the star; how many hundreds had contemplated it ; how many as learned as themselves had watched it, and traced its laws. How had these been discussed,—how had the object to which it tended been gradually made known to many. Yet how few had acted. The question further would present itself, " Why should we go ? why should we move ? It is true we see a star which seems to point to another kingdom; a new religion perhaps may spring up in the West; but our first duty is to our own country and people; why should we run the risk of following a light which, after all, may mislead us? Why need we consider ourselves bound to abandon our homes, our families, our kingdom, perhaps all that belongs to us, to make forfeiture of whatever is precious to us, and follow a star of which we know not the past history, and are ignorant of the present purpose? It is better for us to remain; let us wait a while and see whither it may go ; let some one else try the experiment, and when he reports, it will be time to move." No, they simply considered that it was a sign addressed to them from heaven; and they determined at once without hesitation to follow.

They did so ; and they had no reason surely to repent of their obedience to the call of this voice from heaven. And we shall find this to be the history of conversion, in every other part of the world. God may be said to have used two distinct methods, and to have allotted them to distinct periods of the world. One is when through performance of wonderful works, through miracles, through signs in heaven or on earth, by supernatural grace, eloquence, and power bestowed on a few chosen servants, men came into the Church in multitudes. Such was the course in the first conversions in Judea; such was the effect of the preaching of the great apostle of the Anglo-Saxons, St. Augustine ; such, too, was the case with St. Boniface, who carried the faith to Germany ; and such was it, likewise, when St. Francis Xavier went and bore its light and truth to the East. But, with a few brilliant exceptions such as these, the work is slow, and gradual, and individual.

For, after the first foundation of the Roman Church, it was the consolation of Christians day after day to hear,

D

now that a member of the senate, now that one high in
the state, and again, that an officer of distinction in the
army, or perhaps a simple knight, had joined the Church.
Their ranks then swelled slowly ; God was thanked
heartily as each soul came in, and this slow increase went
on for three hundred years before Christianity was sufficiently great to take on itself the government of the world.
Such has been often the case, and is now ; and if we see
that, through our humble ministry, God works thus, if
we discover that one by one we gain souls, we must not
be astonished or dejected, but feel that this is the course
which God has generally pursued.   Should it please Him
to rejoice our hearts with one of those splendid religious
phenomena, which He has permitted only from time to
time, then, indeed, we will thank Him in the fulness of
our hearts ; but in the mean time let us be content to go
on sowing and scattering silently in the furrow, and with
tears, those seeds of His word, of which we know that not
one can fall in vain.

But whither are the wise men of the East led ?   Does
the star at once conduct them to the point at which they
aim ?   No, Providence has been pleased to give us here
a further lesson.   God wished that, in addition to that
guidance which their own reason, reflected on the word of
prophecy, had till now given them, they should receive
stronger testimony still, and that from unwilling teachers,
—from the very enemies of Him towards whom they were
journeying.

It was natural that they should go to Jerusalem.   The
King of the Jews was born.   They are come to seek Him ;
and where more naturally could they expect to find Him

than in the royal city? They expect, on approaching Jerusalem, to see signs of gladness, rejoicing, and jubilee, and thanksgiving; they expect to find the Temple garlanded, the priests in their noblest robes, and the Levites leading the chaunts of the multitude; they expect to find the roads filled with pilgrims on their way to pay the same act of religious worship which they are about to render. How different is the reality! Not a pilgrim is wending his way towards the city. They enter in, and find it the same as usual; its business of every-day life, its traffic and its litigation, its disorders and its military oppression, are all going on, as if no great event had occurred to excite curiosity in the population, or increase the tide of ordinary joy. Jerusalem shows no symptoms of consciousness that He is come into the world, of whose coming they have no doubt.

The faith of the wise men may waver, but they cannot doubt they are right in their search, and here they must discover all they wish to know. Yes, whither shall they go but to the chief of that priesthood which is in close alliance with the state, which gives it information on all that relates to religious duties, which expounds articles of faith, and is supported and maintained in pomp and greatness by the monarch of the Jews? It is among them naturally—it is with the national religion firmly established by the law of the land, that they must expect to find all that their star has brought them to seek. " Where is He," they ask, " that is born King of the Jews ?"

Jerusalem is dismayed. Herod and his city are troubled, and at what? They fear that a disturbance is going to take place in the quiet and unruffled course of affairs in the kingdom; that men are come from a distance to ask questions which it is troublesome to answer; that a rival power is about to arise which will disturb the church and state in Jerusalem. But they receive the testimony which they seek. If that King is to be born, if there is to be such a manifestation, it is not in great and noble Jerusalem they must look; they must go to little Bethlehem, a mean and poor city at a distance, and there, perhaps, if He has been heard of, they may find what they desire.

How is this the history of many a soul, of many a one who is here present, and who had pursued that reasoning which I have described—who had felt in his mind the assurance that there must exist on earth a living Church— a body that can teach, a body that can guide, a body that is the depositary of truth—one which is plain and simple, one which makes no doctrines, one which unites the extremes of great and little within herself; one, also, that opens her maternal bosom to give nourishment to those that want it, and cleanses from sin, and strengthens to life in Christ, which the soul requires. Many a one who has reasoned thus, and, studying the Word of God, has said, such a body, such a kingdom, such a society must exist, and must have these great characteristics of unity, firmness, and infallibility in teaching; many a one who pursues this reasoning, this star that guides him, goes at once there where all his feelings, all his sympathies, where all his natural prejudices even would carry him: and he has thought that there it must be found—there where all is so noble, so great, so learned, that it appears outwardly to contain within it all the elements of which he is in search. They have gone to the priests of that Church, to the high priests, to the scribes and learned men, and have asked for the solution of their doubts, for the direction which they have sought. What has been the answer they have received? "Do you come to seek for exemption from doubts as to your faith? do you seek to avoid the painfulness of inquiry? do you come to us to reconcile conflicting opinions by proposing to you a certain, fixed, and definite mode of belief? We profess to have nought of the kind among us; we claim not the power thus to exempt you. Do you come to us for an infallible creed, for an unerring guide who will teach you authoritatively and with certainty, that if you believe every word it teaches, you believe only the Word of God? Go to Rome, you that want doctrines like these; they are found in the Vatican, they are taught and maintained in the Catholic Church, not in the Apostolic Church of England. You have come to ask for the power of approaching nearer to your Saviour incarnate. You have an idea in your mind which is the result of your reading, but which is false and heretical. If you wish to approach and worship Him nearer, go to despised Bethlehem—go to the Catholic Church : you will there be told that put before you on the altar is truly that same child as the kings found: but in our Church we pretend to have no such object of adoration."

Thus baffled, they may have turned away disappointed and humbled, with broken hearts and broken hopes, and for a time they have faltered, whether or no they should give up the search for ever; for they from whom they expected comfort and direction, they to whom the star had guided them, have coldly cast them away. But no, they go. forth, turning their backs on those false leaders. Their star will re-appear ; the same force of convincing reasoning will tell them that truth is still to be found on earth. And it may be that they think where indeed are they to find it ; but be certain that the guide which has brought them thus far, will not lead them wrong. Yes, they have turned their backs on the noble cathedral, and on the pealing anthem, and its sweet and ancient recollections, on its elegant discourses, on its respectable worshippers, and they must move away sorrowing, until they come hither where the star directs them.

Then they say, " Must we enter here ? is it here that we are to find what has appeared so great and noble in our minds, greater than what we have left behind ?" They enter, and they enter precisely as did the wise men of the East. For if, my brethren, you might happen to be in some country place in England, what I have said would be literally true ; and, after all you had abandoned for ever, it might be you would have to pause for a moment on the threshold of some garret, or loft over a stable, in which alone the Catholic Church is allowed to offer worship. And then you would go in with those wise men ; you would bend lowly to pass under the humble door ; you would indeed have lost sight of the star, but you would then truly believe for the first time, you would then for the first time fall down and adore. There is around you nothing but what is mean and humble. There are shepherds in their coarse attire ; there are reapers from the neighbouring island, an assembly of people of lowly and poor condition. But there for the first time you feel that you have become associated with the Saints, with the patriarchs and the apostles of the Old and of the New Law, who bring you into communion with all that is great and holy in the Old and the New Testament. There, for the first time, you become acquainted with her who is both Mother and Virgin, the very thought of whom speaks tenderness to the heart of the Catholic. There, for the first time, you are truly introduced to the joy of earth and heaven : for you are in the presence of Him whom the wise men of the East saw and adored ; and with them you believe and adore. To believe, and to adore,—these are the two great objects to which the star guides every one that is brought to the Church of God ; and these two words are all that I need explain ; to bring this discourse to its conclusion.

"To believe !" you will say. "Have I not believed till now? Is belief more than a sincere, deep, and earnest conviction of the truths we hold ?" I know not how I can better describe the nature of true belief or faith, in distinction from every other sort of conviction or opinion, than by reference to that figure of light which has guided us till now. During the time that you have been seeking after the Church of God, you have been following the guidance of a star. That star diffuses no light around you ; it is a luminous point at a distance, and nothing more. The ray between it and you is dark ; you can only direct your course towards it. But it enables you to do nothing more ; it lights not even your path on your journey ; it helps you not to read the inspired book that you bear with you. You want a very different light when you have reached your goal. To illustrate my meaning, I suppose that it is your wish to become acquainted with all that God has done for man in the system of nature, and in the system of grace ; man's destiny and end ; what He has done to make him what he is, and what he is to be ; in fact, the whole system of religion, natural and revealed. It is as though you had entered in the dark into a great and magnificent edifice—let it be one of those old cathedrals to which I have already alluded.

You have determined to make yourself acquainted with the whole interior ; so you light your lamp, and go from place to place, and examine it on every side. The moment you cast your light on one spot, and have briefly illuminated it and studied it, you move on, and it returns to darkness : that shifting light only gleams upon single objects. You raise high your lamp, and in vain endeavour to reach the loftier parts of the structure. You lower it into the crypt below, and it only discovers impenetrable gloom ; and there are parts on every side, with which it seems impossible that you can become acquainted. It is a work of endless search ; and, in the end, you have no idea of the bearing of its parts, of its relative proportions, of the talents of those who designed, and the skill of those who erected, the structure.

Then, you may say, I will not be thus content with my own small light ; I will collect the brilliancy which others wisdom and experience have cast on it. I will concentrate the lights which skilful and learned men have thrown upon it. In one part, it will be a torch burning with single but with brilliant splendour ; in other parts, there will be collected a multitude of tapers, diffusing their joint radiance in every direction. And what is the result? In proportion as I have produced a dazzling glare, I have deepened the shades ; there are places which the light cannot enter ; it cannot soar to the highest and most delicate portions of the structure ; it cannot find its way into the gloom below ; while graceful objects are cut in two by the light and shade, and made to appear monstrous by the relative forces of dark and luminous. In fine, I have made myself no better acquainted with the edifice than I did by my own unaided efforts.

Then what shall I do? Sit down and weep, and complain that God has made religion so laborious, such an endless task, that it is impossible, by the combined genius and efforts of men, ever fully to explore it? No! the foolish wisdom of this world, is not that the light that you have kindled? Wait with patience until the sun shall arise, and then you will find it illuminate the whole magnificent edifice. It will not be a ray, but a light which will not strike with partial intensity some points, but will diffuse itself throughout the building ; it will creep into every nook and cranny, it will find and bring every beauty out. The whole will be steeped in a uniform and cheering brightness, and you will be able to comprehend the harmony of details, and the grandeur of the entire structure.

Those lights represent reason endeavouring to grasp and comprehend the works of God ; that sun that has risen is faith, which convinces you more than any speculation or argument can do, that it is a true light which God has given you. It is to us a universal radiance which makes us acquainted with the whole system of religion. It is not necessary for us to give up three or four years to the reading of ancient authors, in order to discover that God has established His Church with its mighty prerogatives on earth. We need not devote several years to convincing ourselves of the existence of a sacramental system. We have no necessity to come and study the historical monuments of Rome, in order to satisfy ourselves of the supremacy of Peter, and his successors. We have not to satisfy ourselves that the intercession of saints may be safely practised ; we have no need of studying point by point the system of religion; but the whole of it, under the light of faith, coheres, and is so equally lighted, that it is as instinctively clear to us as are the objects which we see by the light of the sun.

And it is like the light of the sun to us, for we enjoy its rays as it comes direct to our souls, or as it is reflected by earthly objects ; by it we walk ; in it we recruit ourselves ; under it we refresh ourselves ; we enjoy it, even as we do the air of heaven ; we bask in it ; we inhale it in our hearts ; we feel it in our inmost principles and souls. The whole of religion to us is so natural, so simple, that faith supersedes every other inward light; it often supersedes those intellectual lights which others use to relish the beauties that surround us. And we find ourselves in the full possession and understanding of that knowledge which to others has been the object of endless research.

The wise men, as soon as they entered the stable of Bethlehem, believed far more than when the priests of Jerusalem instructed them, or when the star first appeared. For the sight of the infant and the smile of His countenance, enkindled within them the light of faith; so that each was ready at once to die for that little which he had seen. And so those who have laboriously toiled, and found their way into the Catholic Church, experience a new sense developed within them,—a sense which as naturally takes in the spiritual light, as the eyes of those whom our Lord miraculously cured received the light of heaven. Thus they find themselves on a level with those who, from their infancy, have been nurtured in the Church : for faith, which is bestowed by the sacraments, enables them to receive, without doubting, every doctrine that is taught them.

And once believing, they for the first time adore. For adoration is not what may be considered the privilege or possession of any one who believes in God ; it does not consist in an act of worship, whereby we acknowledge Him as God, whereby we express our gratitude to Him, or entreat His mercies. It consists in an awful, yet sweetest feeling, that you are in the immediate vicinity, in very contact of God, yea, of God in the flesh, like as they felt of whom we read that they cast themselves down at His feet and worshipped Him. It consists in the annihilation of the very powers of the soul, which leads to the prostration of the body, its natural representative, on the very ground beneath Him. It consists in the assurance that His hand is extended over us, that His eye is fixed on us, that His heart darts rays of compassion and love to our hearts, as if they were beating the one on the other. Then we feel as St. John must have felt at the Last Supper ; or as St. Peter, when he begged Him to depart from him, a sinful man ; or as the wise kings, when they kissed His feet, an infant in His

mother's arms ; with a love which burnt up self in sacrifice, pure and unreserving.

This is, then, the course which God has always followed, from the first manifestation of the star to the
individual, until he is united to that mass of worshippers and believers who stand around His altar, without
distinction as to their arrival earlier or later, whether
they have come to venerate at the dawn of day, or not
until the setting of the sun.

Nothing now remains, my brethren, but to address
to you a few words of exhortation, that you study well
the lessons which our Gospel gives you, and to endeavour
to arrive at what it points out.

To you that have recently received, and are now in
possession of, this faith ; to you who have gone through
the course which I have inadequately described, who have
had to part with your homes and to turn your backs on
all that was dearest to you on earth ; to you who manfully
set out on the search, and, having crossed the shifting
desert of speculation, having wandered through many
regions of theory, came at last to what you deemed the
true Jerusalem, and were pushed aside, and left to go
on your way sorrowing ; to you who, having experienced
the pang of separation from whatever seemed holy, and
was dearest to your best affections, and having felt a
painful shudder at stooping over the threshold of a very
stable, now find yourselves associated with those whom
you had previously despised,—to you, as to ourselves, I
can only speak those splendid words of prayer which the
Church repeats in the Collect of this day, "that we, who
have known the only-begotten Son of God always by

faith, may be led forward on the further part of our pilgrimage, to attaining the contemplation of His sublime dignity in heaven."

You who have now your path before you clear and distinct,—who are no longer guided by the doubtful light of a little star, but walk in broad daylight, in the sunshine of the faith, which shows you every danger, and lays bare every snare, which shows you at every step the hand of your directing mother, guiding you to the altar of God,—you I exhort to go on rejoicing, till you obtain that reward which the Lord has in store for faithful combatants.

But you, who do not feel yourselves yet arrived at this place of rest, I bid you look around, and say if no star has appeared to you. Mark well its laws: it may be found in the secret reproaches of conscience, or in the discomforts of an unsettled faith ; it may be met in what you see, in that which you know of what God is working, by the great direction that He is giving so many good and learned men towards one point. But if you find that there is any slight proof—one least sign which tells you, that there must be something better than what you now enjoy, or even that there may be, then take into your hearts the courage of the wise men of the East, and set forth, with humble offerings, to seek your King. You will find Him infallibly here, where alone He is to be found. It will not, indeed, be your final resting-place ; you will not find a lasting and enduring city. No, you will have still to aim at another. You will go from your Jerusalem to Bethlehem ; but from Bethlehem your way lies to the Jerusalem that is above. You will rest for a

few moments here below ; you will receive peace of conscience through forgiveness of your sins ; you will be
refreshed with the bread of life :—and then you will rise
up again,—and join the pilgrims who have passed that
way before you, onward to heaven, forward to God.

SERMON III.

Our Saviour in the Temple.

LUKE, ii. 46, 47.

" And it came to pass, that after three days they found
Jesus in the Temple, sitting in the midst of the doctors,
hearing them and asking them questions. And all that heard
Him were astonished at His wisdom and His answers."

THE Gospel of to-day, from which I have drawn these
words, relates how our Saviour, when twelve years old,
was unwittingly left in Jerusalem by His blessed parents,
and after three days' fruitless search, found by them in
the Temple, conferring with the doctors of the Jewish
law.   With the exception of this incident, the inspired
records have concealed from our knowledge all the events
of His life between His return from Egypt and His final
manifestation unto Israel.   And if we inquire wherefore
this anecdote alone has been withdrawn from under so
close, and, doubtless, so mysterious a veil, I would suggest,
that the purpose of the Gospel-history is only to record
those events which belonged to our blessed Redeemer's
public life.   And though no doubt many lessons of pure
and holy wisdom were to be learned from His domestic
and retired life ; though His meekness to His companions, His cheerfulness in poverty and distress, His assi-
duity in the work of His humble calling, His kind charity

to the poor, His tender attention and dutifulness to His parents, must have appeared to us exceedingly beautiful, and most profitable, too, had we been shown how well they became, in Him, the winning age of childhood, yet were they directed rather to the edification of a few more favoured souls than to general instruction.

But on the occasion alone described in this Gospel, He Himself emerges from the obscure retirement which He had voluntarily chosen ; and, like His father David, who came forward, yet a stripling, to vanquish Goliath, and then returned to his homely life, as if to give earnest of the prowess he should display when called at manhood to greater endeavours, so did He come forth at this tender age to meet, and skirmish with, those whom He should later encounter with sterner and more fixed determination.

And, wherefore, we may still further ask, this interruption of His unpretending course, and this premature exposure to the jealousy of His future adversaries ? Not surely from any of that forwardness and petulance which not seldom disfigures that age, nor from the ambition of display which blemishes too often precocious genius, nor yet from the zealous desire to hasten His day of manifestation, which even a virtuous soul might well have felt; but rather that He might exhibit, while only in His own person He could, the strong contrast between the old dispensation and that which He came to establish ; inasmuch as, standing, a child, amidst the aged and hoary elders of the synagogue, He aptly brought together, and opposed to each other, the chosen types and emblems of the old and new covenants.

For, in the Jewish law, old age was the favorite symbol of wisdom and virtue, to which were to be paid all deference and submission. The young were commanded greatly to reverence and stand in awe of its slowly-gathered experience, and exhorted to imitate the gravity and sedateness of its deportment. In its books of wise counsels, natural want of grey hairs is always mentioned as a defect to be partially remedied by superior sense; while throughout the old legislation, the child's estate is hardly attended to, save as one of restraint and thraldom, so that he is scarcely raised a degree above a servant or a slave.

But the religion of Jesus has precisely reversed this standard and its emblem. It was to be the religion not of harsh restraint and severe authority, but of filial love and of brotherly love ; not of acquired wisdom, but of infused grace ; not of virtue with much toil hardly purchased, but of innocence preserved unstained; not of imposing and venerable exterior, but of free and fresh, natural and unpresuming perfection.

Hence, His apostles and followers were especially charged to preserve the virtues of His little ones, as being the dearest portion of God's flock. And, instead of the child being exhorted, as heretofore, to shape its conduct after the model of age, the old and experienced are commanded to copy the child, and imitate its artless virtue and unconscious innocence. And, as such a type of His own religion, and such a model for our study, doth Jesus appear before us this day, in mild and beautiful contrast with the sterner features of the aged religion, representing in Himself all the guileless sim-

E

plicity which was to be the characteristic of His own in
doctrine and in practice ; He stands as the child placed
in the midst of all, however venerable, however learned,
however holy, like unto whom must necessarily become,
whosoever wishes to enter into the kingdom of heaven.

Two-fold is this characteristic of simplicity in the child,
and therefore two-fold must it be in the Christian : as it
affects the understanding, and this is docility; as it affects
the heart, and this is innocence. Docility will direct his
belief, and innocence will sanctify his conduct.

Our blessed Saviour, after He had severely reproved
their folly who refused to listen to His words, thus
solemnly exclaimed in prayer : "I give thanks to thee, O
Father, Lord of heaven and of earth, because thou hast
hid these things from the wise and prudent ones, and
hast revealed them to little ones. Yea, Father, for so it
hath seemed good in thy sight." (Matt. xi. 25.)

What, my brethren, mean these awful words ? What
is faith (some would say) but a strong conviction which is
the offspring of knowledge; and is not this the acquisition
of the wise and of the prudent? Shall not the philosopher,
whose mind has been trained by long exercise to habits
of deep thought, dive into the abyss of truth more easily,
and bring up thence its hidden treasures more securely,
than the dull illiterate rustic, who can scarcely raise his
thoughts above the clod which he tills ? Shall not the
subtile jurist, accustomed to weigh the force of evidence,
and the justice of legal decisions, more fully apprehend,
and more highly value, the beauty and perfection of the
Divine law, than the unlettered artisan, who has never
even heard of the principles whereby such investigations

are ruled? At least, shall not the theologian, versed in the knowledge of sacred Scripture, and in the maxims of ecclesiastical antiquity, more accurately penetrate, and more deeply reverence the holy dogmas and dispensations of religion, than a foolish, unsteady, unreflecting child?

No, my brethren, not one of them, except inasmuch as, scorning his dear-bought acquirements, he brings his reason to the same standard of docility as characterises that child. For, so far from faith being like what we call knowledge, it is both in its objects and its mode of acquisition every way very different. Our study and knowledge here below is but that of the perpetual captive, who scans and explores the walls of his prison cell. To beguile the time, he will, perhaps, oftentimes measure their height and breadth and massive proportions; and he will calculate the hours of his nightly darkness and of his daily twilight; or he will watch in their toil or their sportiveness the insects that share with him his narrow abode; or he will sometimes be glad to hear consolation from some one whose chain sighs echo to his own. He will amuse himself, perchance, awhile, by many ingenious devices and new arrangements, that bear a mocking semblance of novelty and variety. Then he has, too, his sculptured monuments and written records to study, rudely carved upon the walls around him; their annals who have inhabited his prison-house before him, the lords of the dungeon, who thought their names and deeds worth inscribing for their successors to decipher. And after these occupations his head, too, may ache, like any philosopher's, and his eye become dimmed, and his face look pale, and his limbs be languid. Alas, poor captive!

could thy eye but for one moment pierce the low-browed vaults of thy bondage-house, and plunge with the dove into the deep blue ocean of heaven above thee,—couldst thou but for one instant gaze, even at the risk of being dazzled, upon that glorious throne of brightness, whose sidelong ray lights up, and cheers, even thy sorrowful dwelling, or commune with those happier beings who inhale to the full its warmth and radiance, how would that one glance, no longer in imagination but in reality, be worth all the lonely and wearisome lessons of thy captive hours! and although the fetters might still gripe thy limbs, and the iron of captivity still be fixed in thy soul, thou wouldst no longer feel bowed by the weight of the one, or tortured by the other's smart.

Now, my brethren, as these vain beguilements of a prisoned life is human knowledge, and such as that glance would be, is heavenly faith. After you have studied nature in its grandest or minutest parts; after you have condensed into one small mass the experience and wisdom of ages, you have but studied, and learnt at much cost, the qualities and prerogatives of your place of durance; and it is only by plausible conjecture, or delusive fancy, that you can pass beyond its bounds. But faith comes in by her own power and energy to our relief, and makes a bright light of heaven to shine around our place of thral-dom; and not so content, strikes our side, bidding us to arise and gird our garments around us, and shake off our fetters, and shows us through the iron gate, that will open as we approach—the holy and heavenly Jerusalem—the place of our true abode. For, "Faith is the foundation of things to be hoped for : the demonstration of things not appearing." (Heb. xii. 1.)

Faith, therefore, belongs in its objects to another sphere of things from knowledge, and, consequently, is not to be acquired by the same means ; the one is a bread prepared and made by the hands of man, the other a manna which comes down to us from heaven. Knowledge is the pro-gress of the understanding, as it marches forward erect, panting and proud, on its toilsome path: faith is its breath-less prostration before the wisdom of God. In it, reason, purely passive, must be cast on the ground, like Gideon's fleece, to drink in the soft calm dew which falls unheard from heaven, and penetrates and fills, and aliments it thoroughly with its celestial principle. Or rather the entire soul lies as earth without water before God, dilating its wide capacity, rending itself open on every side, and distending every pore, till it draws in, with deep thirsty draughts, the life-giving wisdom which He rains upon it, and mingling its whole being with the pure element descending from above. It is as of old, when the Divine Majesty was to be revealed to the prophet's spirit ; it is only with our heads closely veiled, and our foreheads buried in the dust, and our entire frame in still and mo-tionless adoration, that we shall abide the approach and passage of the awful revelation ; yea, and even when gladder visions of joy and salvation are displayed, as on Mount Thabor, we must sink upon the ground with the chosen three, nor dare to raise our heads, to pry too curiously into the light and voice which are communicated to us.

Such, my dear brethren, is faith in its acquisition : it

is the union of the soul's intellectual powers with the
wisdom of God, just as charity is of its affections with
His goodness ; it is the obedience of the understanding,
it is the humility of reason.

Hence is a child-like docility the principal disposition
to obtain and to keep it. So soon as the child Samuel
answered the voice he had twice heard, by saying " Speak
O Lord, for thy servant heareth," (1 Reg. iii. 10) the
mysteries of God's counsels were laid open to him. So
whoever, becoming a child like him, shall call out in like
words, may well hope the same favour, if he happen to
be in a state of ignorance or delusion.

And in this docility of the youthful prophet we see exemplified its principal manifestation—prayer. Whoever
feels that his faith is weak or insecure, whoever is conscious of uneasiness in his belief on any point, of a desire
to inquire more deeply into doctrines which he has been
formerly taught to despise, or of a certain habitual uneasiness and restlessness of mind, such as accompany the
forebodings of coming evil, though we know not for what
cause, let such a one turn himself to God, and entreat
Him, with all earnestness and humility, to lay open unto
him His ways, and to guide him along them, and assuredly
he will thereby profit more, and learn more, and receive
more sure directions, than by all his study and inquiry.

Directly opposed to this youthful docility is every system which introduces pride or self-confidence among the
ingredients of faith. The idea that our creed must be
the production of our own genius,—that because we are
gifted with better abilities, or have received superior education, our religion must be of a more enlightened order

than others can hold, who are less highly accomplished,—
that in short we must, by our individual study, decide
what we will believe and what we will reject : all such
principles as these are in direct opposition to the symbol
of true Christianity : you become not as a child when
you reason thus, and therefore you enter not thus into
the kingdom of heaven.

And might not I say, that to speak of each one's
having to make out by study his own creed, is in reason
as absurd as to speak of each one's having to arrange, in
like manner, his own system of astronomy ?   The laws
which regulate the moral world are not less fixed than
those which govern the visible ; only one system can be
true in either ; and whoever undertakes to fabricate that
one by his own unaided skill will assuredly fail.

No less opposed to the docility of Christian faith is all
obstinacy and pertinacity in clinging to our own opinions,
the moment they have been satisfactorily confuted ; all
unchristian heat and acrimony, and uncharitableness in
religious disputation ; all lurking desire, in fine, that
we may triumph and not the truth.   For, how do you
imagine to yourselves the blessed Child, of whom this
day's Gospel speaks, to have looked and conversed among
the Jewish doctors ?   Do you fancy Him a lively, ready,
forward boy, with keen, restless eye, and unsteady gait,
eagerly watching the moment when He could thrust in His
remarks, ever studying, by perplexing questions, to confound, or by smart repartee, to shame, the venerable elders
who surrounded Him ? For my part, I would rather represent Him as a sweet and gentle and bashful child, whose
downcast looks and clear open brow, and mild calm

features, should appear to the bystanders to cover such a
heaven of innocence, and such an abyss of wisdom, as
neither child nor sage had ever before singly, nor angel
unitedly, possessed.   And I would suppose Him listening
to their discourses in modest silence, and with an air of
respectful deference, putting His questions as one who
deeply venerated the authority He interrogated ; teaching
those around Him as one who only learnt, and astonishing
all by the art with which He in reality scattered flowers of
heavenly wisdom, while He appeared only to be gathering
those which were of earth.   Such, then, is the Christian's
type who seeks for religious wisdom, that is *faith*.   He
must be as a child; and the child Jesus hath been pleased,
in this instance, to stand in person as his model.

   In fine, this having been given us as the type of Christ's
religion, it may often serve many to correct the severe
judgments they are tempted to pronounce on others'
practises and conduct.   Are your eyes unused to see marks
of respect and devotion shown to religious representations,
or to material objects consecrated by holy recollections ;
and does the practice, as you witness it here,* strike you
as offensive to God ?   Why, study how a child shows
its affection to those whom it loves, and see if it does not
treasure up any little record of their kindness, and lavish
its affections upon their portraits and images.   Wherefore, they who do these things thereby become as little
children, rather than you who reprove them.

   Are your ears sometimes shocked by the warm and
enthusiastic forms of supplication which you hear, and do
you feel tempted to pronounce, when you see such un-

---

* In Rome.

checked outbreaks of devotional feeling in the poor and
simple, that there is too much of passion and emotion in
their religion, and too little conviction and reason? I
will only ask you, are you then offended when you hear
the child express its love in the artless poetry of passion,
and pour out its feelings warm and rich as they flow from
its unspoiled heart ; or can you think that He who gave
us the child as the symbol of the Christian's belief, wished
thereby to denote that intellect and not feeling, reasoning
and not rather emotion, was to be its principle, its guide,
its security, and its very soul ?

Are you scandalised, perchance, at the apparent levity
which this people seems sometimes to mingle with its
most serious duties,—at the absence of those demure looks
and that formal exterior, which in our colder north is considered essential to piety, or at the cheerful gaiety which
makes their Lord's Day a day of mental as well as bodily
rest ? Go and preach to the child, that, when rejoicing
before its parent, it must look sad and mournful ; and
when you shall have succeeded in plucking from its young
heart, in stripping from its smiling features, the quality
which makes its age the most amiable, then may you try
to convince the natives of the golden south, that all the
natural buoyancy of their disposition is to be repressed,
yea, cut out and seared by religion. Take the child once
more as your model, and putting aside all intentional
irreverence and neglect, see whose practice in other
respects comes nearest to its ; and that, be you assured,
cannot be unpleasing to God.

Much more instruction might be drawn from the consideration of this attribute of docility, which has been

shown to be a characteristic of the Christian's faith ; but I must hasten to a few brief remarks upon the second quality of our model, which is innocence. The great advantage of the standard proposed by the New Law over that of the Old is, that we have all of us experience, to guide us to its attainment. The wisdom and gravity of age, which in the elder dispensation was to be studied and copied by the young, these had never possessed ; nor had they, consequently, any guidance of internal feeling to lead them to its acquisition. But we have all been children ; we have all passed through that state of pure innocence ; and I will venture to say, that no one looks back upon that spring of his life without a soft regret, that he should not have fixed any of its charming traits in his character, before they passed away for ever. You must become as little children if you wish to enter the kingdom of heaven ; that is, study only what you your- selves were, and strive to your utmost to become so once more ; and, without fail, you shall be saved.

You were then mild, and courteous, and affable, to all. You asked not after men's opinions, or party, or rank ; but Nature guided you, by her own instincts, to judge of what was amiable and virtuous, and taught you to love and esteem it wherever found; and, at the same time, to despise no one, to hate no one, to treat no one ill.

You were then obedient to all whom God had placed over you, you felt towards them respect and affection; you dreamt not of schemes to overthrow or diminish their authority; you received their instructions with attention; you submitted to their correction without resentment. And how beseeming the character of the child this con-

duct is, our blessed Saviour was careful to show us in
this day's Gospel, which concludes by telling us that " He
went to Nazareth with His parents, and was subject to
them."

You were then unambitious, content with the lot which
Providence had given you; for, as St. Chrysostom remarks,
if you should present before a child on one side a queen
clothed in embroidered robes and bearing a jewelled
crown, and on the other its mother clad in tattered
raiment, it would remain undazzled and unseduced ; but,
following the voice of Nature, cast its arms round its
parent's neck, and mock at the allurements of ambition.

You were then, too, unsolicitous about the future and
about the world, enjoying the simple innocent pleasures
which the present afforded you, knowing that there was
a parent who ever thought of you, and took care that all
was provided for you at the proper season.

You were sincere, open and unsuspicious; you spoke
your sentiments with artless candour, respecting not the
person of man ; you knew not that the truth was to be
studiously concealed or disguised; you laid open your
wants and little sufferings whenever you thought you
might obtain assistance ; you laughed and you wept as
Nature's impulse taught you.

You were pure and undefiled in heart, in desire, in
affection, and in thought ; you had not even heard of
that monster-vice which, when once it has fastened its fangs
in its victim, and cast round his loins its fiery chain, drags
him unresisting, through storms of passion, into the
bottomless abyss.

Your virtue then, as your bodily health, was not the

result of unremitting attention, and of repeated recoveries, but consisted in the unconsciousness of disorder,
the fearlessness of any danger, unattended by any effort
or precaution. Nature, restored by grace to something
of its primæval purity, created round you a paradise for
its preservation, a paradise of delight, and cheerfulness,
and joy, where every thought was as a new flower
springing fresh into instant bloom, and every wish was
a tempting fruit which might be plucked without danger.
And love was the fountain in its centre which you seemed
ever to drink,—love towards all who associated with you,
to all who caressed you, to all who served you, to all
who looked upon you ; and, breaking through even these
bounds, its waters parted, and diffused your kindliness
and affectionateness even over the irrational and inani-
mate objects of creation. And the gold and precious stones
of that land were rich ; a blessing there was which bound
your head as with a diadem over which angels watched
as you reposed; graces which made your soul more bright
and precious before God than the golden ark in His
tabernacle ; a treasure of eternal promises sealed up with
His own signet in your bosom, which the powers of evil
repined at and envied. Such were you once: alas! what
are you now ? You have since tasted of the tree of
knowledge of good and evil, and its fruit, too, fell from
your hand into that beautiful fountain, like the bitter
star which St. John saw ; and it is well if only a third
part of its sweet waters have been turned into wormwood.
(Apoc. viii. 11.) How has the unruffled peace of innocence been dashed from your soul by the wild broad
sweep of boisterous passion ? How hath " your silver

been changed into dross, and your wine been mingled with water ?" (Is. i. 22.) I will leave to each one's conscience to draw his portrait, and hang it by the one I have faintly sketched, and then say if in the two he recognizes the same original. And yet, certain as is the infallible word of truth, so certain it is, that only the first resembles him who shall enter into the kingdom of heaven.

What then remains, but that you mould yourself anew upon the model which memory holds up before you. At every year of your life you remove a step further from that happy age : God grant that you depart not as much from its happy disposition. Why is our Saviour's age so carefully recorded in this day's Gospel, and at other great periods of His life, except to teach us to keep count of our years, and be able to remember them by some consoling record of signal virtue. But, alas ! can we do so ? Shall we, for instance, remember the year which has just elapsed by any new step in virtue and grace, which may refresh and comfort us when summoned to depart ? Look back upon it and see before it is too late; for perhaps you have already begun to forget it. You have flung it away from you, like the stone which the wayfarer used to throw from habit upon Absalom's grave, without pausing to reflect on the odious corruption it covered deeper from his sight. It passed by just as did its fellows before it ; its garb was motley as the fool's, chequered alternately with good and evil, though I should marvel much if the darker hues did not prevail. In it you laughed, and you sighed ; you feasted for those who came into the world, and you put on mourning-weeds for those who left it ;

you transgressed and you repented, you made resolutions
and you broke them, you had quarrels and reconciliations,
illnesses and recoveries ; you did, I trust, much that was
virtuous and good ; and very much we all did that was
evil and sinful before God.   But as the serpent at its
annual term glides out of its speckled coil, or as the bird,
when its yearly period comes, shakes off its variegated
plumage, and scatters it to the winds of heaven, so have
we cast off and left behind us, as far as we could, the
state and habit of the past year, retaining no more accurate recollection thereof, than we do of the lights and
shadows which played on yesterday's landscape.   But
yet every fragment of your past condition has been
carefully picked up as it dropped carelessly from you,
and nicely joined together and treasured up, as a record
of what you have been and what you have done.

How will you be dismayed, when one day this shall be
produced and unrolled as a huge sheet before you, where
you shall see registered how every month, every day,
every hour, yea every minute hath been passed; how many
have been given to indolence, how many to dissipation,
how many to transgression, how many to vice, and how
few to God.   And then, too, you shall see all those with
whom you have associated during this term, all who have
shared in your varied fortune,—the many who laughed
and the few who wept with you, yea and they too who
have preached to you, arrayed and sworn as witnesses
against you.   Their course has resembled the frantic
dance of those Grecian matrons who, joined hand in
hand, whirled round, as they moaned the death-song on
the mountain's brow, so that whoever at each revolution

came to the edge, loosened her grasp and fell into the
abyss below. But the circle reclosed and the dance continued.

Alas ! who fell from our circle in this its last revolution ? We have forgotten him, perhaps : be it so ;
but there is to be some victim in each round ; some one's
turn is approaching, some one is bounding towards the
precipice, perhaps you, perhaps I,—it may be only one,
but oh ! let us all be forewarned and prepared. And how ?
Become as little children, and return to that innocence
which you have lost ; for to sum up in the appropriate
words of St. Peter : "this is the word which hath been
preached unto you. Wherefore, laying aside all malice,
all guile, and dissimulations, and envies, and all detrac-
tions, as new-born babes, desire the rational milk without
guile ; that thereby ye may grow unto salvation." (1 Pet.
i. 25 ; ii. 1, 2.)

SERMON IV.

The Holy Name of Jesus.

St. Luke, ii. 21.

" His name was called Jesus, which was called by the Angel
before He was conceived in the womb."

It is not uncommon, nor I think unwise, my brethren,
for those who undertake what seems beyond their
strength, to shelter themselves under the protection of
some great name, by the authority of which they may
ensure success. It was thus that, a few centuries ago, in
times of turbulence and oppression, the feeble would put
on the cognizance of some powerful lord, as whose vassal
they would not fear to repel the attempts of an unjust
and stronger aggressor. It is thus that, even at the
present day, the obscure scholar hopes to win some more
partial favour, if he can prefix to his labours the name of
any one, whose reputation and acknowledged merit may
give consideration to his humble efforts. Now, by the
blessing of God, as I think, it has this day befallen me to
open our annual course of instructions, in the full
consciousness of inability and unworthiness, but under
the sanction of that Name, besides which there is none
other on earth given to men whereby they may be saved.
For you are not ignorant, brethren, that on this day the
Holy Catholic Church commemorates the blessed and

adorable Name of Jesus. Amidst the joyful festivals of our Lord's Nativity, the mysteries of this holy Name could not be forgotten. But so many and so various have been our motives for joy, that we scarcely have had time, during their celebration, to pause upon this. Even on the first day of the year, on occasion of our Lord's Circumcision, there were too many other mysteries of faith and love, to allow the mind's dwelling as it should upon the tender glories of the Name then given. Worthily, then, has there been allotted to it its own proper festival; for it is a Name to us full of delightful suggestions,—one that will amply repay the devout meditations of our hearts.

But on this occasion it presents itself in connection with the circumstances under which you are addressed. It is impossible to overlook the consideration that we are here assembled in the Name of this our Lord : and that for a purpose which can have no virtue if performed not in His Name. In this Name I summon you to hear the word of God ; under this I mean to seek protection and virtue for my feeble efforts. Of old, when this city (Rome) was the abode of every evil passion, they who called themselves clients of patrons, wicked as themselves, would, under the sanction of their name, run into every excess of violence and injustice, and foul the name, which they affected to honour, with reproach and public infamy. But we, blessed be God, have chosen for the name to be invoked upon us, one which can only be the symbol of peace, and charity, and joy. They who reverence that Name must reverence His laws who bore it ; they who love it, must love the boundless treasures of benevolence, mercy, and charity, which it records.

F

Let us, then, prepare our hearts this day for the receiving of His law when declared to us, and for the practice of His commandments; by considering the force they must derive from the holy Name that sanctions them,—a name of mighty power with Him who proclaims it, a name of boundless sweetness to those that learn it.

When God had decreed to achieve the wonderful deliverance of His people from the Egyptian yoke, the first step which He chose towards its accomplishment, was revealing to them a name, whereby they should know Him, and worship Him as their deliverer. Moses, in fact, asked Him by what name he should declare Him to the people of Israel, when he communicated to them his commission. Then, "God said to Moses, I AM WHO AM. . . . This is my name for ever, and this is my memorial unto all generations." (Exod. iii. 14.) And afterwards He reappeared to the holy law-giver, and said to him, "I am the Lord, that appeared to Abraham, to Isaac, and to Jacob, by the name of God Almighty; and my name Adonai" (or Jehovah) "I did not show them." (vi. 3.)

God then began His first work of deliverance by the assumption of a new name, unknown to those who had not witnessed His salvation. And that Name was a name of power. Yes, a name of terrible power. Not by it were the blind made to see, but darkness such as might be felt with the hand, was brought over the entire land of Egypt. Not by it were the lepers cleansed, but foul ulcers and sores were brought to defile and disfigure the bodies of its inhabitants. Not by it were the sons of widows and the friends of the poor restored to life, but all the first-born of Egypt, from the heir of Pharaoh who sat with his father on his throne, to the eldest son of his meanest subject, were struck in one night with death. Such was the power of this delivering Name,—a power to make the proud and obstinate quail, to scourge kingdoms, and to destroy their princes,—a power of angry might and avenging sway.

And such it ever continued, even to those in whose favour its power was exerted. It resembled, in fact, the protection of the cloud that guided them through the desert, which, whether by · day with its overhanging shadow, or by night with the red glare of its fiery pillar, must have excited feelings of awe and terror, rather than of love. So great, in fact, was the fearful reverence paid this dread Name of God, that it ceased to be ever uttered until its true pronunciation was completely lost. And, moreover, such is the measure of power attributed by the Jewish teachers to this now ineffable Name of God, that they scruple not to assert, that whosoever should discover its true sound, and according to this utter it, would thereby perform any work however wonderful, and find no miracle too great.

But leaving aside these opinions, which, as of later growth, deserve not as much notice, it is sufficiently obvious how through the sacred Scriptures the Name of God becomes the symbol of Himself, so that to it all power is attributed which to Him belongs. It is the *Name* of the Lord which men are invited to bless ; it is by calling on His *Name* that we shall be saved from our enemies ; it is in His *Name* that we put our trust, when others confide in chariots and in horses; His *Name* is holy and terrible, or glorious and pleasant. In the Name of

God victories are gained, and prophecies spoken, and the evil threatened, and the perverse punished, and the good encouraged, and the perfect rewarded. It receives the homage due to God, for it is the representative of God : it is as God Himself; spoken by the lips, it is to our hearing what were to the eye the angels that appeared to Lot or Abraham, or the burning bush of Horeb to Moses, or the dove to John,—a sensible image of Him, whose invisible nature can only be manifested through such imperfect symbols.

When the covenant of new and perfect redemption was made, a new name was requisite to inaugurate it; and it needed to be, even more than the former, a name of power. For it was not any longer a bondage under man that was to be destroyed, but slavery to the powers of darkness and of wicked might. They were not chains of iron or bolts of brass which were to be broken insunder, but the snare of death and the bonds of hell, which had encompassed and straitened us on every side. We were not merely condemned by an earthly tyrant, to make bricks without straw, but we were deeply fixed in "the mire of dregs," as the Psalmist expresses it (**xxxix.** 3, and lxviii. 15); that is, in the filthy corruption of vicious desires ; or, as Ezekiel describes the foolish devices of the wicked, we were as "a people that buildeth up a wall, and daubs it with clay in which there is no straw." (xiii. 10.) So much as spiritual wretchedness is deep beyond the bodily, so much stronger was the power required to drag us from the abyss.

Now, to do this was the great work of our salvation, and He who came to accomplish it was to bear, as in the former deliverance, a name of power. And that name, as brought down from heaven by an archangel to Mary, as communicated by an angel to Joseph, and as solemnly given eight days after His birth, by a priest, was the Name of JESUS.

If, during His life, He concealed the glorious might of His Name; if He bore it meekly as another might have done, and as though it but formed a name to distinguish Him among the children of His people, who shall thereat wonder, seeing how He shrouded from the eyes of men the fulness of the Godhead that resided in Him, and reserved, for a later period, the completer manifestation of His true character? For no sooner had His prerogatives as the Saviour of man been finally asserted, by His triumph over death, and His return to the right hand of His Father, than the "Name which is above all names" became, in the hands of His apostles, the great instrument of all their power.

There are few incidents in the apostolic annals more beautiful and interesting to a loving Christian, than the first public miracle after the Paraclete's descent. It was wrought, as you well know, upon the lame man at the *Beautiful* gate of the Temple, by Peter and John, when they entered it to pray. I know not whether, humanly speaking, we can fully realise their feelings, I mean apart from the consciousness of power which they had just received. During their divine Master's life, they had occasionally failed in their attempts to work miracles. Now they are alone, the entire cause is in their hands; any ill success on their parts will be ruinous to it, for they cannot now fall back upon the certain might of Him

who sent them. We might have supposed some slight
fluttering of the heart, some creeping anxiety coming over
the mind, as they decided upon putting the power of their
Saviour's Name to a great public test. But no; mark the
calm decision, the unwavering confidence with which they
proceed. The cripple asked them, as he did every passer-by,
for an alms. " But Peter, with John, fastening his eyes
upon him, said : Look upon us. But he looked earnestly
upon them, hoping that he should receive something of
them. But Peter said : Silver and gold I have not, but
what I have I give thee. In the Name of Jesus Christ of
Nazareth, arise and walk. And taking him by the right
hand, he lifted him up, and forthwith his feet and soles
received strength. And he leaping up, stood and walked."
(Acts, iii. 4–8.) It was in virtue of no personal power,
that the holy apostles expected or claimed this dominion
over Nature, as spoilt by the fall of man ; it was the
virtue of His Name who had conquered sin, and plucked
out the sting of death, that wrought through their hands.

So necessary did some such sanction appear to the very
priests, that when they had apprehended the two apostles
and placed them in the midst of them, they asked them
" by what power, or *by what name*, have you done this ?"
Peter, filled with the Holy Ghost, replies, that " by the
Name of Jesus Christ of Nazareth," whom they had
crucified, even by Him that man stood there before them
whole. Then they " charged them not to speak at all,
nor to teach in the Name of Jesus." But when they had
been let go, and returned to the assembly of the faithful,
they lifted up their voices in one unanimous magnificent
prayer, concluding with these words—" And now, Lord,

behold their threatenings, and grant unto Thy servants that, with all confidence, they may speak Thy word, by stretching forth Thy hand to cures, and signs, and wonders, to be done by the Name of Thy holy Son Jesus." (Acts, iv.)

And what was this first public triumph of that glorious Name, but only the first of a long series of victories over earth and hell? Yet, terrible as it was to those leagued powers of evil, it was ever wielded for the benefit of men. It was as a healing balm for the sick and the halt; they were anointed in this Name, and were raised up from their infirmity. "The Lord Jesus Christ healeth thee," said Peter to Eneas; "and immediately he arose" from his eight years' illness. (Acts, ix. 34.) It was a savour of life to the dead in Christ, whom it raised, when expedient for them, from the grave. It was, moreover, a bright and burning light to them that sat in darkness. It overthrew the dominion of Satan; it destroyed the empire of sin; it brought forth fruits of holiness, and diffused over earth the blessings of heaven. Soon did it become "great among the Gentiles, from the rising of the sun to the going down of the same." (Mal. i. 11.) As the first discoverers of unknown lands, as the conquerors of hostile countries solemnly pronounce that they take possession thereof in the name of the sovereign who commissioned them; so did the twelve, whether explorers of the distant seats of barbarism, beyond the flight of the Roman eagles, or as valiant warriors against the active resistance of worldly principalities, register their discoveries and settle their conquests in no other name than that of the Lord Jesus.

Often was the world distracted by the rival claims of
pretenders to the empire ; often was province in arms
against province, through the wide extent of Roman
domination ; often was the empire itself engaged in cruel
war with the nations without its pale : still there was
one empire, vast, interminable, and indivisible, ruled in
peace over all the world, Greek and barbarian.   The
dominion of Jesus was undisturbed by rivalry and
undistracted by conflict.   It could allow no competition,
it could fear no jealousy among its subjects.   One Name
was called upon by them all ; and it was a name that
drew from all an undivided homage.

So secure were the early Christians of its power, that
they hesitated not to attribute to it an efficacy, so to
speak, sacramental—that is, a virtue independent of all
peculiar privilege in the individual who employed it.
They were not afraid of incurring the guilt of superstition, by believing its very sound to possess a resistless
influence over the powers of darkness.   Saint Justin, in
his Apology, only fifty years after the death of Christ,
appeals for a testimony of the truth of His religion to the
acknowledged fact, that any Christian, by pronouncing
the Name of Jesus, could expel the evil spirit from any one
possessed by him.   And Tertullian goes even as far as to
challenge the heathens to the experiment, with the condition that if any Christian failed in it, they might
instantly put him to death.

But now, alas ! my brethren, the first fervour of faith
has long waxed cold, and with it have been withdrawn the
wonderful prerogatives it had obtained and secured.   We,
the servants of Christ, may speak His word with all confi-

dence in His Name, but the cures, and signs, and wonders, which may ensue by the stretching forth of His hand, will be in the inward soul, not upon the outward flesh. And in whose name else can I, or any other that shall fill this place, address you ? In what other name were we admitted into His ministry, in what other name have we received commission to the flock of Christ, if not in His, the shepherd's ? In His Name alone are the sacraments of life administered to you ; in His Name alone is the adorable Sacrifice of His Body and Blood offered by us ; in His Name alone we can admonish you and threaten you, upbraid and encourage you, forgive you or retain you in your bonds. When the prophets spoke of old, they contented themselves with the simple preface, " thus saith the Lord of Hosts." Seldom was it a prologue to words of peace or comfort, but rather to menaces and warnings, and woes. And yet they that heard them looked not on the meanness of the speakers, but considered the majesty of the God who sent them, and they rent their garments before them, and humbled their souls with fasting, and covered their bodies with sackcloth and ashes, and did penance.

And when the minister of the New Law stands before you saying : " Thus saith the Lord Jesus," shall there be less heed taken of his words, because he speaketh in the name of One who is gracious and full of mercy, and comes to communicate " thoughts of peace and not of affliction"? No. Did we come before you in our own names, and speak to you "of justice and chastity, and of the judgment to come," you might, like Felix, send us back and say, " For this time go thy way." (Acts, xxiv. 24.) Did

we, as of ourselves, preach to you the resurrection of the
dead, ye might, as they of Athens, mock us to scorn.
(xvii. 32.) If, in fine, we presumed to command you to
be continent and chaste, meek and forgiving, penitent and
humble, to distribute your goods to the poor, or to afflict
your bodies by fasting, you might, perhaps, resent our
interference with the concerns of your lives, and chide us,
not unreasonably, for exacting duties hard and disagree-
able. But when we speak unto you these things by the
power and in the Name of Him who is King of your souls
and Master of your being,—when we claim from you
docility and obedience for Him whose livery we bear and
whose heralds we are, refuse ye at your peril to receive
our words, and honour our commission.

But, good God, what do I say? Shall I misdoubt me
of the power and virtue of the Name of Thy beloved Son,
—of that Name, at the sound whereof "every knee shall
bow, of things in heaven, of things on earth, and of things
under the earth"? Shall I fear that the neck of man
redeemed, will be more inflexible than the knees of Thy
vanquished enemies, and refuse to take up Thy gentle
yoke? Shall I apprehend that the soul of the captive,
who hath been ransomed by the power of this Name, will
adore and love it less than the angels, to whom it brought
no tidings of salvation?

No, my brethren, from you we hope for better things.
For know you not that we are engaged together in a holy
warfare, for which we have no other strength than that of
this holy Name? In "a wrestling, not against flesh and
blood, but against principalities and powers, against the
rulers of the world of this darkness, against the spirits of

wickedness in high places"? (Ephes. vi. 12.) And if you fight not under the Name of the God of Jacob, how shall you prevail? Anciently when armies rushed to battle, a name was put into the mouth of each, as a watchword and cheering symbol of the cause in which they struggled. Glad was the heart of the commander, and flushed with confidence of victory, when one unanimous shout of the name of their king or their patron rung clear and joyous from his men, as they rushed to the onslaught, and drowned the feeble response of the rival host. And so, in the Name of Jesus, will we strike boldly at our spiritual foes; and bravely will we sound it forth together, to the terror and discomfiture of hell, and the overthrow of its might.

It is the Name of ten thousand battles, and of countless victories. It echoed of old through the vaulted prisons of this city, and filled the heart of the confessor with courageous joy. It broke from the martyr's lips, when Nature could no longer brook silence, and was as "oil poured out" upon his wounds. It was the music of the anchorite, when in the depths of the desert the powers of darkness broke loose upon him: and it dissipated his temptation. And so it shall be the signal of our combat, the watchword of our ranks. See, it is written in broad letters upon the standard we have followed, "Jesus of Nazareth, King of the Jews." Shame and confusion to the dastard who deserts his banner, or refuses to follow where that Name leads! Victory and glory to the chosen ones, who shall confide in its power, and combat in its cause!

"Out of the strong," said Samson, in proposing his

riddle to the Philistines, "out of the strong came forth sweetness." "What," they replied, in solving it, "is stronger than the lion, and what is sweeter than honey?" (Jud. xiv. 14, 18.) Surely, we may reply, "His Name, who, as the lion of the tribe of Juda, hath prevailed over death and hell, and hath been found worthy to open the book and loosen its seals: and who yet in proposing to us its precepts, makes them to us sweeter than honey and the honey-comb."

It would seem to have been a special privilege of patriarchal foresight, to understand when a child was born what character it should bear through life, and to name it accordingly. Thus was Noah so named by Lamech, because he said : "This same shall comfort us from the works and labours of our hands, on the earth which God hath cursed." (Gen. v. 29.) When the Saviour of mankind received from God himself a name, it could not fail to be one descriptive of His high and gracious office; and the Name of Jesus doth, in truth, signify a saviour. In this its meaning is treasured up its sweetness. It is a name as pregnant with merciful recollections, with motives of gratitude, with assurances of hope, with heavenly comfort, and with causes of joy, as to be the abridgment, as it were, and essence of whatever religion has brought of blessing down from heaven.

Who does not know what choicest delicacies of feeling may be condensed within the small compass of a little name? How the name of *home* will bring to the exile's heart more ideas than a volume of eloquent description? How the title of child or parent, wife or sister, will stir the affections of a bereaved survivor? And in this Name

of Jesus, we shall find it to be so, if we duly meditate
upon it. It is the name more especially of His infancy,
and the name of His passion. During the important, but
to us less dear, interval of His life, while engaged in the
task of preaching His doctrines, men addressed Him as
Rabbi, or Master; He was saluted with titles of well-
deserved respect.

But while yet a child, and when abandoned by human
favour to the ignominy of the cross, we know Him by no
name, we read of Him in the Gospel by no name, but that
of Jesus. And those surely are the two portions of His
life wherein principally he proposes Himself as the object
of our love. No ; think of Him by that Name, and you
cannot present Him to your imagination as an object of
awe or dread, as just or terrible. He smiles upon you
as an infant in the arms of His maiden mother; He seems
to stretch forth to you His little hands from the manger
of Bethlehem ; you see Him reposing, on the way to
Egypt, amidst His blessed family ; or you think of Him
lost to His parents, and found again by them in the
Temple. Through all these scenes, what can you do less
than love Him,—the God-like child that bears the griev-
ances of unnecessary infancy for love of you. During
all this time He answered to no other name than that of
Jesus,—a Name rendered to us doubly sweet by the lips
of her who first addressed it to Him.

As you will think on His Name in hours of deeper
meditation and repentance ; and straightways you shall
see Him transformed into the man of sorrows, the bearer
of our griefs. You shall see Him cast upon the ground
in the prayer of agony, swallowed up in mortal anguish;

you shall follow Him through steps too painful to be here rehearsed, to the great sacrifice of Calvary. When you behold Him there stretched upon His cross, and expiring in cruel torment, you will ask of any who stand gazing upon Him, by what name they know Him, and all will answer, "by the Name written above His head, 'Jesus of Nazareth.'" No other name will suit Him in these passages of His life but this. We cannot bring ourselves to call Him here our Lord, our Messias, the Christ, our Teacher. They are but cold and formal titles of honour, when given to Him at Bethlehem or on Calvary. One name alone, the adorable Name of Jesus, satisfies the desires of our heart, and utters in a breath its accumulated feelings. Hence, the Seraph of Assisium, as St. Francis has been called, than whom no other on earth ever more closely imitated or resembled, as far as man may, the Son of God, ever cherished with peculiar devotion the early infancy and the passion of Jesus, and by a natural consequence, never, as St. Bonaventure tells us, heard that sacred Name pronounced, but a bright glow of gratitude and delight diffused itself over his countenance.

St. Bernard, too, the warmth of whose devout outbreaks the coldness of our age would almost deem extravagant, overflows with the most affectionate enthusiasm when he comments on this blessed Name. It was, as he says, to him, "honey in the mouth, music to the ear, and jubilee in the heart." "If thou writest, I find no relish in it unless I read there Jesus. If thou discoursest, it hath no savour for me unless the Name of Jesus be heard." (Serm. xv. in Cant.) Yet even we, with all our lukewarmness, will not occasionally help feeling some small portion of

this holy ardour. Never will our secret prayer warm
into fervent and loving supplication, without this Name
frequently escaping from our lips. We shall dwell upon
it with a tenderer emotion than on any other whereby we
address God, our salvation. It will, when often pronounced, unlock the more recondite stores of our affections, too seldom opened in the presence of God; it will
be as wings, to the soul, of aspiration and love soaring
towards the possession of our true country.

And now, applying this quality of His ever-blessed
Name to this preaching of His word,—what more can we
require to recommend it, than its being proclaimed in
that His Name? Who shall be able to resist a summons
addressed to him under this most winning sanction?
Who will refuse his heart, when claimed by One who
bears such a title to his love? When we shall address
the sinner, immersed in his vices or enslaved to his passions, what shall we need to say, beyond the eloquent
appeal of this most blessed Name? We will place before
him all that his Saviour has done to raise him from sin,
and gain his love. On His behalf, and in His Name, we
will conjure him to answer with a generous heart the
call upon his affections. We will paint as best we can
the dark ingratitude and enormous guilt of making this
Name, as far as he can, an empty sound, without character or meaning as regards him. Or we will show him
how that Jesus who ascended to heaven, will one day
return bearing the same Name, but as an outraged title
that pleads for vengeance, to punish his unfeeling conduct.

When we shall see the slothful, faint-hearted Christian,
whose desires are good, while his efforts are weak, stag-

gering along the right path, but scarce standing upright
thereon, how better can we address him, to arouse and
strengthen him, than by recounting to him the earnestness of purpose which the very Name of Jesus imports
in Him that bore it, to save and win his soul. It described an office of painful and arduous discharge,
through suffering and death; He who undertook it,
would fain keep the thought of it ever before His eyes,
by bearing, even in the apparent thoughtlessness of
infancy, the name which must ever have recalled it.
And at the sight of such steadiness in love, such earnestness of perseverance in care of him, will he refuse an
earnestness of gratitude and a steadiness of requital?
Will he refuse anything which in that Name is required?

If ever it be necessary to offer consolation to the
virtuous, in affliction and distress of mind, in temptation
or desolation of spirit, what will be required but to repeat
to him this dear Name, so often a source of refreshment
to his soul, so often his shield in time of conflict, so often
his reward in heavenly contemplation. It will be to him
as manna in the desert, or as dew to Hermon—a quickening food, a fertilizing influence, by whose vigour he
shall be restored to comfort and inward joy.

Such shall be, with God's blessing, "our speech and
our teaching, not in the persuasive words of human
wisdom," but in Jesus Christ and Him crucified. (1 Cor.
ii. 4.) Nothing else shall we judge ourselves to know.
But if we address ourselves to you in His Name, in this
Name do ye also hear. Remember, that this Name was
given Him for you, that is, for each amongst us. It was
one which without us He could not have borne; for it

expresses His relation to us. To each of us ought it to be dear, by each of us ought it to be cherished, and lovingly pronounced. Speak it in trouble, and it shall bring you comfort ; speak it in temptation, and it shall give you victory ; speak it in times of relaxing fervour, and it shall throw fire into your hearts ; speak it in devotion, and it shall perfect you. There is no time, no place, where it is out of season, if to the lips at least to the thought; there is no action so blessed which it will not improve; there is no forgetfulness so deep from which it will not arouse you.

But, my brethren, there are two periods when its sweetness seems doubly sweet. For as we have seen that this is peculiarly the name of Our blessed Saviour in His infancy and in His passion, so are they two corresponding periods of our lives, when it best appears to become us. It is a sweet Name when lisped by babes and sucklings, joined, through early suggestion, with those first names dear to parental affection, which form so firm a root for filial love. It is good to teach your little ones to utter it as they do your own, that He who became an infant for their sakes may grow up in their hearts as the first companion of their dawning attachment, and have His love implanted as deeply at least as any earthly affection. But oh ! it is sweeter still to the tongue of the dying who in life have loved it and Him who chose it. Insipid to the ears of such a one will be the catalogue of his titles, his honours, or his possessions. Without power to help will their names be, whom the bonds of the flesh have knit to him, to be separated from them at that hour. He will search his soul for some affection which can

G

stretch across the grave, for some link between the heart of flesh and the disembodied spirit. He will earnestly desire some token to show that he was fore-chosen here below, some pass-word which angels shall recognise, some charm which evil spirits shall dread. He will want some name written upon his garment and upon his forehead, which at first glance may establish his claim to the mansions of bliss. And all this he will find in this holy Name of Jesus, the God of his salvation. If through life he have received it and loved it, as the summary of what under it was wrought for his salvation ; if he have often fed his heart upon its sweet nourishment, he will find in it an object of his affections, imperishable and unchangeable, enduring beyond his dissolution, and even more powerful in the next world than in this. It shall seem written in letters of light over the gate of eternity; it shall seem graven with a pencil of fire on his heart; and even from very habit and strengthened practice, his lips will struggle to arrest his last parting breath, and form it into that sacred Name, inaudible save to angels, whispered now only to Him that bore it.

Oh, be this Holy Name called down upon us all ! be it our protection through this our earthly pilgrimage; be it the assistance of this our ministry and of your patience and profit. Be it our comfort in death, and our joy in eternity.

SERMON V.

The Two Great Mysteries of Love.

" And Jesus took the loaves, and when He had given thanks,
He distributed to them that were sat down."

THERE were supposed conjunctions of the heavenly bodies,
my brethren, which in ancient times were considered
of favourable augury, as promising great blessings to all
beneath their influence. And if such speculations were
mere vanity, springing only from the foolish fancies of
men, you will forgive me, if I own to myself to discover
something similar in the peculiar concurrence of two
most holy mysteries in the celebration of this day. For,
on the one hand, the incident related in the Sunday's
Gospel,—the feeding of five thousand persons with five
loaves,—and the subsequent discourse thereon held by
our Redeemer, forcibly turn my mind to the contemplation
of that divine Sacrament, wherein He feeds us in this
wilderness with bread truly descended from heaven,—His
own adorable Body and Blood. But at the same time,
the festival which has fallen upon this same day, commemorative of the angel's annunciation to Mary, necessarily
draws our thoughts to another still greater mystery on
that occasion, wrought in favour of man ; for no sooner
had the spotless Virgin given her consent to the heavenly

message, by those blessed words, "Behold the handmaid of the Lord, be it done unto me according to thy word," than the Incarnation of the Son of God took place in her womb, through the power of the Most High, and the Word made flesh entered on that course of blessing, which ended in our salvation.

Either of those two mysteries, my brethren, is a rich theme for discourse, but richer still for meditation. Each of them presents to us an act of self-devotion on the part of our dear Redeemer, whereby He gives Himself up unreservedly to us, and makes His own abasement a means of our sanctification. The more they are considered together, the stronger and more numerous the analogies they present, till one seems to be but the natural consequence and accomplishment of the other. Nor is it merely in the fancy of the moderns that this close resemblance between the mysteries of the Incarnation and the Eucharist is to be found. It has been remarked by the wise and venerable teachers of the ancient Church. For not only in matters of controversy regarding one of these mysteries, is the other employed to afford illustration or argument, but they are often compared together by the Fathers, as similar in grandeur, efficacy, and love.

St. Ambrose, after clearly stating that the words of consecration change the bread and wine into the Body and Blood of Christ, as much as Moses changed his rod into a serpent, proceeds to say : " We will now establish this mystery by the truth itself of the Incarnation. Was the order of Nature followed, when Jesus was born of a Virgin ? Plainly not. Then why is that order to be looked for here ?" (De Initiandis.)

" You believe," says St. Ephraim, the glory of Edessa and the light of the Eastern Church, " you believe that Christ, the Son of God, was born for you in the flesh ? . . . . Believe then, and with a firm faith receive the Body and Blood of our Lord." (De Nat. Dei.)   In like manner, St. Augustine writes, " Christ took upon him earth from the earth, because flesh is from the earth, and this flesh He took from the flesh of Mary; and because He here walked in this flesh, even this same flesh He gave us to eat for our salvation." (In Psalm.)

In like manner, not to multiply authorities, St. Peter Chrysologus says, that Christ is the bread which, first sown in the Virgin's womb, is finally brought to the altar, to be our daily food. (Serm. lxvii.)   St. John Chrysostome compares the altar to the manger, in which Christ lies not wrapped in swaddling clothes, but surrounded on all sides by the Holy Spirit, and where we, like the wise men, adore Him. (Orat. de S. Philog.)   And a later writer, the Patriarch Dionysius, though belonging to a separated Church, says, that the altar is the symbol of the Virgin's womb, on which the Holy Ghost descends, transmutes the bread and wine, and makes them become the Body and Blood of Christ. (Hor. Syr. p. 58.)

These examples, which might with little trouble have been multiplied, are sufficient to prove, that it is no result of scholastic ingenuity—no fanciful reasoning of modern theology, to discover a marked parallelism and resemblance between the two mysteries, which the circumstances of to-day have brought together before our consideration. Unwilling, therefore, to give up either, I will unite the two ; and, after the venerable authorities I have quoted,

will endeavour to unfold them united to your pious contemplation, treating of them both, first as a two-fold mystery
of humiliation, and as a double mystery of grace. The
whole struggle between faith and weak yet haughty reason, should, methinks, be directed to the conquest of a very
narrow point, which if faith has won, there remains no further room for contest. All the difficulty of belief should
seem to rest upon the admission of only these two words :
" Ecce venio,"—Behold I come. And well are they said to
have been inscribed by the Eternal Word in the very head
or frontispiece of the Book, wherein are registered the
merciful counsels of God. For they are as a seed from
which fruits of incalculable abundance as well as sweetness
must spring; they are as the theme from which the richest
strains of harmonious music may be developed; they are
a summary of deep incomprehensible wisdom, from which
a successive series of heavenly truths may be evolved.
Nay, if they are but on the first page of that blessed book,
there must be much to come after them to fill the volume.

Admit these words, and where will your faith come to
an end, or where shall you be able to say, " I have believed
enough" ? When the Son of God, the consubstantial to
the Father, hath once consented to take upon Him the
nature of man, frail, disfigured, and disgraced by sin, it
is not surely for man's reason to calculate what more He
may be impelled to do. After the first step, from the
glory of heaven and the bosom of the Father, into the
womb, however pure, of woman, the step from this to the
cross, and from the cross to the altar, must seem but as
comparatively short in His gigantic career of love. For,
whatever may befal His humanity, insults, injuries, tor-

ments, death, is but as a mere nothing compared with what He Himself assumed to His divinity.

What is a cross upon the shoulders of the man, compared with the burden of the flesh united to the Godhead? What are blows upon His cheek, or thorns upon His head, compared to the humiliation of feeling, the cravings of human wants in the person of a God-Man? What were nails through His hands, or a spear in His side, compared with the ignominy of submitting to the temptations of the Evil One? What was death compared with the imputation of guilt to which His Incarnation brought Him,—yea, of the guilt of the entire world? No, when once that first plunge into the abasement of human nature had been made,—when the entire abyss of its misery had thus been absorbed into Himself, the rest must be as mere drops and sprinklings, concerning which a loving heart will not condescend to calculate.

Nay, there seems to be something ungenerous and unkind, in the attempt to establish anything like a proportion between our belief, and our powers of comprehension, or our powers of love, when once we have seen that the very first stride went so infinitely beyond our measurement. There should seem to have been laid in the first mystery of Christ's earthly existence, such a strong foundation of confidence, as would allow a superstructure of any extent and of any mass. There should appear, in His first words, a promise of so much, as should prevent all surprise at whatever might follow in fulfilment. Man should listen to its unfolding wonders, to its tale of love, with the simplicity of a very child, who, upon each recital of a marvellous incident, only craves

and expects another still more strange, and is only disappointed and grieved when the history is closed.

And, in like manner, when a man with a heart disposed
to love, has learnt and believed, that out of affection to
him, a God of infinite power and majesty has become a
helpless infant, seeming completely as the children of men
in a similar condition, yet possessing all the fulness of
the Godhead ; then that this infant, grown up to man's
estate, has died an ignominious death, impelled by the
same love, to save him lost, at the expense of His own
life,—will it any longer seem strange, or incredible to him,
that even after these efforts of incomprehensible love, this
untiring benefactor had discovered and adopted a new,
unheard-of way to complete His scheme of benefits—has
submitted to a new act of humiliation, so as to become
our food ?

It would be indeed too inestimable a benefit for him to
admit without proof ; but against this his heart, at least,
would not allow him reason to start objections.   For any
of us might be called upon to give satisfactory evidence,
that an affectionate Father has left him a magnificent
legacy, but we shall think it nothing strange or wonderful if we were told that, being able, He had done so.

But the resemblance between the two mysteries of the
Incarnation and Eucharist will bear a closer investigation.   In both there is an outward veil, hiding from the
eye of flesh a precious and divine deposit, visible only to
that of faith.   When the wise men came from the East,
under the conduct of a miraculous star, there can be no
doubt that they were but little prepared for what they
were to discover at Bethlehem.   The very circumstance

of their inquiry at Jerusalem for Him who was born King
of the Jews, shows that they expected to find His birth
treated as a public event, and His entrance into His
kingdom hailed with festivals of joy. Yet they find
Herod ignorant not merely of the occurrence, but of the
place where it was likely to happen, and obliged to summon the priests to meet their inquiries. What a shock
was here to their expectations! Still, encouraged by the
re-appearance of the star, they prosecute their journey
with undiminished ardour, and arrive at Bethlehem.
Their miraculous guide points to a poor dilapidated shed,
not likely to be tenanted by any but outcasts of human
society; yet, strong in faith, they enter in.

What do they discover? A little babe, wrapped up as
the poorest infant would be, and laid upon a bundle of
straw! And is this all that they have crossed the deserts
to see? Is this all that they abandoned their homes and
palaces to discover? When they set off from their homes,
their friends derided them, perchance, for undertaking so
long a journey, and on the guidance of a wayward meteor,
that might abandon them in the midst of some frightful
wilderness. Many probably thought it little better than
madness to go so far in search of a foreign sovereign,
only yet an infant. What an account will they have to
give on their return of their success, and of the employ-
ment made of their precious gifts! Will not their very
attendants ridicule them for their credulity, in coming so
far to find only a child in a manger? Will they dare to
report what they have discovered to Herod? In spite of
all such obstacles, which pride must have raised to a simple faith, without any new assurances to encourage them;

without any miraculous splendour, round the humble
group they have found, to overawe them; without any
evidences to convince them, they trust implicitly to the
sure guidance of that star, which having led them safe
through all their journey, first to Jerusalem and then to
Bethlehem, they do not conceive likely now to turn traitor
and mislead them; they prostrate themselves before that
child, they adore Him, and by their gifts do Him supreme
homage, acknowledging Him as their Lord and their
God.

If we then have in like manner been led by the light
of God, through all the obscure paths of faith, shall we
hesitate to trust our guides to the utmost ?   If His word,
which told us how His Son became man, and has been
believed, tells us no less, that He has assumed another
disguise of love, and shrouded His glories still further for
our benefit, shall it not be equally believed ?   If His
Church, which hath been our principal conductor through
the mazes of early tradition, whereon alone the belief in
the Divinity of the Incarnate Word can be solidly built,
fixing its directing ray, in the end, upon that humble
tabernacle, assures you, with the same voice that till now
you have believed, that therein dwells the God of your
souls, your dear Saviour, no longer under the form of
flesh, but with that same flesh, in its turn, concealed
under the appearance of bread, why will you hesitate to
prostrate yourself and adore ?   If He Himself, of whom
reverently we treat, whose words we unhesitatingly receive, when he tells us that He and His Father are one,
taking up this bread, solemnly declares it to be His Body,
shall we make difference between word and word,--reason

away the glorious announcement of the one, and not fear that we are weakening the testimony of the other ? No, like those Eastern Kings, we will hush and subdue every suggestion of pride; and if the humiliation of our blessed Saviour in either mystery shocks our sense, let it be honoured the more with a corresponding humility of our hearts.

But if a few, like the wise men and the shepherds, worshipped Him devoutly in the disguise of a child, there were many who, then and afterwards, refused to acknowledge Him for more than He outwardly appeared, a mere man, however privileged. And so should we not wonder, nor should our faith be shaken, if many now refuse to raise their belief above the range of their senses, and admit more to be contained in the Eucharistic species than they outwardly exhibit. For it is easier to abstract from the influence which our senses exercise upon our judgments, when they are not immediately called into use, than where the object of inquiry falls directly under them. Thus we find that the preaching of Christ's Divinity was more easily received from the Apostles in distant countries, where His person had not been seen, than in Judea and Jerusalem, where men had been familiarised with His human form. And so may it be that many who, able to use the testimony of their senses in discussing the inquiry concerning the blessed Sacrament, prefer it to every other, would have acted similarly in regard of our Saviour's Godhead, had the same test been within their reach. Contrary to Thomas, they believe because they see not ; peradventure, had they seen, they would not have believed.

But all this is only in the course of God's ordinary dispensation. It would seem that the love of our blessed Redeemer towards us would never be sufficient for His heart, unless, in some way, it involved His suffering. The humiliation of the manger was but preparatory to the humiliation of the cross : and all the intermediate space was filled by privation, poverty, and sorrow. He became man, to all appearance, that He might become the reproach of men. And so is it no small enhancement to His graciousness, in thus again abasing Himself in the adorable Sacrament, that thereby, even after returning to His glory, He has remained exposed to the insults and ingratitude of men.

I speak not of those ignorant blasphemies uttered against it by those who believe not, and know not what they do : still less of those frightful outrages which heresy and infidelity, in moments of impious frenzy, have committed. But I speak of our own conduct,—of the treatment which He receives from us who believe. Do you not sometimes think the world must have been stupidly blind to its own happiness and blessing, to have allowed Jesus for thirty years to live hidden in a poor carpenter's cottage, and not to have discovered the jewel it possessed, and begun, much earlier than it did, to enjoy His instructions, witness His example, be benefitted by His miracles, and be blessed by His presence ? But there at least was a deep counsel of God that He should lie concealed.

What, then, shall we say of ourselves, who have Him ever in the midst of us, humble, indeed, and retired, yet ever accessible, day and night within the reach of our homage and petitions, and yet do so seldom visit Him, so seldom turn towards Him our eyes or thoughts? The churches, which should be crowded all day with adorers, are comparatively empty; if here, in Rome, what shall we say of our own country? And we seem to make over our duty to the lamps that burn day and night, as our hearts should do, before the altar. Oh! it is too true that God seems to have made Himself too common,—that we act as though we thought He had demeaned Himself too low! For, as a devout author observes, had He appointed but one place on earth wherein the adorable sacrifice could be offered, and but one priest who could administer it, what eager devotion would drive crowds of believing Christians to adore at so privileged a place! And even so, it would be nothing more than He formerly did for the ark of His covenant, of settim wood and gold. But now that He has unreservedly made Himself over to us,—that He dwells in every part of our cities and in every hamlet, as though but one of ourselves, we pass by the doors of His temples without a thought of Him, we enter them often without respect, we admire them and their riches, but their real treasure we heed not. And would to God, that only in this, our neglect, did Christ suffer from us in this blessed mystery, and not in a way which, in His Incarnation, was spared Him! When, on this day, He descended into the womb of Mary, He found His chosen place of confinement strait, indeed, but pure and holy; He dwelt with one whose heart was entirely His, whose soul was free from every stain, whose desires, whose thoughts were in every respect devoted unto God. But when, in this blessed Sacrament, He comes into our breasts, alas! what does He find? A chamber, perhaps, but lately tenanted by His hateful enemy, sin, ejected thence a few hours before by a hasty repentance. Its paltry furniture is yet in the disorder and confusion which this foe had caused there, bearing on every side traces of the riot and havoc committed within it so long and so late. A few shreds and tattered scraps of virtuous protestations collected together in half an hour, out of the stores of our prayer-books, have been hung around it, to cover its habitual bareness. The remains of many a once precious gift, presents from God's bounty, the torn fragments of contracts of love and promises of service, lie scattered about, patched up for the moment, by its passing fervour. And, perhaps, even in the corners of this den yet lurk, skulking from his sight, irregular attachments and dangerous affections, which we have not had courage to expel when we turned out his full-grown enemies, but still to his eyes monsters of hateful shape and nature. Into this cell, this dungeon, we invite Him, the King of Glory, and have the courage to introduce Him, the living God; and He remembers the first time he visited it, how clean and fair it was, how cheerful and pleasant a dwelling, and how He then decked it out for us with those gifts, and many others, long since broken or lost, or flung away. And we, oh, do not we feel our cheeks burning with shame, when we have thus received Him, to think what He has found within us; and to what a degradation we have dragged the Son of God! What was the hall of Herod, or the court of Pilate, or the house of Caiphas to this? And what, if when He is once there, you are so wretched as to strike and buffet Him by sin ? If, as too often happens, on the very day that you have received Him into your bosom, you offend Him: and thus betray Him in your own house to your enemies, while dipping your hand with Him into the same dish, and feasting at the same table ? Oh, how has our dear Saviour drunk to the dregs the cup of humiliation and self-abasement, that He might enable us to drink of the chalice of His salvation !

If Jesus hath twice humbled Himself so low, it was love that constrained Him. For the moving cause, the active principle of both these mysteries was affection for us. When John, in the sublime preface to his Gospel, describes to us the Divinity and Incarnation of the Word, he sums it up in these terms : " And the Word was made flesh, and dwelt amongst us." Here was a double bless- ing, in first assuming our human nature, and then re- taining it. We frequently read in Scripture of angels appearing to the patriarchs in a human figure. But they merely put on this outward form as a garment, or dis- guise, which they threw off again as soon as their mes- sage had been delivered and their commission discharged. One might almost imagine that it would have been an intolerable hardship to those pure spirits, had any of them, who were sent on such errands to earth, been obliged to retain, for the rest of their existence, that body which they had joined to themselves for the occasion.

In like manner, might not our Saviour have appeared in the flesh to teach and instruct us, or by some act of graciousness, save us, without assuming it so as for ever to retain it ? But His object would not have been thus attained, of dwelling and conversing among men, and truly being as one of us. It was not merely for the one momentary act of redemption that He put on our nature; it was to procure thereby for us that abundance of grace which on every side flowed from His sacred humanity. The excellence of His example, the model of His prayer, His conduct under temptation, His suffering of hardship and distress, His resignation, His obedience and other virtues would have been lost to us, had he not become truly man, dwelling upon earth. That pleading which His wounds, still open, keep up in our behalf; that light and joy which the presence of His humanity sheds over heaven; that glory which the exaltation of His flesh secures to man; that headship of His Church on earth which He retains; that mediatorship which He holds between His Father and us; these, and many other immense prerogatives, we should not have enjoyed, had He contented Himself with less than the absolute and permanent union of His manhood with His Godhead.

But then, how comparatively short of the object of His great design would the execution have fallen, had but one short visit to earth comprised the whole of his commerce with His new brethren here below! And still more, what an undue advantage, so to speak, would they have enjoyed over us, whom accidental circumstances brought to live in the same time, and country, with Him. Were they to possess the privilege of touching His sacred body, and we not be allowed to touch even the hem of His garment? Was the women of Chanaan to be admitted to partake of the fulness of His benefits, and we who are the children of the kingdom, be denied what she ventured to claim—the right of feeding on the crumbs from His table? Was He to place His hands upon the heads of children, some of whom, perhaps, joined in the outcries against Him, and be to us like Isaac, who had no blessing for Esau, when Jacob had anticipated him? Such is one motive assigned by the great Father of the Eastern Church, St. Maruthas, for the institution of the Blessed Eucharist.

No, my brethren, our dear Redeemer was too impartial in His love to treat us so. We who were to come eighteen hundred years too late to enjoy His company in the flesh, had as large and as warm a place in His heart, as they who entertained Him in their houses. It was but natural for us to expect from Him some ingenious contrivance, some institution of almighty love, whereby His sojourn upon earth should be prolonged until the end of time. Even in the Old Law, His presence by visible emblems, which gave assurance and promised mercy, was made permanent in His holy place. While Israel dwelt in the wilderness, His cloud overshadowed the tabernacle; and both there and in the Temple, the Holy of Holies contained a mercy-seat, whereon He sat between the cherubim, to receive the supplications of priests and people. And if this was a figure or symbol of Him, who alone has wrought propitiation for many, was it otherwise than reasonable to expect, in that Law when realities succeeded to shadows, truths to figures, there would be some provision for a corresponding token of God's presence, securing, however, its reality and truth? Such precisely was supplied us in the Blessed Eucharist, in which Christ is with us, our true Emanuel, ever residing in our sanctuaries. There we may visit Him hourly, and pour our entreaties before His feet, assured of His listening to us with graciousness

H

and sweetness. There we may grieve over our sins, sympathise with His sufferings, and protest to Him our love. And thus does the Sacrament of the altar hourly appear what it is—the full accomplishment of His manifestation in the flesh; the firmly securing to all ages and all places, of one of the greatest blessings of His Incarnation, His "dwelling amongst us." It is, indeed, the completing of this ineffable mystery.

Further, the Incarnation of Christ Jesus, was the preparation for Redemption; the Eucharist is its application. He became man that, as man, He might suffer and die, and so procure for us all grace, inclusive of eternal salvation. He became our food, that so the remembrance of His passion might be ever kept before us; that His precious blood might be applied to our souls, and that we might be filled with all grace, by contact with its very source and author.

But, finally, the great and true analogy between those two mysteries, consists in the communication made in both of God to man. The love which inspired the Eternal Word to take upon Him our human nature, was in the form of an ardent desire to devote Himself to man, to sacrifice Himself for him. He became one of us, so to acquire an interest in all that concerns us. He gave to us, so far as he could, participation in that divine nature, which He associated to our humanity. He gave us heirship with Himself in heaven. And, after this, He gave up to man, and for man, all that He had acquired, if it could be considered an acquisition—His time, His mind, His strength, His happiness, His blood, His life.

But then all these communications and gifts were made to our race in general; and only through their connexion with it, to the individual man. Whatever He thus bestowed, was bestowed upon mankind. Not, however, there would His love rest; but it sought to communicate all this and more, individually and personally, to each of us; and this He accomplished in the divine Eucharist. But strange as at first sight it may appear, there was a corresponding ardour of desire on the part of man for such a union, traceable among the ruined traditions of heathen superstitions. For, in many countries of the old and new world, did the idea prevail, that by partaking of victims offered to the Deity, man did become actually united and incorporated with Him; and many were the vain follies devised, whereby wiser and holier men were supposed to arrive at a close, and most intimate, union with God. Wherever nature, even in its degradation, has preserved a craving after anything good and holy, we need not be surprised if it be gratified.

And how, in this mystery of love, it is gratified, they who love their Saviour alone can tell. When, with a conscience cleansed by penance, of the lesser transgressions to which all are subject, and a heart at peace with itself, free from rancour, from anxiety, from disturbing fear, they approach their Saviour's feast, they feel their hearts so divided between eagerness and humility, love and a sense of unworthiness, as to tremble, they scarcely know if from hesitation or hope. But, when they have drawn nigh unto the altar, and received the pledge of their salvation, he seems to come into their souls as rain upon the fleece, in calm and sweet serenity. Their hearts are too full for

analysing their feelings ; but there is a sense of silent
unalterable happiness—an absorbing overflow of tranquil
joy, which disdains the feeble expression of the tongue.
The presence of their God is felt with sufficient awe to
depress the soul into humble adoration—the presence of
our loving Redeemer is experienced with an intensity of
affection, that burns in the heart, rather than breaks forth
into a flame. But this deep paroxysm of heavenly feeling,
this foretaste of future bliss, cannot last long, but that the
outburst of contending affections must take place. It is
as though so many different inmates of the heart, the
children of the house, scarce restrained for a time from the
presence of a brother they revere and love, at length
broke open the door into his presence, and poured forth
their tumultuous emotions upon him. There hope seems
to seize upon his strengthening hand, and faith to gaze
upon his inspiring eye, and love to bury its face in his
bosom, and gratitude to crown his head with garlands,
and humble sorrow to sit down at his feet and weep. And
amidst this universal homage and joy, of every affection
and every power, the blessed Jesus sits enthroned, sole
master of the heart and of the soul, commanding peace
and imparting gladness, filling with sweetness, as with a
heavenly fragrance, the entire being. True, the vision
soon dies away, and leaves us to the drearier duties
of the day, its burthen and its heat ; but the dew of the
morning will lie upon that Christian's soul, long after
the bright cloud that dropt it hath faded away.

If, my brethren, there were any one point whereon I
could concentrate the zeal of every order of men who have
our dear country's true interest at heart ; if by narrowing

the sphere of our exertions, I could hope to increase
their intensity, yet so as to neglect no claim, I own that
I could turn the thoughts and hearts of all to the restoration of the belief, the knowledge, the worship of the
Blessed Eucharist amongst us. I would beg that,
comparatively small stress should be laid upon other
matters contested between us and our fellow-subjects; but
that every energy of clergy and laity should be devoted
to the vindication and adoration of this incomparable
Sacrament. Three hundred years of public rejection of
its true doctrine is idolatrous; three centuries of privation
of the blessings which it alone can bestow upon man, so
much written and spoken against the noblest institution
of Divine love,—these things are a fearful weight upon a
nation's soul, not to be expiated but by many tears and
much loving reparation by those that believe. Let the
laity be ready to concur in every measure that may be
proposed for man's public homage, a bolder worship, and
a more frequent use of it in our country. Let us, who
have dedicated ourselves to its ministry, whose standing-
place is by God's altar, consider ourselves the apostles of
this mystery of love. Let us be willing to suffer every
extremity to promote its honour and glory, and diffuse its
benefits among men. Happy they, who having collected
thousands to hear them, shall take care not to let them
depart contented with their words, but shall send them
home nourished with this heavenly bread, divinely multiplied so as to suffice for all, possessing every savour of
delight, medicine, food, sweetness, and strength, source of
our hope, fuel of our love, security of our salvation, and
pledge of a blessed eternity.

SERMON VI.

Thabor and Olivet.

MAT. xvii. 1, 2.

" And after six days Jesus taketh unto Him Peter and James
and John his brother, and bringeth them up into a high mountain apart; and He was transfigured before them."

LAST Sunday we contemplated our beloved Saviour on
the mountain of temptation : we are this day called to
consider Him on the mountain of His glory. He was
then under trial, lonely and unfriended, without a disciple
to witness His struggles—without an admirer to sympathise in His sufferings ; He is now in triumph, surrounded and supported by faithful followers, and by the
venerable representatives of the older saints, who feel a
deep and affectionate interest in the majesty and splendour which, for a time, invest Him.   In His life of sorrow this is a solitary event, a suspension, for a few
moments, of that course which He had chosen—a course
of toil and travail, of persecution and affliction. Can
we, then, be surprised that His disciples, amazed at the
unusual spectacle, and overpowered by the newness of its
delights, should have longed that it might become perpetual?   Their divine Master is no more such as they have
known Him till now ; no more walking in meekness

among men, as though He were but one of themselves,
He is raised up in majesty, His face is bright as the
sun, His raiment white and glittering as snow ; Moses,
the great legislator of their nation, hath broken from the
confinement of death ; Elias, the mightiest of the prophets, hath abandoned the seat of his temporary rest, to
do Him homage, and bear Him their testimony. He is
no longer harrassed by the malicious and teazing questions of Pharisees and scribes, nor blasphemed by the
scoffs and jeers of an unbelieving multitude ; but heaven
speaks its approbation of their faith, and utters a powerful witnessing to His divine authority. Yes, the beauty
and majesty of the better world appeared for a moment
to have descended upon this lower state, and Heaven
seemed, through that mountain's top, to have imparted
unto earth the thrilling kiss of reconciliation and love.

Who, then, shall wonder if Peter, ever ardent and
uncalculating in his affection, should have exclaimed,
" Lord, it is good for us to be here !" Nor was there in
this exclamation aught of selfish desire, or a care of his
own enjoyment ; inasmuch as forthwith he added, " If
thou wilt, let us make here three tabernacles, one for
thee, and one for Moses, and one for Elias." For himself
and his two companions, whose hearts in his own he could
comprehend, he asks not that provision should be made.
He and they would gladly brave the rage of mountain
storms, and the summer's scorching ray, unsheltered and
unheeding, so that they might witness the glory of their
Master and the happy companionship in which He was
engaged.

But, alas ! " he knew not what he said." He knew

not that he and his two fellow-apostles were reserved to
witness, upon another mount, a spectacle sorrowfully
contrasting with what they now saw ; on Thabor he was
mercifully kept in ignorance of the desolation of Olivet ;
the splendour of the one dazzled him into forgetfulness of
what had been foretold of the other's anguish ; and the
cruel contrast between glory and agony, adoption and
abandonment by God, which the two were intended to
present them, were withheld from their loving souls.
But not so be it with us, to whom our Saviour's life in
its entireness has been proposed for an example and a
lesson, and who may well temper the variety of emotions
it has a power to excite, by the comparison of its diverse
parts.   And therefore, of the many and moving instructions, which this day's Gospel may well suggest, I will
fain choose the one which seems to me most touching,
that of discoursing on the mountain of His glorious transfiguration, " concerning His decease which He should
accomplish at Jerusalem."   Thus it is, that in the words
of the Psalmist, " Thabor and Hermon" are brought together to " rejoice in His name;" (Ps. lxxxviii. 13) that
Hermon of the New Law, on which the dew of life, our
dear Redeemer's blood, first trickled down, and thence
descended over the hills of Sion. (Ps. cxxxiii. 3.)

For whosoever shall diligently and lovingly consider
the scenes of these two mountains of Thabor and of
Olivet—the transfiguration unto glory, and the transfiguration unto abasement which occurred in each—will
not fail to be struck by the notable resemblances and the
nicely balanced differences which they exhibit ; as if intended by the Spirit of God for the working out of some

great and mingled instruction. And it is in the joint contemplation of the two, that my humble endeavours shall strive to engage you this day : showing you, through God's grace, how upon the former Jesus publicly received the glorious title, which He of right possessed, of the true and " well-beloved Son of God," and on the latter made good His claim to that other, more endearing, title " of the Son of Man."

Twice, then, did our blessed Redeemer summon Peter, James, and John, to be the witnesses of a great change in His outward appearance and in His innermost soul : once to see Him exalted into a glory more than human ; another time to see Him sunk into the deepest abyss of wretchedness whereof humanity should seem capable. On the first occasion, when lifted so high, earthly attendants are sent to remind Him of His future sorrows, and check, in a manner, the torrent of delight which is poured into His soul; on the other, a heavenly messenger comes down to temper the bitterness of His cup of sorrows with consolation, and nerve Him to His trials and griefs by the prospect of their glorious end. On Thabor, as St. Luke has recorded, " Peter, and they that were with him, were heavy with sleep ; and waking, saw His glory, and the two men that stood with Him." (Luke, ix. 32.) On Olivet the same drowsiness overtook them, and drowned their senses, till they awoke only to see their Master in the hands of His cruel foes. In His first transfiguration, the voice of the Father was heard proclaiming Him His well-beloved Son ; in the second, He entreated " with a strong cry and tears to Him that was able to save Him from death," (Heb. v. 7) and seemed to be rejected. In

that He was raised above the earth, His garments were
changed into a raiment of glory; in this He was stretched
upon the ground, and those garments were steeped in His
own blood!

Need I, my brethren, ask you, wherefore these contrasting spectacles were presented to the three favoured
apostles, and, through their witnessing, to us? For, who
can doubt that the two natures in our Lord's sacred person
was thus intended to be exhibited, each on its proper
stage. His divinity raised aloft to receive the homage of
the most exalted saints, and be the object of a well-assured
faith. His humanity abased to all that It, and we, can
suffer, as to our proper and common sphere. And by this
two-fold change which *He* undergoes, *we* are led into a
suitable, but yet inverted, variation of feeling : in His
exaltation, our pride should be humbled into lowly
docility; and through His humiliation we should be
cheered into a patient and resigned endurance.

The mountain of Thabor is, without doubt, the representation, united in a lively scene, of all the evidence
which God's holy word, in sundry places, hath given of
our blessed Redeemer's divine authority, and divine
nature. The written word is but a dead letter, liable to
misapprehension, possessing no vital power to vary its
evidences according to our wants, no voice to shape a
fitting answer to our specific inquiries. There is, moreover, a charm in the sound of man's tongue; there is a
spell in the enthusiastic flash of his eye, when earnestly
striving to convince; there is a power to win in the solemn
interest which he exhibits, when uttering the secrets of
his mind. And who shall doubt but that when the

prophets spoke of old, the inspiration which beamed upon their countenances, as well as enlightened their minds, the spirit which thrilled through their frames, as it filled their hearts, the hand of the Lord which seemed to play a sweet music through the very gesture of their bodies, as truly as it came upon their souls, did give to their sublime words an energy and a feeling, a life, and a wonder-working might which, written, they but feebly retained?

Who hath not often longed, with the eloquent Chrysostom, that he could have beheld the apostle Paul addressing his defence to Festus, or preaching before the wise men of Athens? Who hath not wished that his happiness it had been, to witness the divine power of our Lord's appeals, when crushing under His indignant eloquence the pride of the Pharisees, or when mildly unfolding to his apostles, in their charming simplicity, the moral doctrines of His law? Nay, so natural does this superiority of the living testimony to the written appear, even where no proportion exists between the authors of the two, that the rich glutton in hell, pondering on the experience of his own impenitence, hesitates not to say, that his hardened brethren will be sooner brought to faith and repentance through the preaching of the ulcerous and ragged Lazarus, returning from the dead, than through the reading of Moses and the prophets. (Luke, xvi. 28.) How much surer then would he have felt of the desired conviction, could he have carried his presumption to such a pitch, as to hope, that Moses, and the prophets themselves, might be allowed to break their cerements, and testify in person to his obdurate generation?

And precisely, such is the evidence here given of our

Saviour's dignity, authority and character. When addressing the Jews, He had appealed to these very witnesses
as speaking through the organ of the written word. But,
alas! they had ever read them with a crooked mind,
forestalled by preconceits concerning the temporal glories
of their Messias, and the worldly conquests which He
should achieve. They misunderstood their evidence; and
remained in unbelief.

But to the chosen few, it was given to know the mysteries of God's kingdom in the full and clear light of
living evidence, and to hear them speak whom others had
only read. For here their most extravagant desires were
more than fulfilled; their most unreasonable hope of
proof must have been incredibly surpassed. Moses, whose
face had shone so brightly as to terrify his countrymen,
now standing overshone and eclipsed, as the lamp before
the mid-day sun, by the presence of their divine Master,
whose countenance truly rivalled the source of earthly
light! Elias, who had ridden, of all men alone, upon
the fiery chariot of the Lord of Hosts, and whose cloak
imparted to him that inherited it, prophecy and miracles,
now receiving a light and splendour from the dazzling
brightness of *His* garment! These two, the greatest
men, without exception, whom the arm of God had ever
strengthened for the manifestation of His Almighty power,
now as humble attendants, ministers, and servants, honoured and privileged by standing at His side, must have
produced a briefer, deeper, and more indelible conviction
of His superiority, than the painful and repeated perusal
of whatever prophecy had written. They seem to say
that the law and the testimony are now sealed up, and all

the mighty things accomplished, which they had foretold and foreshown. They stand as shadowy forms beside the reality of Christ's presence, as faint, indistinct, and dusky images, receiving light, and reflecting glory, from the brightness of His truth.

But, in the choice of witnesses thus called in, there were personal considerations which greatly would add to the interest of their testimony. Both of them had been purified before God by a fast protracted through forty days, even like our blessed Saviour's, not long before. Both had been admitted to a closer view of the Divine countenance than any other of the human race. In this manner did they approach nearer to His perfection, and were far livelier types of His surpassing excellence, than any others among the Fathers of the Old Law. And that the figure might afford still fuller measure of comfort to the disciples who witnessed it, they had in their generation, like Jesus, been lovers of their people, zealous for their fidelity to God, and unwearied in doing good.

Such are the great and holy men who return to earth to confer with their Master and Saviour, as though deputed, by it and its inhabitants, to hold solemn council with Him, touching their dearest interests. And, ah! how truly does their discourse prove whose representatives they are; and what little else than pain any embassy from our fallen kind could bear Him! No glad tidings do they bring of His chosen people's being repentant, and seeking reconciliation; no promise or hope of His reception among them as their King and Redeemer. No; they too had been liberators of their people, and were familiar with its reward: it is concerning His decease at

Jerusalem, from the hands of *His* people, that they come to treat! Oh! who can imagine the shame and sorrow that hang on their countenances, struggling with their kindling gratitude, admiration, and love, which a topic so disgraceful to their nation, yet so necessary to man, must have excited in their bosoms! But think, on the other hand, what a new idea of the grandeur of Christ's redemption must have flashed upon the wondering apostles' thoughts, on finding that subject, which was their scandal and distress, chosen as the meetest theme of conference, at this unusual and magnificent meeting. How must the ignominy of the cross have, for a moment at least, been forgotten, on hearing it the subject of praise and thanksgiving, chosen by such men, at the very instant that heaven itself seemed opened visibly before them.

But then, let me ask, what was all this witnessing compared with that, which the eternal gates burst open to communicate? What was the testimony of the past compared with that of this very moment; what were the asseverations of men, beside the proclamation of the Most Highest : "This is my beloved Son, in whom I am well pleased, hear ye Him"? To the two earthly witnesses that stood by, what a marvellous contrast with other scenes must this simple utterance have suggested! Moses had stood upon Sinai, when the law of fear was delivered to the people. It came forth from that mountain, as an infant giant, swathed like the ocean in a stormy cloud, (Job, xxxviii. 9) its first accents were in the thunder, the first glance of its eye, was in the flashing of the winged lightnings. The earth shook beneath its tread, and the people hid themselves in terror, before its manifestation. And yet, as St. Paul assures us, only by the ministration of angels was this law of fear given. (Gal. iii. 19.) Elias, too, had stood on Horeb, when the Lord passed through the cavern ; and, though He came to comfort him in the whispering of a gentle breeze, a mighty wind, an earthquake, and a raging fire announced His approach. (3 Reg. xix.)

How characteristically are all things here changed, on this mountain of the New Law, whereon its evidences are uttered by the voice of God Himself. A bright cloud overshadowed them ; to the husbandman on the plain below, nothing new or strange appears over the mountain's top ; he notices perhaps but a brighter wreath upon its brow; and from this glad and glorious, though mysterious, canopy, issue the comforting and assuring words, which proclaim Jesus to be God's only Son, and settle our faith and decide its objects, by reference to His infallible word. Here then is Jesus constituted our great and everlasting Law-giver, the author and finisher of our faith, our model and our guide unto life eternal.

This union of evidence, this homage of earth through its holiest of saints, this proclamation of heaven through its Lord and God, forms, in sooth, the solemn mystery which Christ's glorious transfiguration was intended to set forth. To us, it is a blessed and joyful spectacle, to contemplate Him, for once, such as to our affection it seemeth that He ever should have been, treated so as became His divine nature, by God and by men, elevated above the reach of enemies and transgressors, shrouded from the gaze of such as love Him not, surrounded only by adorning disciples, escorted by His blessed saints, enshrined in his own brightness, majesty, and loveliness, and crowned by His Father, with the unfading eternal glory which He possessed in Him from the beginning. Such is Jesus, the Son of God, exhibited to us in his transfiguration upon Mount Thabor, and such will every soul that loveth Him, think that He ever should be seen.

But now turn we to another mountain, and see Him whom we thus love, alas! how transformed in truth! The brightness and glow of the overshadowing cloud are exchanged, for the bleak and dreary darkness of night, within an olive garden's gloomy shades. The same three disciples are near, but buried in a sluggish weary sleep, from which no warning of danger, no expostulation of love can rouse them to consciousness. Instead of being elevated above the earth, surrounded by a halo of glory, Jesus is sunk upon the ground, unable to support His own weight; His face then so splendid, is now pale, haggard, and bedewed with tears; and His garments hang upon Him clammy and damp, through the blood that steals out at every pore. The brightness of heaven is fled from His soul; the calm prospect of future suffering is exchanged for the torture and anguish of present woe; and an angel, one solitary comforter of the countless host whose joy He is, comes to support and encourage Him in the work of His own love!

Can He be the same whom we have so lately seen on Thabor? Is this the well-beloved Son of God, whom we are commanded to hear? Has there been any diminution of love in His heavenly Father, or any change in His own high dignity here below, that He should now appear so sadly altered from what erst He was? Most assuredly not; but He is now making good another title, a title to our love as before to our faith; He is proving Himself to be, even more than we are, the Son of Man. For it is not as engaged in the painful work of our redemption that I wish here to consider Him, but as merely incorporating Himself the most completely amongst us, by the participation of our sorrows.

When men of powerful minds have been thrown, by accident or chance, into the society of hostile or barbarous tribes, they have easily discovered, that the surest way to win their confidence, and secure their friendship, is to show no abhorrence of their most repulsive usages, but to adopt whatever practices are among them reckoned most peculiar to their race. They have quaffed with seeming delight their most noisome beverage; they have clothed themselves in their most fantastic attire; they have humoured them in their most capricious moods; and they have even outdone them, in the apparent fervor with which they have copied their habits, and adopted their sentiments.

It would seem as though, with nobler ends, our blessed Redeemer had in like manner sought to captivate our love, and establish His claim to brotherhood amongst us. He entered on earth with the rights and privileges which His Godhead bestowed on Him. He possessed thoughts, virtues, perfections that belonged to a higher sphere than we could ever aspire to. Frailty was not His characteristic, death was not His desert, sin was not His tyrant. There seemed to be a hedge of separation between Him and us, which would prevent all true

I

feeling of fellowship and brotherhood, and mingle ever too much awe and reverence with our sentiments towards Him. When the angels appeared to Abraham in human form, though he had prepared a most abundant banquet, yet would he not venture into familiarity with them, and only stood by while they did eat: (Gen. xviii. 8.) and thus would our humanity have gladly welcomed, and hospitably entertained, our divine Guest, who had condescended to assume our nature, but would only have presumed to wait upon Him as a servitor or menial, glad to do homage, but fearful to claim a closer tie.

But such cold and measured relations with us, the deep and ardent love of Jesus spurned; and He resolved to give proof of His consanguinity with our frail race, by bearing the heaviest burthens which can be its lot, in their most unexampled aggravation. Sorrow and affliction are the portion of man, and He laid them upon Himself, in this Garden of Olives, until they crushed Him to the ground. In the sweat of His brow was man, in the earliest curse, condemned to till the earth; and a sweat of blood was that wherewith He watered it. Tribulation and anguish were the bitter ingredients of man's cup; and He made His chalice bitter, till His own heart sickened at its contents, and prayed that it might pass away. The wretchedest of men may find a name for his most grievous sorrow, but His alone could be termed a living agony, the struggle of death in the midst of health and vital power. And did He not thus fully establish His right to be the Son of wretched outcast man? Yea, and if suffering be the true badge and characteristic of our race, hath He not justly become the

very type of suffering humanity; and if the name of man
in sacred speech doth signify " the afflicted,"* who shall
deny his right to the name and its miserable privileges,
who on that evening won the emphatic title of the " Man
of sorrows" ?

And who will, after this, venture to say, that in the
willing abasement of that hour, He forfeited one tittle of
that exceeding glory, which he had assumed upon Mount
Thabor ? Who will assert that He dimmed in the least,
the evidence of His greatness and His divinity, by His
momentary humiliation ? For, rather, as the eclipse
which for a time hides the sun's disc, and withholds his
light, proves best the magnitude of his orb, beyond all
other heavenly bodies, and demonstrates him to be the
centre of the entire system, even so doth this partial,
apparent, obscuration only present the surest proof of the
sublime dignity and divinity of our Redeemer. No. Did
I wish to convince one whose feelings are alive to the
noble, the beautiful, and the perfect, but whose belief in
Him was weak, I would by no means take Him to Mount
Thabor, where the spectacle was meant for friends ; but I
would sooner lead Him to the other scene of the Mount of
Olives. The idea of one who is considered God-man,
represented as arrayed in glory, is too analogous to natural apprehension, to have so convincing a force. But
the conception of such a Being presented to us, " bowed
beneath sorrow till His pale forehead chilled the earth,
with a body bedewed with blood, and a soul steeped in
unutterable anguish—the conception of such a One hon-

---

* In Hebrew.

ouring the inferior nature which links Him with sorrow, by assuming its characteristics as fully as He ever bore those of the sublimer, embracing and caressing the cruelest realities of His manhood, with equal love and earnestness, as He did the magnificent prerogatives of His Godhead:—surely this is a thought, an idea, which the boldest invention never could have dreamt, and which none but one truly possessed of the two could ever have practically realized.

No; had the Redeemer of man been Himself but man, He would have been screened from every infirmity of his nature.   He would have required the investment of every outward attribute of perfection, even in appearance, to raise Him above the rest of men ; to make Him seem worthy of His immense elevation, and give Him a claim to the love, the obedience, and the veneration of His fellow-men.   Only one, who was truly God as well as man, could afford to sink beneath the lowest level of human wretchedness, and hope to secure love and admiration by becoming, to appearance, even less than man.

And if our very faith may thus be strengthened by visiting Olivet even after Thabor, what shall we say of love, whose very home and harbour is in community of suffering? Who hath even linked his heart to the stoics, cased in a mail of false philosophy, proof against the griefs of humanity ?   Who hath not, like Jonathan, loved one that with David, bears unmerited persecution with meek endeavourance ?   And who then will not love Jesus in the garden, even more than on the holy mount? I speak not now, as I have already forewarned you, of the endearing circumstances that all his suffering was for our redemption.

But only consider Him as one of ourselves, rendering beautiful and dignified, that which ordinarily degrades man; embracing, as a part of His being, that which all must suffer, though not so severely as He; and then in His higher character consecrating, and canonising, in His own person, the most disesteemed portion of our human lot. For in assimilating Himself thus completely to us, and involving Himself in all that beats down the heart of man, He wished to give proof of the holiness of mind which may sanctify the strongest bursts of uncontrollable anguish. Fortitude had been ever a virtue among heathens ; contempt of sufferings had been a boast among savages : both of them blunted the edge of the infliction; the former strained the sinews, the latter hardened them, into resistance.

Resignation was taught by Christianity alone; the virtue which bears the entire weight of calamity, bows down without opposition beneath its force, feels to the utmost the pain it inflicts, and then rises to praise God for what He hath permitted, and trusts more than ever in His love. And of this holy feeling, the purest and perfectest example was here given, in the cruel agony endured without mitigation, and without repining; and that too as a foretaste only of more grievous suffering. Can we for a moment doubt, that Jesus in this His second presentation to His chosen apostles wished thus to appear, not merely as asserting a claim to brotherhood with us, but as indicating the dignity of suffering, considered as that badge of humanity whereby He principally claims our love?

For is it not spoken of in the sacred volume, as though all that intensity of woe were but a state proper and belonging to Him, while the glory of His first appearance is described as unusual and unnatural? Would He, whose countenance giveth intelligence to the angels, and splendour to heaven, have otherwise been said to be transfigured, when it shone forth merely as the sun; and not rather be deemed then transfigured, when defaced and defiled, bruised and smitten? Would He, whose body was untouched by sinfulness, whose mind, when busied amidst a wicked world, was purer than the chastest virgin's holiest meditations, have been said to undergo a transformation, when the raiment that covered Him, caught the colour of His purity, and looked white only as the snow; and was He not to be called transformed, when His robes were red with His own blood, as though He came from Edom, having dyed His garments in Bozra? (Is. lxiii. 1.) Would that have been called a transfiguration of the Lord of glory, where the saints surround Him, to pay their court, and the heavens tell of His glory; and not rather then, when stripped of all marks of dignity, cast off and abandoned at once by earth and heaven?

No; in all this He wished us to consider Him as in His own chosen state. He cared not to extort our admiration, by a display of His surpassing majesty; He spoke of it as of a momentary extraordinary glimpse, a change which, for momentous reasons, He allowed to remove Him from our society; but He strove to win our love, by tasting more earnestly of the fruits of humanity, even than we, by joining us in the most trying allotments of God's dispensation, and proving to us the dignity of our nature, by not disdaining to assume its most humble and most abject forms.

But shall the more endearing lessons of this second transfiguration destroy the recollection of the first? God forbid; but let the one ever be by the other tempered. The princes of earth have their winter and their summer residences, that pleasure may be enhanced by variety, and each season have its fitting dwelling-place. And so be it ever with the Christian who loveth Jesus. Let him have in Thabor and Olivet a two-fold retreat, suitable to its various states. When his faith is cold, or his thoughts begin to grovel and creep on earth; when heaven seems too distant, and its acquisition too painful; when dejection and pusillanimity assail him, let him ascend the mountain of glory, and basking in its splendours, and hearkening to its evidences, and gazing on its enticements, there refresh and strengthen his mind and his belief.

But in the softer and the milder hour, when love reproaches you in your silent breast, that it is neglected; when tears of penitent sorrow begin to gush from the eyes; when the world and its afflictions lie wearily upon the heart; when your soul feels sorrowful even unto death, oh! repair to the Mount of Olives, the hill of unction and of rich abundance, there to weep and to pray, to sympathize and be comforted.

Upon both these sacred mountains it is good for us to be. Let us make upon each a tabernacle, wherein we may in spirit dwell; and then we may with well-grounded hope expect, that the third, not made with hands, our lasting dwelling shall be prepared for us on the holy mount: that Sion which is in heaven, on which is the city of the living God, the true Jerusalem, where we shall meet not one solitary angel of comfort, but " the company of

many thousands," of those messengers of salvation; not a few
saints of either covenant, but the array of the " spirits of
the just made perfect," with Jesus above all, and amidst
all, the Mediator, and the Head of " the Church of the
first-born," with that humanity which was by turns glorified and abased on earth, now permanently shining with
the splendour of Thabor, yet retaining "the sprinkling of
blood," which purified and fertilized the earth on Olivet.
(Heb. xii. 22.)

SERMON VII.

On Coming to Jesus for Refreshment.

MATT. xi. 28.

" Come unto me all ye that labour and are heavy laden, and I
will refresh you."

HAD the blessed Jesus proclaimed, Come unto me all
ye that are poor, and I will enrich you, or all ye that are
oppressed, and I will redress you, or all ye that are sore
and sick, and I will heal you ; and had He appointed
certain visible treasure-houses or dispensaries, where these
blessings might be dealt out to such as sought them, I
believe, my brethren, that He would at no time have
wanted a crowd of eager and zealous followers, and that
long trains of pilgrims would be daily seen starting to
give proof to the heavenly promise, by seeking therein
the remedy of their evils. And yet in any such hope,
had He proposed it, there would have been but scanty
measure of relief for the ills which oppress us ; nor could
He have well attempted to number each of these, however
large His discourse, with a provision of suitable remedy,
without leaving some sore place in man's estate without
its balm, and some uneasiness of his nature without its
consolation. But in the gracious speech quoted, He hath
comprehended in two words all the evils and distresses
which can vex or afflict us, (for all are a *labour* and a

burden,) and in another, in that short sweet invitation *come*, which the last page of the inspired volume puts into the mouth of the bride and of the spirit, (Apoc. xxii. 17) He hath condensed all the wisdom of consoling aphorisms, and all the treasures of spiritual pharmacy, together with many heavenly philtres and charms of a most marvellous operation.   And note, I pray you, how much more comprehensive and effectual is the simple and general prescription.   For as to its comprehensiveness it thus comes to reach to the heart, to the mind, and to the soul, embracing all the thousand indefinable ailments and sicknesses of each, though offering one only universal cure: which, without danger of error or excess, acts upon each according to its own peculiar need, and bestows everywhere comfort, relief, and increased strength.   Then as to the virtue and efficacy of this divine promise, if you feel inclined to doubt thereof, I know not what I can say other than did Philip to Nathaniel, upon his mis- doubting the praises uttered of our Saviour upon His being first discovered: whereupon Philip was contented to answer, "Come and see." (John, i. 46.)   And so do I say to you, come ye all and see, and make proof thereof, bringing your respective burthens and labours to His feet, and cast them down before Him, and He will bless them: and ye shall take them up again, and find them no longer heavy or distasteful, for they will by that blessing have been changed into *His* burthen, which is light; and into *His* yoke, which is most sweet.

It is my wish to aid you in this experiment, by point- ing out the way wherein each one may best come unto Jesus, according to the peculiar relief which he requires at His hand, showing the fittest season, as it were, and attitude wherein he should approach Him, how he should commune with Him regarding his distress, and how he may expect to receive His blessed assistance.

And first, I would address those on whom the various ills of life do seem to weigh with undeserved rigour, those who imagine that God hath dealt hardly with them, because they are but scantily supplied with earthly goods, or because their life is a continual suffering from accidents or illness, or because unjust calumnies and bitter injuries keep them in constant disturbance, or because the world has refused to do justice to their merits, but has rejected and illtreated them, though its signal benefactors. Or, I will suppose, all these various evils, each sufficient to embitter one particular life, united in the same person; and he will undoubtedly consider himself as arrived at the uttermost point of human wretchedness. Now, wishing to lead this sufferer to Jesus, for refreshment, such is the overflowing richness of consolation in Him, and so mean is all that we have rehearsed in the scale of true unhappiness, that I would not take him higher to drink than the first gushing forth of this wellspring of true comfort, reserving the fulness of its waters for more grievous sorrows. I would bid him approach his infant Saviour, and ask for consolation at the crib of Bethlehem. There he shall see all those evils whereof he, in the power of manhood, complains, combined in ten-fold strength, to afflict a tender child; and what he considered the winding up, and final consummation of accumulating misfortunes, here chosen as but the prologue to a bitter, and touching mystery of love. There will he see a royal babe exposed so soon as born, to the biting frost of a cruel winter, without the comfort of a decent roof, or sufficient clothing to protect it, seeing and touching around it, on that first night of life, and suffering, nothing but the plainest tokens of rudest poverty; then undergoing, with full consciousness, the degradation of a painful rite, and scarcely recovered, sought after by a prince who would give the diadem from his brows, to him that should slay it. Then He is forced to fly with but sorry attendance, through a long winter journey, into a foreign land, the banished and proscribed, poorer even, and more abject than he would have been in His own cottage at Nazareth ; and thus within a few days of His birth does He bear all the burthen of temporal evils, which the most wicked, or the most persecuted, of men could well incur in the course of a very long life. And surely if the power of sympathy is so great in relieving sorrow, if we bear with greater cheerfulness when we see others, equally worthy, sharing the same load, what consolation must we not derive from seeing who is here the companion of our misfortunes, of our poverty, the King of kings ; of our persecution, the Holy One ; of our rejection, the anointed of God ; of our pain and sorrow, the innocent Lamb, the world's infant Saviour.

Then too you may go nearer and reflect. You suffer by a dispensation over which you have no control, and to which you must perforce submit. But this tender sufferer, wherefore doth He endure so much, seeing that He is the Lord of all things, and the author of every blessing? Why does He not give the word to the shepherds that came to worship, and they will proclaim Him to the world ; and presently He shall see the whole country

aroused and bringing forth its best gifts, and His crib
surrounded with nobles, and warriors, and priests, and
tetrarchs, "and all the people of the land," who shall be
proud to carry Him on their shoulders, unto the city and
palace of David, even as they did the infant Joas, merely
because He was to be His forefather, and bear Him
through the gate thereof, and place Him on the throne of
the kings ?   (4 Kings, xi. 19.) Why doth not the angel,
in warning the wisemen against visiting Herod on their
return, tell them that he sought the infant's life, and give
it into their charge; and presently they will wrap Him up
in costly furs, and place Him in a jewelled cradle, and bear
Him away on their camels as a priceless treasure into their
own country, where He shall be tended and cared for as befits
so great and mighty a Lord? Or why doth He not ask of His
Father a legion of those angels who have come to sing
" glory" above His birth-place; and they shall be flattered
by the charge to bear Him up in their hands, and defend
Him against all the powers of earth, and minister unto
His wants, as they did afterwards in the wilderness ?

Dost thou who sufferest ask thus ?   Does not thine own
heart tell thee that it was in order that He might be like to
thee, and thou like unto Him ? that He might show thee
how wretchedness and pain are more akin, and, as it were,
foster-brethren to Him, sucking the breasts of His own
mother, rather than riches and happiness? And art thou
not more than consoled, yea, filled with joy and delight,
to think that thou, whom others despise, art, therefore, the
dearer to Him, and closer to His heart, and mayest presume the more upon His kindness; that the gifts thou
presentest Him are a thousand times more precious and

acceptable in His sight, than the offerings of those eastern
kings; that thy prayer is, according to His own word,
truly as frankincense which pierceth the clouds, and departs not till the Most Highest shall behold; that thy patient
endurance is a myrrh, bitter, indeed, in the mouth of him
that tasteth it, yet suffusing a precious savour, like the
Magdalen's spikenard, before Him whose feet thou wipest
in humble resignation; that thine own heart, thine own
self is as burnished gold, proved and annealed for Him in
the furnace of tribulation ?   And thus will you not wonder why His blessed mother, poor and persecuted, like
Himself and you, should be said to have laid up all these
words in her heart, as holy stores of joy and comfort for
all sorrow and misfortune.   And thus early doth Jesus
begin to afford refreshment.

But beyond this first class of worldly wretchedness
rises another still more difficult to bear, and requiring a
riper grace,—the sufferings of the spirit.   Some there may
be, though probably they are few, who have to deplore the
early ruin and destruction of all religious principle or
feeling within them, and after having yielded to the wiles
of some tempter, find themselves now to have been driven
from a paradise of happiness and peace, to which all return
seems inexorably debarred.   There can hardly be conceived a deeper wretchedness than the consciousness
and conviction of truth, without the power to embrace
it, than this feverish longing after a blessing, once within
our reach, but now withheld for our ill deserts.   No one
can describe the pangs of remorse, the racks and hooks of
jealousy and envy towards others, the perpetual scourge
of self-reproach, which such a person must endure; and

truly it is a burthen beyond all the outward evils of this world.

But besides this grievous burthen of interior tribulation, there is a labour which causes much uneasiness and pain, when the mind hath not been wholly shaken from the foundation of its early religious conviction, but finds itself unsteady and wavering on them; when, like the covering cherub, it hath not been cast down from God's holy mount, but walketh up and down thereon among the stones of fire, (Ezec. xxviii.) uncertain which to choose for its badge and signet. And in this age, when a keen and restless spirit of inquiry has descended among the children of men, and in this country where every year, every month, every day detects some new fallacy whereby they or their forefathers have been misled into hasty and unjust opinions on the subject of religion, the number of those cannot be small, who, either by their attention to passing events, or by the force of their own reflections, or by the clearer and bolder announcement of doctrines which, for three centuries, have been only whispered in the ear, have been led to entertain some doubts touching much which they have been taught, or at least some fear or surmise sufficient to break or flaw the illusion of previous security, and inoculate its constitution with a principle of restlessness, which must sooner or later break out into activity. Nor, if once a solemn doubt of what till now has been held as certain, presents itself before you, so long as you admit not a controlling or deciding power with authority at once to quell it, can you calm the mind or lull it to peace, by arresting or checking its onward course. Nor would it, indeed, be just or generous in any

one, who begins to find error mingled with his early prepo-
sessions, to arrest the eagerness for further inquiry, which
such a discovery must awaken.   Every mistaken opinion
reflecting on the principles or practice of others, is an
injustice to them however involuntary ; and to be
alarmed at finding early prejudices shaken, or believed
representations proved erroneous, and to turn the mind
from prosecuting investigation from fear of its being
farther undeceived, is as unjust as to suspend the exami-
nation of our accounts with others, for fear of discovering
farther errors in our reckonings, that might oblige us to
reparation.

But for either of these troubles of the mind and spirit
there is refreshment in Jesus.   Come unto Him when, now
entered upon His heavenly mission, He teaches the multitudes, or opens to His apostles the mysteries of faith.
And how are ye to come to Him ?   By deep and earnest
study of His holy word, wherein as it were His whole image
is reflected, read in humility, docility, and disinterested
readiness to obey His calls, rendered fruitful by fervent
and persevering prayer ; by listening to His word, as
expounded to you by His ministers, gladly receiving such
lights as may serve to guide you towards the settling of
your doubts, seriously weighing such evidence as may be
laid before you in candour and charity, however opposed
to your former opinions, thankfully accepting such explanations and representations as may correct the preposses-
sions instilled by ignorant or mistaken teachers.   For thus
we learn, that even in His lifetime they who wished to
come unto Jesus with advantage, were not content to
stand aloof, following Him in the crowd, nor yet ventured

to approach directly, and of themselves, before Him, but rather "came unto Philip, who was of Bethsaida of Galilee, and desired him, saying: Sir, we would see Jesus." (Jo. xii. 21.) And thus, likewise, will the ministry of His servants, however unworthy, often procure a speedier and happier acquaintance with Him, and readier access to the peace and refreshment of His knowledge, than your own direct and unaided efforts.

And from His holy word we may easily learn the dispositions and feelings wherewith you should come unto Him.

Come not as did the Sadducees, determined to doubt and to dispute everything, even to the first foundations whereon faith may be built; nor as the Herodians, putting to the test of captious and irrelevant consequences, and of political considerations, the pure dogmas of religion. (Mat. xxii.)

Come not as did the Pharisees to catch Him in His words, (Mar. xii. 13) by merely laying hold of expressions rather than things, and taking offence and scandal at words, without attending to the spirit which directs them, and the meaning they enclose.

Come not, as did the doctor of the law, and many others, tempting Him. (Mat. xxii. 35.) By which expression two different things are meant in Holy Writ. First, demanding of God some definite and specific line of evidence, or laying down some self-willed terms of conviction, upon which alone we will yield to what is proposed to us as His truth ; in which sense, Achaz said, " I will not ask (a sign), and I will not tempt the Lord," (Is. viii 12) and Judith reproached the rulers of Bethulia, saying, " who are ye that this day have tempted the Lord," (Jud.

K

viii. 12) by fixing a day for His deliverance? And St.
Luke tells of some who "tempting Jesus, asked of Him a
sign from heaven." (Luc. xi. 16.) And again, by the same
phrase is signified the constant recurrence and repetition
of the same difficulties and dissatisfaction, the returning
to them once answered and removed : in which sense the
Jews are said repeatedly in Scripture to have tempted or
provoked God, or rather His Word in the wilderness, by
ever murmuring anew, and refusing to be content with
what He had done for their satisfaction, rejecting ever the
proofs of divine mission given to His servant Moses. And
in either of these ways, beware ye tempt not Jesus.

Come not as did the young man, eagerly asking what
he should do to be saved, and upon finding that the terms
of salvation touched him in his worldly goods, and must
bring with it their loss, went away again sorrowful.

Come not, in fine, as did the Jewish multitude, following Him even into the wilderness to hear His word, and
then when His doctrines shocked their prejudices, and
attacked their national religion, took up stones to insult
and injure Him ; nor like those disciples who first eagerly
cleaved unto Him, and followed Him over all the land ;
but as soon as they heard a proposition which wounded
reason's pride, exclaimed, " this is a hard saying, who can
hear it, and went back and walked no more with Him."
(Jo. vi. 61-67.)

But rather come unto Him as did the father of him
possessed, " crying out with tears : I do believe ; Lord,
help thou my unbelief." (Mar. ix. 23.)

Come like Nicodemus who, not content with the general
instruction he might receive by standing in the Temple's

porch, or attending Jesus in the crowd, sought to have private speech of Him, to propose his own particular doubts, and consult in the silence of night the interests of his own salvation, receiving with meekness the severe reproof given him for his ill-timed objection, and becoming one of those few steadfast followers, who feared not to own Him as a master immediately after the ignominy of His cross.

Come to Him as Peter and the eleven, who, after they had heard, on His sufficient authority, doctrines incomprehensible to their reason, and repugnant to their senses, surrendered their belief into His hands without reserve, exclaiming : " Unto whom shall we go ? Thou hast the words of eternal life." (Jo. vi.)

Come to Him like Mary Magdalen, leaving to Martha, or those of your household, the cares and anxiety of domestic and worldly concerns, and heedless of their reproof, cast yourself at His feet, sit there in lowly and respectful attitude, in teachable and humble mood, looking upwards into a countenance whose calm majesty stamps truth on all He teaches, and whose winning smile can engage any one to embrace and practise it.

Or rather aim at still nobler feelings ; and if the solemn rite which I have interrupted form, as it generally does, the great stumbling-block of your unsettled faith, come with John the beloved unto Him, when instituting the mysteries of unspeakable and unimaginable charity at His last supper, and lean in childlike love and abandonment upon the bosom that conceives it.   Hear well its throbs and sighs after your redemption, the throes and pangs of this your birth-hour unto life ; take well the measurements of this deep and full cistern of mercy and graciousness, that " ye may be able to comprehend, with all the saints, what is the breadth, and length, and height, and depth of the charity of Christ, which surpasseth all knowledge ;'' (Eph. iii. 18) consider the majesty of divine almightiness, the ineffable energies of creative wisdom, and the boundless efficacy of redeeming love which dwelt therein together as in a holy temple, now joined in solemn counsel how to leave some last Godlike legacy to man worthy of them all ; feel that bosom, as you repose thereon, swelling and heaving with this great and majestical birth, this crowning work of love ; and then assuredly will your doubts change into confidence, your hesitations into assurance, your perplexity into peace, and nothing will appear too bold, too mighty, too divine, for such love to have given at such an hour, or for a soul like yours to believe in such an attitude.   There, there at length in that belief, you will have opened the full fountains of life ; there you may slake your burning thirst, and feel in Jesus refreshment after the weariness of anxious doubt.

Yet is there a heavier weight, and a more grievous labour, than any of these,—one to which we all are subject, and under which we all must groan,—the weight of sin, as the apostle justly calls it. (Heb. xiii.)   Under this we all walk from our childhood bowed down to the ground, and with our own hands we have added burthen unto burthen, heaping it up, until its load almost prevents us from looking up into the face of heaven.   And who amongst us hath not experienced the sorrows and miseries of this sad state? who hath not felt the anguish and torture of a rejection by God, and the loss of His holy

favour, and withal the ignominy, the helplessness, the
entire wretchedness which it must produce within the
soul? And it hath seemed some time to us as if a gulf
was placed between us and His mercy, between our spirit
and His,—a wide, deep, impassable gap in our attachments
and habits, in our affections and adopted nature, which
no power could enable us to surpass ; and we were thus
tempted to consider our case as hopeless, and our sore as
incurable. And yet, my brethren, it was not so. It is
such as are in this most miserable state that Jesus principally had in view, when He promised refreshment to
the troubled and oppressed. Draw nigh, come unto Him
all ye that labour with sin, and are heavy laden with
iniquity, and He will refresh you. Come to Him at that
blessed hour when His teaching finished, He is made a
sacrifice for sin, and has laid upon Him by God the
iniquities of us all.   .

Have you already felt within you the sorrows of a
loving repentance; have you already been at His feet, and
washed them with many tears, and poured out on them
the precious ointment of holy love? Have you heard,
through the voice of His minister, the consoling words,
that much hath been forgiven you, and do you feel within
you the blessed assurance, founded upon His first promises,
that you are a forgiven sinner, though one feeling that
much remains undone, to perfect the great work of
salvation? Come boldly forward ; your place is in His
chosen train, and near His cross, with her whom you have
imitated, with the centurion, and those who struck their
breasts in compunction at His death, and nearer still with
the disciple of love and the Virgin-mother. There, under

the shadow of that tree, and of your beloved that hangs thereon, in calm and feeling meditation on the graces purchased for you, and the charity displayed, you shall find sufficient to strengthen your weakness, to ripen your conversion into perseverance, and to inflame your luke-warmness into burning love.

But alas! does thy conscience still reproach thee that thou art unforgiven, and does thy courage fail thee to undertake the awful work of repentance? Art still staggering under the weight of the flesh and its lusts, and sinking under their load, as under that of a most heavy cross? Art thou not thus, as yet, like one of the evil-doers with whom Jesus was reckoned? Away then with thee unto Calvary, and bear thither this burthen of thy sins, and be crucified to them, beside Him. Stretch forth thine arms in earnest supplication, and let thy love nail thee to the cross. There transfer to thyself, for a moment at least, in mind, the pangs and tortures which He endured for thy salvation; count the wounds and bruises which should have been thine, for they were inflicted for thee; feel if thou canst the overflowing bitterness of sorrow and hatred towards sin which filled His breast, the abandonment by God, the forlorn desolation of soul, the universal unhappiness which overclouds Him, and there, hanging as it were at His side, read the handwriting which was against thee nailed upon His cross, read His title of thy Redeemer inscribed above His head, read the decree of thy forgiveness traced by His bloody diadem upon His brow, engraven by the soldiers lance upon His heart, and see if thou canst longer doubt that there is pardon even for thee, if with the penitent thief thou wilt cry out to Him in that hour, making confession and acknowledging thy guilt, even according to His appointed ordinances, and casting thyself with unbounded confidence upon His mercy, sole fountain of reconciliation and forgiveness. And amen, I say unto thee, in what day thou shalt thus come unto Jesus, thou too shalt be with Him in an inward paradise of peace and refreshment.

And ye, few indeed and chosen, who have long since found in Jesus relief from all the world's troubles ; whose minds, settled and at peace in Him, know not the anxieties and perplexities of religious doubts ; who trust in Him, that the load of your sins has been taken off, and that your course of virtue is regular and steady, is there for you no further refreshment in Jesus ? Oh, surely, there is ; for the tear is not yet wiped from your eye. Ye, too, have yet your burthen to bear ; the flesh is a load upon your spirit, which clogs its flight towards God, and makes you long that it be dissolved. You, likewise, then, must come to Jesus for your refreshment, but to Jesus, now no longer persecuted and suffering, but risen from the dead and in glory, sitting at the right hand of His Father. Thither you must already ascend in spirit, and there dwell ; thither must your sighs and longings daily rise ; thitherward must your looks be turned, as the captive prophets' were to the earthly Jerusalem. In the contemplation of that glory, now enjoyed by your beloved, ye may well forget the teasing claims of selfish interests; in the view of that calm ocean-like blessedness wherein His just are lost, ye may drown the impertinent tumults of all worldly uneasiness ; in the sight of that tenantless over-hanging crown, which your humble hope tells you may be reserved for you, ye may, indeed, feed unto fulness the richest, and purest, and holiest energies of your souls. And when the end shall come, then lift up your heads, for your salvation is at hand. Not for you is the last hour one of clamour to rouse the sleeping virgins, nor of despair to find your lamps untrimmed. It is, as Job describes it, the wished-for evening of the labourer's day, the remembrance of toil and travail finished, the casting on the ground of load and incumbrance, and the immediate prospect of rest and home. Not for you will the invitation of Jesus then sound as one of excitement to the laggard, or of encouragement to the faint-hearted, or of animation to the desponding, or of promise to the diligent; it must be as a watchword between Him and you on the confines of your two worlds, a signal repeated from one to the other, at that last strait pass into His kingdom, well understood and welcome unto both. "For the spirit and the bride say, come : and he that heareth, let him say, come." Then will He once more say, "Surely, I come quickly," and ye shall reply even as the gate is unbarred before you, "Amen, come, Lord Jesus, come." Then, at length "your joy shall be complete, and your joy no man shall take from you." (Apoc. xxii.)

Let us then all, the afflicted and the perplexed, the sinner and the righteous, "come and taste how sweet is the Lord, and how blessed is the man that hopeth in Him, (Ps. xxxiii. 9.) When on earth He allowed publicans and sinners to approach Him so familiarly as to bring censure on Himself ; once, when little children would have drawn nigh unto Him, and His disciples would have

withheld them, He rebuked them for it; when the
Pharisee was shocked at His allowing Himself to be
approached and touched by a woman notoriously infamous in the city, He commended her boldness, and received her into special favour. Thus did He show that
none is excluded from His all-embracing mercy and
kindness, and that His invitation to all that labour and
are heavy laden, is not a mere display of liberality, but
the true manifestation of sincere and gracious love.

But how shall we come to Thee, oh blessed Jesus!
unless Thy Father, who sent Thee, draw us unto Thee?
(Jo. vi. 44.) Our desires are too faint—our powers too
weak, ever of themselves, to reach Thee. Thy blessing,
then, be upon our unworthy efforts; a blessing upon the
lips of him that teacheth, and upon the hearts of them
that hearken; a blessing upon Thy word, and upon the
soil which shall receive it; a blessing upon our beginning, and upon our consummation; a blessing upon our
seeking and following Thee here, and upon our finding
and reaching Thee hereafter; a blessing upon our warfare, and a blessing upon our crown—in the name of the
Father, and of the Son, and of the Holy Ghost. Amen.

SERMON VIII.

On the Character and Sufferings of Christ in His Passion.[*]

JOHN, viii. 42, 46.

" Jesus said to them, . . . Which of you will convict me of sin."

THIS Sunday, my brethren, opens the annual commemoration of our dear Redeemer's sorrowful passion. It commences a week of preparation to the more solemn procession, through which His Church will soon accompany Him in spirit, from Gethsemani to Jerusalem, and from Jerusalem to Calvary. It therefore begins gradually to initiate us into the deep and unsearchable mystery of our redemption, which forms the ground of our hopes and the object of our belief; by the important and interesting appeal made by our Saviour in this morning's Gospel : " Which of you will convict me of sin ?" He is just going to be slain as the victim of sin, and yet He openly protests His immunity from it : He is soon to be treated as a culprit by the justice of His heavenly Father, and He seems, in this question, to appeal from this sentence to the conviction of His hearers, when He defies them to allege against Him one of those offences for which He is doomed, and justly doomed,

* Delivered on Passion-Sunday, 1830.

to suffer.   Yet, my brethren, there can be no contradiction between the justice of the Father and the appeal of
the Son ; for they are one, and can be but of one will.
Both therefore are truths, and, when united, they concur
to form the hidden mystery of redemption.

It is my wish to engage your attention for their consideration, as both demonstrated in the painful survey of
the close of our Lord's life.   Jesus by His passion vindicated from the slightest charge of even venial transgression ; Jesus in His passion, justly bearing the combined
punishment due to the sins of the whole world : these are
the two conflicting portraits of the world's Redeemer
which I wish to sketch for your edification, and thus
represent to you in its full grandeur, that most astonishing device of Almighty goodness, the innocent Lamb of
God, who yet should bear the sins of the world.

It had been foretold by king David that his great descendant should be treated as " the reproach of men and
the outcast of the people :" (Ps. xxi. 7) and such He
appears, in the most aggravated manner, in the history of
His passion.   Betrayed by one of His apostles, denied by
His greatest friend, abandoned by all His disciples, accused
by His own people, judged to die by the rulers and priests
of His nation, condemned to the cross by the Roman
governor, outraged with impunity by the vilest of men,
insulted publicly by the flagrant criminals with whom He
was associated in death ; surely any one who beheld this
spectacle must have concluded, that all those discordant
characters could never have conspired, in pitiless persecution, against any being stamped with the human figure,
unless he had been the most flagitious and remorseless of

his race. In fact, my brethren, this forms the scandal of the cross, "to the Jews a stumbling-block and to the Gentiles foolishness ;" and, alas! the apostle might have added, to modern unbelief a blasphemy and a scoff. But to the true Christian this scene brings triumph and joy ; for he sees, in it all, the noblest victory of Him whom he reveres, over the malice of man and the frailty of his nature, as he reads at every step, the attestations of his adversaries to His spotless character, and views the sublime perfection of it, exhibited in His own conduct.

For three years the Son of man had exercised His mission in every portion of the land, from Dan to Bersabee, and from the coast of Tyre to the parts beyond the Jordan. At every step His conduct had been narrowly watched by vigilant and keen adversaries ; their emissaries had beset Him with ensnaring questions, had assailed Him alternately with flattery or abuse ; by turns, the Pharisees, the Sadducees, and the Herodians, had employed their wily arts against Him to destroy their common reprover. His political principles had been tried, as on the question of tribute ; His religious opinions searched, as in the inquiry on divorce and the punishment of adultery. He, on His part, had acted openly and without disguise; had taught in the Temple, had debated in the synagogue, and healed in the streets and public places. He had mingled in every class of society ; had joined the publicans and the poor at their humble repast, or reclined at the more sumptuous table of the rich Pharisee. He had been placed in the most opposite situations ; now seized to be King against His will, now assailed with stones, or dragged towards the brow of the hill to be cast headlong from it. Do I wish to insinuate that through all these trials His character had never been assailed? Quite on the contrary : whoever adhered to Him had been solemnly excommunicated ; (Jo. ix.) He had been publicly denounced as a transgressor of the law, and a contemner of the Sabbath ; and His very miracles had been in His presence attributed to the co-operation of Beelzebub. Now at length the time is come, when through the treachery of His apostle He is in the hands of these foes ; now is their hour and the power of darkness. They have plotted His death and have determined upon cloaking it under the forms of justice. Some charge is necessary against Him: and we may therefore expect to hear an indictment of real or pretended offences, collected through this long course of unceasing investigation, and embodied into at least a specious form of accusation, in the frequent councils held by the entire Sanhedrim. (Matt. xxvi. 3, 4.) He stands then before them, on the last night of His life, without an advocate or a friend, to hear, in silent meekness, their charges against Him. Let us watch the course of this interesting inquiry.

The accusations are many, and witnesses are not wanting to support them. Yet all were such as even this partial tribunal could not admit: " they found not, though many false witnesses had come in," (Mat. xxvi. 60) " their evidence did not agree." (Mar. xiv. 56.) Was there then not one of His numerous miracles against which the charge of imposture could be artfully insinuated; was there no doctrine which could be ingeniously distorted into a contempt for the law ; no action which could be misrepresented into a transgression of public or private duty ?

Instead of any charge of this sort, after hearing and rejecting numerous depositions, the council is compelled to receive only one which exhibits a shadow of truth. Two witnesses attest that He had said, "I am able to destroy the Temple of God, and in three days to rebuild it." (Mat. 61.) From the accusation thus selected, we may judge of the futility of those which were discarded. It consists in an altered version, and palpable misapplication of an allegorical prophecy of His resurrection. Asked to reply to this accusation, our blessed Redeemer preserves a dignified silence : and this silence proves a sufficient confutation.   His very enemies become ashamed of the charge; and finding that they have even yet no grounds to slander His character, the high-priest rises, and .solemnly adjures Him in the name of the living God, if He be the Christ, the Son of the living God.   He answers in the affirmative; the high-priest rends his garments and exclaims: "He hath blasphemed.   What further need have we now of witnesses ?   Behold now you have heard the blasphemy.   What think you ?   But they answering said : He is guilty of death." (Mat. 65.)

Such then is the charge upon which, at length, they have agreed to rest the sentence of condemnation. From this preliminary trial before Annas and Caiphas follow them to the tribunal of Pilate, where the result of the night's deliberation has to be urged against their prisoner. Of what crime is He now accused? Of having excited contempt against the temple of God, or suggested its destruction ? Or perhaps of blasphemy in calling Himself the Christ the Son of the living God ? Nothing of the sort. Though these were the only accusations upon

which the assembly had voted Him guilty of death but a
few hours before, they are not even mentioned now before
the governor. They have changed their ground once
more, and that in the most infamous manner. " We have
found this man perverting our nation, and forbidding to
give tribute to Cæsar, and saying that He is Christ
the King." (Luke, xxiii. 2.) " If thou release this man
thou art no friend of Cæsar's ; for whosoever maketh
himself a king, speaketh against Cæsar." (Jo. xix. 12.)
" Truly iniquity hath lied against itself." The Jews and
their rulers were anxiously expecting their Messias as
a great Sovereign and universal conqueror, who was to
crush the diadem of the Cæsar's beneath the sceptre of
David ; and yet they pronounce the very desire to do so,
a crime worthy of death. But even this new charge is
amply confuted. After inquiry into the nature of the
sovereignty claimed by the accused, Pilate returns to the
Jews and answers " I find no cause in Him." (Jo.
xviii. 38.) " No nor yet Herod ; for I sent you to
him, and behold nothing worthy of death is done to
Him." (Luke, xxiii. 15.)

Such is the result of this keen investigation. Accusers
all in their turns rejected by His own enemies ; charge
after charge discarded by them as untenable, and the
last fully disproved by the judge whom they had
chosen; sentence pronounced by him with a protestation
that it fell upon the innocent ; this is the process of the
Son of Man. And while His enemies are thus baffled in their
search after some plausible accusation, their victim
challenges them earnestly to the inquiry, and calls upon
them to collect every evidence. When they ask Him " of

His disciples and doctrines," He answers, " I have spoken openly to the world ; I have always taught in the synagogue, and in the Temple, whither all the Jews resort. Why askest thou Me? Ask them who have heard what I have spoken to them : behold they know what things I have said." (Jo. xviii. 20, 21.)

This want of evidence could not arise from the difficulty of procuring it ; and it surely was not from the faintest lingering of a sense of delicacy in their minds, that the unjust adversaries could neglect the witnesses who were at hand. Their whole conduct shows them incapable of such a feeling. Crowds of unlettered and timid women have followed Him from Galilee; they are initiated in His doctrines, and have witnessed His actions: how valuable might their testimony be, when elicited by the crafty subtlety, or extorted by the imposing authority, of those who sat in the chair of Moses ! His disciples have fled, and deserted Him; they have proved their timidity or rather their cowardice : why are they not seized, and summoned to depose against Him ? Peter is in the hall with the servants of the high-priest. He has denied his Master upon the harmless accusation of a maid, and in the face of one who had seen him in the garden : how much greater terror might be struck into him by the threatening adjurations of the high-priest, speaking as the minister of God, and as the organ of supreme authority ; and how easily from denial might he be forced into accusation ! But, above all, where is the traitor Judas ? The man who could betray his friend, after having dipped his hand into the same dish with Him, an action in his country equivalent to a solemn oath of perpetual fidelity—

that man, surely, will not hesitate to accuse Him.   The traitor, who sold his Master and Benefactor for thirty pieces of silver, will not scruple, were it only for his own credit, to bring some charge which may justify or palliate his deed, in the face of the world.   Instead of this, he restores the price of blood, protests in the face of the tribunal that he has betrayed the innocent, and hangs himself in despair.   The enemies of Christ, then, must well have known, that even from such witnesses as these, not the slightest accusation was to be hoped.   Oh surely, of all the children of men, none other could have passed through such a trial from the hands of sworn enemies, with a character not only unwounded by the imputation of crime, but even unsullied by the breath of slander.

Suppose that this iniquitous tribunal could have arraigned their great law-giver, the pride and boast of their nation, Moses, and had determined upon his conviction. Of him they might have said, that he had acted with apparent cruelty to his sister Mary ; that he had reduced the people to distress ; that under his government they had been nearly exterminated by plagues, the sword of the Levites, and the bite of fiery serpents ; that his opposers had been devoted to ruthless destruction, and that he himself had disobeyed the Divine commandment at the rock. However false, some charge might have been made out, bearing at least the semblance of accusation. But Jesus had gone about only doing good; had cured every disease, had fed the multitudes, had conferred benefits on His very enemies; and, when assaulted with stones, of all the sons of men, He alone could boldly ask: "Many good works I have shown you from my Father : for which of those works do you stone

L

me ?" (Jo. x. 32.) "If, then, in the green wood, they did these things, what would they have done in the dry?" Even the law-giver of the Jews, must have perished under the doom of such a court, with the name at least of some crime written upon his cross : Jesus alone could die through its sentence, with only His most glorious title blazoned over His head.

With justice, then, could our Redeemer make His appeal to His very enemies. "Which of you will convict Me of sin ?" and it must be a subject of delight to His faithful followers to find that His appeal was fully justified by these enemies themselves. But if from their conduct we revert to His, we shall find that this challenge fell far short of what He might truly have demanded; for we shall there see a character, every trait of which radiates with a perfection, not only unattainable, but inconceivable, by human weakness. It is adversity indeed, that gives the last finish to the moral portrait of man; yet after all it can only mark more strongly His nobler features, and develope an expression of dignity and fortitude. But adversity, my brethren, would be an extenuating term to express the furnace of tribulation through which our Redeemer passed; dignity, and fortitude, would be but mean characteristics of that inexpressible quality of soul with which He endured. It is not necessary that I should enumerate here the varied torments which He underwent; they are familiar to your minds, and we shall have to dwell sufficiently upon this painful topic in the second part of my discourse. At present, I only wish you to contemplate the manner in which they were supported, by contrasting it with every species of endurance wherewith the world has ever been acquainted; to see whether the perfection of our nature alone could have possibly attained to it.

It was a fortitude, for I must call it by the name of some human virtue, which did not result from strength of nerve, or hardihood of constitution. The Son of Man had not been trained to practices that confer these qualities : He had always exhibited a tender and yielding disposition. He had been seen to weep, now over the death of a friend, (Jo. xi. 35) now over the yet distant desolation of His country. (Luke, xix. 41.) When His life had been attempted, He had prudently escaped, instead of facing the danger; when there was conspiracy against Him, He walked alone and trusted not Himself to them. Hence, on the present occasion, He offers no resistance, and yet His enemies dread to seize Him; He uses no menaces nor defiances, and yet His persecutors are baffled. He conquers by submission, He wearies their cruelty by endurance.

It is not the courage of the philosophers. Often has the impious parallel been made between the most celebrated man of that class in his last moments, and the Saviour of the world in His passion. But what a contrast in their situation! The one drinks with grace the poisonous draught, conscious that, however he may be hated and envied by a few, the attention of his fellow-citizens rests on him with reverence, to catch his last words, and that of his disciples, with affection, to inhale the last breath of their master. The other drains to the dregs a chalice of bitter suffering, such as never before or since was prepared for any human creature, scorned, outraged, and insulted by the whole of His nation, abandoned, denied and betrayed by His own dearest followers. What a contrast in their manner ! The one, supported by his numerous friends, defends himself with earnestness and ingenuity, perhaps even with the sacrifice of his real principles, and beguiles his last moments, by the cheering speculations of his profession. The other stands mute through His various trials, with every temptation of innocence to make a triumphant defence ; and preserves an unabated equanimity amidst the desolation and abandonment of His cruel death. And yet His silence convinced Pilate more than the studied eloquence of the other did his judges ; yet, the calm resignation of His agony forced from the lips of the hardy centurion and the prejudiced multitude, that " verily this was the Son of God ;" while the dramatic exit of His rival could only procure for him the praise that he had died like a philosopher.

In fine, my brethren, it was not the fortitude of the martyrs. They were supported in their torments by the example of constancy and love, which He first presented. Yet, even in their virtue, some weak infusion of human frailty might be perceived. The bold tone of defiance in which they sometimes addressed their judges; the warmth with which they overthrew the altars of the false gods ; the eagerness with which they even cast themselves under the stroke of the executioner: these demonstrations of alacrity and zeal were a flame breaking out from the fervour glowing within them, a flame ardent indeed and brilliant, but just sufficiently tinged to show, that some small grains of human frailty mingled with its sacred fuel. But their guide and head, in His passion, evinced nothing of this : not an accent of defiance any more than of complaint escaped His lips ; He sought not to aggravate or hasten, any more than to diminish or retard, His sufferings. Theirs was the daring ardour of the champion,—His the unresisting meekness of the victim.

Yes, my brethren, it is precisely this, which makes the conduct of Jesus during His passion, original in its perfection, and solitary in its sublimity; that His endurance and fortitude was the consequence of those qualities of soul, which, in human calculation, would have led to the very opposite results, but which in Him blended into one divine character the most dissimilar virtues: He alone is strong in not resisting, He alone is courageous in making no opposition. But in the midst of this singular patience there are traits which could not have entered into even the imaginary delineation of human perfection. That kind exertion of power which wrought a miracle to heal one of His captors, though He would not do so before Herod, to save His own life ; that look, which amidst unspeakable torments, could dart at once reproof and forgiveness into the heart of the apostle who had just denied Him; that compassion which could make Him forget His own cruel sufferings, to console the pious women who wept over Him ; that filial piety and zeal, which in the last agony, could provide for the comfort of a parent, and attended to the salvation of His fellow-sufferers; above all, that unheard-of charity which could exhaust His last breath in a supplication for His persecutors' forgiveness: oh, my brethren, these are not the looks, the actions, the accents of man ! How are the ways of God exalted above our ways ! How differently would human wisdom have sketched the character of a God made Man for the redemption of the world! We might have made Him come as the Jews expected Him, a conqueror, overthrowing all who resisted His will, and opposed His religion. But would He then have been more glorious than when, with a strong hand and extended arm, He overthrew the host of Pharaoh, and rescued His people from the bondage of Egypt? We might have supposed Him remodelling the human heart, and gradually adapting it to the infusion of His law. But would He then have appeared in the same magnificence as when He framed that heart from the dust of earth, and by His touch communicated its first vital impulse? No, my brethren, by any of these ways He would have only shown Himself the same as He had always been—the Great, the Terrible, and the Majestic, beyond our imitation as beyond our comprehension ;—but never should we have seen His unlimited perfections acting in the narrow sphere of human relations; never would men and angels have beheld what it would have been deemed blasphemous impiety to imagine—the conduct of a God in suffering and in death.

Hitherto, my brethren, we have viewed, in the person of our suffering Saviour, the " High-Priest, holy, innocent, undefiled, separated from sinners, and made higher than the heavens;" (Heb. vii. 26) we have now to consider Him in the very opposite character, as the Victim charged with the iniquity of the whole people. We have heard His appeal that none could convict Him of sin : we have seen that appeal more than justified in His passion, by the conduct of His adversaries and the perfection of His own character ; we have now to behold Him, in spite of this personal innocence, doomed to die by the decree of His own Eternal Father, as overcharged with a debt for sin. The sentence of men was indeed unjust which condemned Him as a criminal; that of the Father just, as all must be which He commands : and so strong is the contrast between these two simultaneous sentences upon earth and in heaven, that it appears as if even the small particles of equity which lingered here below after the first fall, were now withdrawn from earth, in order that the whole powers of this attribute might be concentrated with greater force in this almighty arm. It fell from heaven undivided upon the head of this devoted Victim.

God, my brethren, abhors sin, with a hatred which it has not entered into the heart of man to conceive. Yet, for four thousand years had He witnessed its increasing ravages over the face of His creation. The first fall had been quickly succeeded by transgressions, without number and without limits. A blindness had dimmed the eyes, a frenzy had seized the heart of man, a perversion of will distorted all his faculties, a feebleness of purpose paralyzed all his desires of good. At every step, the whole race plunged deeper into the abyss of religious ignorance and criminal excess, which proceeded to the absolute degradation of their nature. A thick cloud veiled from their sight the great Author of all good, or, if it occasionally transmitted a few rays from His glory, it was only with a more fierce and threatening glow. The world had even forgot its Maker : the worship of the true God was at one time confined to one tabernacle in the desert, covered with skins, around which only a stiff-necked and rebellious people knelt : the whole of His inheritance scarcely formed more than one speck upon the broad surface of His earth. Alas ! what was to check His vengeance upon His ungrateful creatures ? Was it the faint smoke of the few victims slaughtered upon this one altar, which could scarcely penetrate an atmosphere tainted with abominations, and reeking with crime ? No ; the blood of oxen, or of goats, or the ashes of a heifer sprinkled, could sanctify no more than to the "cleansing of the flesh." (Heb. ix. 13.) Was it the prayers and expiations of the few just who remained faithful to their God ? But not even for themselves could they have deserved mercy, seeing that "the Scripture hath concluded all under sin," (Gal. iii. 22) and that they belonged to the infected race. How much less could they have been propitiation for others ? For, "no brother can redeem, nor shall man redeem : he shall not give to God his ransom, nor the price of the redemption of his soul." (Ps. xlviii. 8, 9.) Hence it was, that the Almighty might have visited the earth with His punishments, but even these could form no expiation and no security. They could only be like the storm, which clears, in its frightful course, the impurities that have gathered under the face of heaven, then leaves them once more to collect, till sufficient to merit the same awful remedy. Had there been no further resource, better would it have been for man, had the great Creator shaken insunder the fabric of the earth ; or if, on His first great chastisement, He had, in the family of Noe, completely cut the chain of human existence, which continued into the regenerated world the crimes and defilements of its predecessor. But no ; in the dread book of the Almighty's decrees, at its very head a mysterious person had entered the solemn and impressive words, " Behold I come." These formed the charm which suspended the exterminating decrees of an outraged Deity, which made Him receive, with complacency, the odour of His sacrifices, and listen with mercy to the supplications of His servants.

When, at length, the fulness of time had come, this voluntary victim who was to expiate the sins of all, Jesus Christ, the Son of God, stands ready to receive the fatal doom. Two things were necessary to accomplish His great purpose; that He should take upon Him the offences which He has to atone, and that He should present an equivalent for the debt due to Divine Justice for them.

In the Garden of Olives the first condition begins to be fulfilled. As the fatal moment prescribed for the commencement of His sufferings arrives, His character and feelings undergo the dreadful change. He is no longer regarded by His Father, as that beloved Son in whom He expressed Himself well pleased, from the cloud of Mount Thabor ; or whom He had a few days before glorified by a voice from heaven. Instead of this, He sees before Him a culprit, upon whose head lie all the iniquities of men; all the foul idolatries, and the horrible abominations of the pagan world; all the rebellions and treasons of His favourite people ; and what is still more grievous, the black ingratitude of those who should taste the fruits of His redemption. Each of the ingredients, every particle of this mass of turpitude, excites His abhorrence in an inconceivable degree; they are now, for the first time, accumulated upon one subject, and bury from His sight, the high dignity of Him whom they oppress. Hence all those feelings which they must excite in Him are no less concentrated against this representative of crime : the indignation which sent a flaming sword to chase our first parents from Paradise, the wrath which drowned in one deluge the entire race of man, the detestation which rained fire and sulphur upon seven cities; these have all at length found one common channel, into which they can pour their burning stream, and so satisfy a craving justice, till now only partially allayed.

Oh ! what a corresponding change does this cause in the soul of our dear Redeemer. He, too, hates sin as much as His heavenly Father; He, too, pursues it with equal detestation, and would avenge the Divine Justice wherever its enemy is to be found. What a prospect then must it be to Him to see the transgressions of the whole world thus crowding before Him, oppressing His soul ! He sees them not merely in mass and indistinctly,—the light of the Divinity, which beams on His soul, shows Him each separate and clear, as if that moment actually perpetrated before His eyes. But, it is not a mere enumeration of these horrors which forms His occupation. The dark and dismal catalogue He has made His own, He has become surety for its amount; and His soul, a few moments before enjoying the " peace of God," serene and tranquil, gradually becomes darkened and agitated by the increasing storm, till it is made one scene of desolation, uneasiness, and distress. "My soul," says He, "is sorrowful even unto death." (Mat. xxvi. 38.) The shame accompanying the commission of crime overwhelms Him, and forms the first ingredient of His bitter cup.

We, my brethren, are but too habituated to the commission of sin, to experience that delicate and fine, but for this very reason, more piercing feeling, which makes us blush and stand confounded before our own consciences, even when there is no witness of our fault. But He sees His pure soul, incapable in itself of the slightest defilement, now hideously disfigured by millions of abominable crimes, more odious to Him than death. Abashed and degraded, He sinks upon the earth. His mental sorrow is necessarily connected with another dreadful suffering, the simultaneous anticipation of every torment inflicted upon Him through His passion. For, as He has to bear the iniquities of the entire race, so must He bear those of His persecutors; and in reviewing them all, He necessarily suffers the pangs, by inflicting which they are to be committed. He feels Himself charged with the treason of Judas, and with the apostacy of Peter. Every blasphemous word to be uttered against Himself, is a stain which now defiles His soul. Thus does He rehearse in His mind every part of the bloody tragedy which has immediately to commence, bearing at once its sufferings and its guilt. Each blow upon His sacred head, not only drives deeper the wreath of thorns which encircles it, but inflicts a far more racking wound, in the guilt of sacrilegious profanation, which it lays upon Him. Every stroke of the guilty hammer, which forces the nail into His tender palm, not only rends its quivering fibres, and convulses His sensitive frame, but transfixes His soul with a keener anguish, by the impiety against God's anointed which it adds to His burthen of sin. He considers Himself a fallen and a rejected creature; and this deep sense of degradation generates an anxious timidity hitherto unknown in His conduct. Oh, how is He changed from what we have always hitherto beheld Him! He has left all His disciples except three, whom He selects to be the companions of His agony—" Stay you here and watch with me." He dreads the eyes of even these three favourite disciples, whom He has selected to be His companions, and He retires from them in order to pray alone. Three times He returns to receive some consolation from them, and to derive some support from their uniting with Him in prayer. Alas! He used to be their consolation and support; He used to exclaim to them " Ye of little faith, why do ye fear." Yet now He must recur to *them* for a like encouragement, and even in this is doomed to disappointment. How different His prayer from that poured forth in the days of His joy! " O my Father, if it is possible, let this chalice pass from me. Nevertheless, not as I will, but as Thou willest." (39.) What, then! is Thy will no longer to do that of Him who sent Thee, that Thou shouldst distinguish between them? Where is now that confidence with which Thou wert wont to exclaim, " Father, I know that Thou hearest me always" ? (Jo. xi. 42.) Why this conditional, this diffident, this so frequently repeated prayer?

Because, He feels Himself changed into another man; He calls out as an unworthy sinner, and as such He is unheard. Even an angel from heaven is necessary to support Him in His excess of agony. Oh what a change again is here! The heavenly spirits did indeed announce

His conception, and sing hymns of joy and glory at His birth : they came and ministered to Him after His rigorous fast. But that they should have to descend upon such an errand as this, to console their Master, and support Him in His sufferings, this surely is a service never anticipated by these faithful ministers of His will. O Lord, what wonder, that with this complicated agony, Thy limbs should fail, Thy pores should break open, and Thy agitated bursting heart should impel its streams with unnatural violence, through Thy trembling limbs and body, till its precious drops gush through the skin, and bathe Thee prostrate on the ground, in a sweat of blood ! " Surely He hath borne our infirmities, and carried our sorrows, . . . and the Lord hath laid on Him the iniquity of us all." (Is. liii. 4, 6.)

The first condition of atonement was thus observed—the second yet remains; and it was fulfilled upon the cross. I will not attempt to lead you through the preliminary sufferings of this willing Victim, nor to describe His torments from the heartless and brutal treatment of the Jewish rabble, or the more studied and systematic mockery of the Roman soldiery. It is the completion of the sacrifice on Calvary, which principally deserves our notice. Of those who beheld the sad procession move towards this fatal spot, and beheld its principal sufferer tottering in the last state of weakness, beneath the weight of His own cross, His hair and beard plucked, His features defaced, His tattered raiment stiffened with gore, His body gashed and welted with stripes, His comely head torn with the thorns which crown it ; if any who saw this spectacle, knew that it was His Eternal Father who com-

manded Him thus to ascend, in order to be immolated, he
would surely have anticipated that the last stroke at least,
would be averted, and have flattered himself, that again, it
would be said with truth, "On the mountain, the Lord will
provide a victim." But no, my brethren, Divine Justice
cannot be eluded; and the heavenly holocaust is cruelly fastened to the altar. Oh who can recount, who can conceive,
the sufferings of His last three hours! All the sores
inflicted by His previous torments retain their former
smart, now aggravated by being re-opened, and gangrened
through exposure to the air. Besides these, four new
wounds, roughly inflicted by the nails which fix Him
to the cross, ever tearing and enlarging, maintain an unceasing and racking pang. A parching thirst, only
aggravated in Him by a draught of gall and vinegar ; a
burning fever tingling through every turgid vein ; a
constrained respiration fruitlessly struggling for ease and
freedom,—such were the ordinary torments of crucifixion ;
but, in this instance, they were the least portion of the
suffering. Even the most abandoned culprit meets with
some commiseration from the multitude; and some expression of sympathy generally soothes his dying ear. But
the Redeemer of the world is pursued with taunts and
scoffs, to the last moment of His life. Not a friend, or a
comforter, raises His head before Him, except those whose
sorrow only aggravates His own—His Mother, and His
beloved disciple. His little property is all in the hands of
His enemies, who are unfeelingly amusing themselves at
the foot of His cross, by casting lots over His wretched
spoils. But what is all this, to the abandonment and
desolation of soul which He now feels ? For Him it was

little that the world should have forsaken Him, or conspired against Him, so long as He was supported by His heavenly Father.   But this consolation is now withdrawn; as He hangs between earth and heaven, He feels Himself placed between man and His offended Deity, abandoned by both, unpitied by both ; and, after looking in vain around Him on earth, to gather some mite of consolation here below, He casts up His desponding eyes towards heaven, and exclaims in His last burst of sorrow, and distress, " My God, My God, why hast *Thou* abandoned me !" But no, this is not enough ; not only does He hold Himself abandoned but accursed of God ; "for cursed," says St. Paul, " is every man that hangeth on a tree."   He considers Himself as one struck by God and afflicted, and abstracting from the malice of man, feels in every wound the poignant stroke of His infliction. The darkness which veils the face of heaven, appears to Him not as the mourning of Nature over His sufferings, but as if the sun refused to shine upon such an object of Divine wrath and execration.   The earthquake, with which the ground reels, as He expires, seems to Him not the convulsive pang of creation in sympathy with its suffering Maker, but the painful throes of the world, unable to support the burthen of iniquity which presses from His cross, and struggling to be delivered of its accumulated weight. Oh are not all these sufferings an adequate compensation to the outraged rights of Heaven, for the sins of the whole world ! If justice demanded, and compassion had granted, that blood of such price should be shed for man, it was not surely necessary that it should flow in such a copious stream. But thou, oh Jesus ! wast not content with less than a complete and unreserved purchase, that we might not be any longer our own, but be Thy people, and Thou our Sovereign King. Oh, and what a throne, dear Lord, hast thou chosen, to reign over us—what a sceptre, what a crown ! Not a seat of majesty like that of Thy predecessor, Solomon, which dazzled by its splendour, and astonished by its magnificence all who entered, but the hard and knotty rack of the cross, disjointing Thy limbs, and grating upon Thy mangled body ! Not the sceptre of Assuerus, which all men dreaded to see withheld, and which saved a life by every touch ; but the weak and despicable reed, which mockery has thrust into Thy wounded hand, and whose strokes only descend upon Thine own venerable head! Not the diadem which Thy father David made from the spoils of Melchom, rich in much gold, and glittering with precious stones, (1. Paral. xx. 2) but a circle of long hard thorns, straining and goring Thy sacred brows, and glistening with the crimson drops which it has rudely torn from Thy veins. Oh be not these sorrows endured for us to no purpose ! Thy blood, which pleadeth better than that of Abel, and which cleanseth us from all sin, be upon us, and upon our children; not as called down upon themselves, by the blaspheming Jews, but as its drops fell upon Thy sorrowing disciple at the foot of the cross, as a dew of mercy, reconciliation, and peace !

My brethren, I am conscious of having drawn for you but a faint etching of these two portraits of the Son of God, where the subject might have been wrought into a rich and glowing picture. But still, I may ask, does not reverence for His sacred perfections, and gratitude for His redemption, impel us, once at least in the year, to commemorate

His sufferings?   The season set apart for this purpose, is now come; and, as the functions therein will have commenced before I address you for the last time, next Sunday, allow me here to inculcate the propriety of a respectful and devout behaviour during their celebration. Many of you have, perhaps, been brought up to consider that all pomp and ceremony should be banished from religion; you have been taught that, while you may employ the richest perfume, which the bounty of God has cast over the earth, in the cause of vanity, or personal gratification, it then only becomes an odour of death, when it ascends in a cloud of homage before the altar of its Giver.   You have been, perhaps, taught that the riches of earth, the gold and silver which He has claimed as His own by His prophet (Malachi), may be lawfully used to deck the tabernacles of clay which we inhabit, but they are cast away in useless superstition, the moment, " in the simplicity of our hearts, we offer all these things" for the splendour of God's house. If, then, these are your feelings, I say to you, "refrain from these men," and leave them to themselves.   Mingle not in a worship which you do not approve.   But if you *will* place yourself in this situation, remember that you are present where the most dignified hierarchy of the greatest Christian Church is assembled to commemorate the sublime benefit of salvation.   Remember that the hymns which you hear chaunted in solemn pathos, are the dirge and funeral song of the Redeemer of the world, when, according to the advice of Jeremias, the daughter of God's people, girt with sackcloth and sprinkled with ashes, makes mourning as for an only son. (vi. 26.)   You pass with gravity and salute

M

with reverence, even the humble bier of the poor, as it moves to his last abode, and you respect the sorrow of those who mourn after his remains : surely it is not too much to expect the same for the whole Christian Church, weeping over the cruel death of her Redeemer and Head.   And if any one, with such a reflection before his eyes, conducts himself with disrespect, much more with insult, that man must be so insensible to the benefit commemorated, that it is not harsh to say, that had he lived at the time, he would have joined in the outcry for the release of Barabbas, and scoffed on Calvary in the face of the cross.   " But from you, my brethren, we hope better things."   We trust that you will show to the world that your faith, your hope, reposes upon the mystery of the cross, and that by celebrating worthily this first visit of the Lord, when He comes in meekness and peace, you will not have to dread His second appearance, in the day of His judgment and His wrath.

SERMON IX.

On the Scandal of Christ.

MATT. xi. 6.

"Blessed is he that shall not be scandalized in me."

THE moderation of our Lord's demands, my brethren, should be the inverted measure of our confusion. In proportion as He, who could claim all things, contents Himself with asking little, as He bates more and more of His just rights and lawful exactions, we, too, should rise, or rather sink in our humiliation, and our blushes should deepen, to see how low an estimate He must have formed of our gratitude and our worth. " Blessed is he that shall not be scandalized (or offended) in me !" Note well the connexion of this sentence. " The blind see, the lame walk, the lepers are cleansed, the deaf hear, the dead rise again, the poor have the Gospel preached to them— and blessed is he that shall not be scandalized in me." What! of such as are thus benefited, is no more asked ? Shall they not be called on to minister with their worldly goods, to Him who has restored to them the blessings of life, yea their very life itself ? Is not the foot, or the eye, which He hath renewed, the health which He hath brought back, His, that it should serve Him for ever ? Shall He not have a room in the widow of Naim's house, as the prophet had at Sarepta; shall not the ruler feast Him, when He passes by his way; and the centurion be called on to rescue Him from the conspiracies and violence of His enemies ?   Could any individual being, in a nation so favoured as that was, with His glorious presence, so loaded with mercies, by the exercise of His great power, be reasonably called blessed, even for showing gratitude, overt, active, unceasing and unwearied towards Him; or for feeling love, deep, fervent, and inexhaustible ?   And yet, He seemeth hardly to dare asking so much. He shrinks in fear of man's corrupt heart, in suspicion of our wayward affections, from overcharging us with such a load of sweetness.   He sets the price and acquisition of blessing at the lowest possible instalment of gratitude. " Blessed is he that shall not be scandalized in me !"   As though He had said : "Happy shall ye be, if ye refrain from showing me aversion and dislike; blessed shall ye be, if, not having courage to welcome me when I arrive at Jerusalem with hosannas, ye will at least abstain from joining in the outcries for my blood !   Well shall it be with you, if, unable to stand by me in my trials, with the faithful few who shall surround the foot of my cross, ye, at least, stand not in the crowd, and wag your heads at me in mockery."   Oh, how poor indeed, must human nature have seemed to Him, when He rated its blessedness so low !

And we, my brethren, what are we but a crowd of blind, and lame, and helpless wretches who surround Jesus ; and all of us are lepers whom He hath cleansed from sin in the laver of regeneration; and many of us have been dead, and raised by Him from the deep and thrice-sealed graves of our iniquities. And yet, of us too, He well may say, "Blessed is he that is not scandalized in me." Doubtless, upon hearing these words, and considering them as addressed to us, we, each of us, exclaim with Peter, "Although all men should be scandalized in Thee, *I* will not be scandalized." (Mat. xxvi. 33.) Doubtless, our hearts revolt at the idea of being so thankless and unfeeling; and we fancy, in the delusions of our self-love, that never should we shrink from owning and professing Jesus, even should temptation come. And yet, alas! my brethren, I say it with pain and with shame, the chances are, that, if but the slightest trial presented itself this day, before the cock shall crow, we should deny him thrice!

In two different ways does our Saviour tell us that we may be scandalized in Him. For first, when some men, thinking His doctrine hard and unpalatable, thereat murmured, He reproved them, saying : " Doth this scandalize you ?" (Jo. vi. 62.) Are you offended at my doctrine, because it does not fall within the narrow circle of your comprehensions or conceptions ? Secondly, when foretelling the cowardice and flight of His apostles, upon seeing Him ignominiously and unjustly treated, He called their conduct by the same name, saying : " All you shall be scandalized in me this night." (Mat. xxvi. 30.) Our scandal, or offence at Christ, may thus have a two-fold direction from a common root : which root is pride. For this one, and individual, feeling, will not let us soar into admiration of doctrines above the hampered flight of our weak minds, nor let us stoop in sympathy and admiration over the humiliations and sufferings of our Lord. St. Paul briefly and energetically, as he is wont, characterises this two-fold scandal, when he says, that Christ crucified whom he preached, was to the Greeks, " who sought wisdom," " foolishness," and to the Jews, who required signs, " a stumbling-block ;" but " to those who are called," " the wisdom of God, and the power of God. For that which is the foolish of God, is wiser than man, and that which is the weak of God, is stronger than man." (1 Cor. i. 22, 25.)   That is, these doctrines, whereat the learned Greeks smiled as fond and extravagant, were the fairest manifestations of uncreated wisdom ; and those humble appearances of Christ's religion, which the carnal Jews contemned, were the mightiest demonstration of in-finite power and glory.   Let us see how far we ever fall into this two-fold scandal.

First, we are scandalized or shocked at the doctrines of Christianity ; we perhaps bear them about us, but we bear them as we should a talisman or charm, in whose efficacy we ourselves believe, at the same time that we should feel ashamed were it discovered upon us by others.   Strange and incomprehensible feeling !   The Jew possessed a law of dark and needy elements, the shadow of our good things ; the adaption of God's truths to the unregenerated, unspiritualized mind of man.   Yet, he was proud of it. He meditated upon its open volume, sitting on the door-step of his cottage amidst the ruins of his ancient cities ; he used of old to write its chosen precepts upon the posts of his gate ; he materialized the commands of attention to it, and bound it in phylacteries, upon his arm and over his eyes, that he might never forget it, and that all men might know the religion to which he belonged.   In this, no doubt, was excess and extravagance.   For woe to the man who only outwardly professes the law of his Lord, and treasureth it not up in his very heart's heart; in whom the visible demonstration thereof is other than the overflowing of a soul that will not contain its fulness.

And here, my brethren, it is meet that "justice should begin from the house of God." (1 Pet. iv. 17.) It is right and wholesome, that before we, the ministers of Christ, chide the coldness and neglect of the faithful, we confess in confusion, our own disgrace, and deplore the seduction of our weak example. For it is too true, that the fervent and glowing language of religion hath escaped from our lips, and that we handle its brightest glories with coldness, and wield the thunderbolts of its judgments, as though they were but for our disport. When are the sublime dogmas of revelation proposed to the minds of the faithful, with that kindred inspiration that passed from them into the hearts of ancient Fathers? Where do we now meet that mysterious wisdom, and deep admiration of the abstruser doctrines of faith, which proceeded from long and fervent meditation upon their sublime worth? Is it not too clear, that our preaching consists rather in the diluting of mysteries as in the softening down of severity; and that, while we affect to make virtue amiable, and revelation palatable, we in truth sacrifice the real beauty of both, and reduce them, though divine, to a human, and an earthly standard?

And if the scandal, thus beginning from the shepherds, have spread to all the flock, is it not humiliating to reflect that the Jews, who felt and showed themselves so proud of their imperfect dispensation, shall one day rise in judgment against us?—they who will themselves be witnessed against by Nineveh and the Queen of Saba, for the price which they set upon *human* wisdom and exhortation. But where, you will perhaps ask me, are the proofs that we appear scandalized with the sublime doctrines of Christianity? I answer they are manifold. And first let me ask you, what do you to prove that you love and value them? I speak not now of the unbeliever; I mean not to contend with such as call themselves unsatisfied with the evidence of our faith.

But we who profess to hold the truth, and consequently to esteem it, do we take much pains to manifest our feelings? Love is a jealous emotion; it betrays itself unwittingly in a thousand ways. It lets no word escape unnoticed which disparages its object: it is ever armed although only defensively; and fears no contest, be the foe ever so dreadful. It is of its nature given to discourse much on those things which it follows and esteems. It is artful and ingenious to discover the way, whereby its own feelings may be multiplied in others, and its own quality become universal. It often wearies people by persevering importunity in its one object and thought. Now, if these be the qualities of a real affection, ask yourselves if your love of God's law and revelation so possess them? Search well, if indeed it be a matter of much investigation, whether your intercourse in society often brings before your notice examples of such single-minded devotedness to this cause. And is God's law then well loved amongst us? Nay, let me probe the matter deeper.

Is there not an habitual shrinking from any notice

of such subjects? is not a barrier placed between the
proprieties of life and all conversation upon them?
And wherefore this? The Greeks and the Romans in
their polished assemblies discoursed together of philosophy grave and severe, and next in dignity and in
wisdom to that of Christ. The Eastern sees no unbe-
comingness in conversing of his false religion before
men, and practising its duties in the face of the world.
We Christians, alone, are bashful and timid in professing
our admiration and love for the glorious revelation which
God hath given us. And this, my brethren, is the first
symptom of our being scandalized with the Gospel,—our
want of interest in its regard.

For our blessed Lord allows of no middle or indifferent state : "He that is not with me, is against
me." (Luke, xi. 23.) Now as he who, during a contest,
makes no demonstration of partiality to one side or
another, nor once either by deed, or word, or look, or
gesture encourages either, but passes by or gazes on, as
an uninterested spectator, will not be allowed to share
the victor's crown, or divide the spoils of the vanquished,
so cannot he reasonably hope to be acknowledged by
Christ for His friend and ally, who stands aloof from
His side in cold indifference, during the daily conflicts
of His faith. But the sentence saith more : that, as in
civil contention, the indifferent citizen who looks on,
when the friends of order and justice have girded on
their swords, hath always been considered a fautor and
abettor of the rebellious, so will the Lord look upon those
as having fallen off from Him, and joined His enemies,
who stand not up for Him and His law.

And live you not, my brethren, in the midst of such warfare, and in the constant duty of actively striving for the faith? Thanks indeed to the Lord of Hosts, who hath strengthened the arms of His faithful servants, the great triumph over crested and rampant infidelity has been achieved ; and our age no longer quails before the hideous pestilence of its blasphemous breath. But if the great and more appalling conflict has ceased, because "the Lord Jesus hath killed the monster by the breath of His mouth," there has arisen, as it were, from its very blood when spilt, a creeping and annoying brood of foolish philosophies and empty theories, which have transferred the war from the open field wherein all the church contended, to the domestic circle, and the intercourse of individuals. Few will now openly combat the great doctrines of faith, but many privately. None, perhaps, would join in the coarse and scornful laugh against all things sacred, which resounded through many parts of Europe in the last century ; but the number is not small of those who smile at the credulity of others, and plausibly condemn their belief, as only linked to less enlightened and more grovelling minds. The rejection of some of the sublime dogmas of Christianity, of the Trinity and Divinity of Jesus Christ, has awfully increased. And has our active zeal in their defence increased in proportion? Have our earnestness and determination to contend for the faith of Christ—to contend I mean with the meek yet powerful arms of the spirit—gained strength in equal measure, with a strong desire to see all men freed from error and bowing in simplicity to the doctrines of truth ? And if not, does not our want of an active zeal effectually prove that we shrink in cowardice from the cause of God: and what is this but to be scandalized thereat?

But pride will ever cloak itself in the outward vesture of some better feeling. We say to ourselves, " God forbid that we should do other than glory in His doctrines and laws ; but they are too sublime and too holy to be mingled with our ordinary thoughts, or paraded before the world. It is our deep awe and veneration for them which make us shroud our feelings towards them from the gaze of men." Ah ! my brethren, did we, like the prophet, retire three times a-day to the silence of our chamber to meditate on the law of our God, and pray for the restoration of His kingdom, (Dan. vi. 10) we might indeed have some pretence for thinking that we separated our reverence and love for them, from the daily feelings and actions of our life, and considered the holy treasures of our spiritual sanctuary too awfully venerable to be exhibited in the profaner precincts of the outer court. Yet no, even thus should we descend from our close and secret converse with the Law and its Giver, as Moses did from the cloud of Horeb, bearing its tablets openly upon our arms, and shedding from our very countenance the mild and cheering light, caught in such close and inspiring a communion. But for us, so to speak, whose meditations are unfrequent and distracted, whose minds are sluggish, and whose hearts are cold, and whose thoughts of God and His commandments form the smallest of occupations, is nothing better than a miserable delusion. Nay, it is much worse. For, so to affect is but to copy the conduct of the Israelites, who so much offended God ; when, loving the flesh-pots of Egypt, and loathing

the manna which came down to them from heaven, they
excused themselves even by the delicacy of the food, as
not suited to their coarser palates. "Our soul now
loatheth this light food." (Num. xxi. 5.) Yes, so it is with
us ; this nourishment of the soul which was not given to
us by angels, as was their manna and their law, but communicated to us by the Incarnate Wisdom itself, is too
ethereal, too pure, too heavenly for us to relish: and we
pretend this as an excuse for not loving it more. "Our
soul hath a loathing of this light food." The knowledge
of God's law and will, the study of His truths and manifestations, the real support of a mind and soul that actually
looks upwards to a higher sphere, are ever postponed to
the frivolous occupations or pursuits of the world: and we
shelter ourselves beneath the paltry excuse, that they
belong to a sphere too elevated for the mind unceasingly
to revolve in.

And is not this to take scandal at that very quality of
God's truth, which renders it most worthy of His Name ?
Wherefore was a sublimer revelation made to man, save
to enable him, by the elevation of his powers, to turn his
thoughts, which sin had bowed down unto the earth,
upwards towards heaven ; to raise the flame of all his
spiritual movements into a higher level, and cause them
to mingle, in glad and easy aspirations, with an order
of intelligence, from which his fall had, till then, excluded him ? It was precisely that we, who believe in
the sublime truths thus revealed, should have ever before
us a more extended view of the providential scheme, devised by infinite love, in favour of man, with all the
stirring motives and principles of action which its know-

ledge must inspire ; and that this knowledge, and its consequent impulses, should pervade the very constitution of society, and form the very spring and regulator of every Christian mind. And yet, thus elevated above the world, instead of our contemplating it with the eye of faith, and considering it a school wherein lessons of the highest order are taught, we busy ourselves with the paltry interests that surround us, and take an active part in their passing pleasures ; thus resembling the recreant prophet, who, neglecting the marvellous work of grace and mercy which was going on in the city below him, was only engaged in watching the growth of the perishable gourd which sheltered him from the heat.

Do you not see how ungrateful is the pretence, that religion is not the constant object of our conversation and thought, on account of its sublimity and superiority to man's conceptions ?—and how paltry, too ! Is not the sun too bright for his eye, and yet, doth he shut it to its lustre, and does he not look at all things through that which, if gazed on, would blind him ? Is not the ocean too deep for his lines, and yet, doth he forbear to seek riches in its gulphs, or to pursue his desires through its billows ? Is not the home of the nearest star too remote for his measurement, and is not the arch of heaven too vast for his span; and yet, doth he not, in soul, fly thither, and love them the more for the expanse of sublime conception and tender feeling, in which he is there lost ? Was not man born to soar, was not his soul created a spirit, and were not his desires winged, that they might aspire, and naturally rise, to thoughts and ideas of that highest sphere to which they are destined ? If, then, in

all things else, their greatness and majesty and incompre-
hensibleness do no ways deter us from attempting or using
them, so should it be with those spiritual elements, that
were made for the spirit's occupation.

But, my brethren, let us now examine ourselves a little
closer. Do you still think, after what hath been said,
that you shrink not from Christ's Gospel, and that you
show no weakness in its cause? you may then place
the point thus clearly at issue. It has, at least, been
shown, how little fervour we display in the cause of religion, how little we speak and converse of it, how seldom
we defend it, how unintentionally we betray our want of
feeling in favour of those very qualities which form its
chiefest worth and recommendation. Now, such we are,
where all that surrounds us is in our favour, where many
even think alike regarding .it, and where the applause
and esteem of the virtuous, at least, would reward our
efforts. If such, then, we be in time of calm, what should
we have been amidst trial and tribulation? Should we
have merited the blessings pronounced on those who are
not scandalized in Jesus, when to own Him brought with
it suffering, disgrace, and death? Would the Gospel
have been preached, or Christianity established, had the
task been supported by no better spirit, by no greater
fervour, than we exhibit, merely to preserve it? Listen
to the apostle of the Gentiles : "I am ready," he saith,
"to preach the Gospel to you also who are at Rome, for
I am not ashamed of the Gospel." (Rom. i. 15, 16.) And
yet that Gospel was to him as a fetter to his feet and ma-
nacles to his hands, and a yoke of iron around his neck,
of which he elsewhere writes, that he laboured in it "even

unto chains, as an evil-doer." (2 Tim. ii. 9.) He was not ashamed of the Gospel, or of preaching it in Rome, where his preaching would bring him not only bonds and proscription, but torment and death. He was not ashamed of the Gospel, nor of preaching it amidst the scoffing sages of the Athenian council; no, nor of openly announcing its most sublime and trying doctrines, or of boldly expounding its stern morality, to the proud and debauched Festus, on his judgment-seat! Ah! he, in sooth, was not scandalized in Jesus; he loved His doctrine, and he cherished it, and he defended it, in the face of men; yea, and in the face of death; for he, moreover, was not scandalized at the humiliations of his Master, or the ignominies of His cross. And this is the second scandal into which I have said we are liable to fall.

If it was a sad reflection that one day the Jew shall rise in judgment against us, because he loved and openly professed the imperfect law which God had given him, while we were ashamed of that sublimer one wherewith we have been blessed, I fear that a bitterer reflection here awaiteth us, regarding the second offence into which we fall : for, here the heathen will justly take up his testimony against us, and say : " The gods which I worshipped were but the likeness of sinful man ; in the vanity and blindness of my heart I clothed them with all the vices of their adorers; I imagined them ambitious, cruel, and revengeful ; given to their lusts, proud, and contentious. But, having thus named them my gods, I was not ashamed of them ; I decked them out in gold, and silver, and precious stones ; I created the arts to embellish them, and left to posterity splendid memorials of my fond belief ;

I sang their praises in my daily songs, and I made them the theme of every laboured composition. But you, Christians; you who had a God among you, pure and without stain—the type of our nature in its most faultless conception—the ideal of all that is noble, exalted, divine in man : how do you honour Him, or even show Him respect ? Is He, or are His virtues and beautiful qualities half as much in your mouths as were in mine the false deities of Olympus or of Helicon? Or rather, is it not too true, and too evident, that when you wish to embody, through art, the ideal of comeliness in feature or in mind, you still go, as I used to do, to the sculptor, and bid him carve, as ornaments to your halls, a voiceless Apollo, or an uninspired Muse ?"

My brethren, even in this lowest form of reverence to our humble and afflicted Lord, do we fall below the ancient pagan in avowed honour for Him. But I must be allowed to distinguish between two classes of Christians differing widely in this respect.

In this capital of the Catholic world, the heathen could not utter that reproach. Its monuments, its public places, and its private houses, exhibit fearlessly the symbols of our religion, and of its Founder in His lowliness and sufferings. The cross welcomes you at the approach to every hamlet ; the *stations* of His Passions represent His ascent to Calvary, at every steep acclivity leading to a church; His helpless infancy, in the arms of His mother, stands forth prominently at the corner of almost every thoroughfare. These and other countless demonstrations of pious faith, show to the stranger that he is not only in a Christian city, but in one which demonstrates its Christianity by these very characteristics that the Gospel describes as truly belonging to it.

For you may wander all day through the squares and streets of Rome, without meeting a single representation of our Lord's resurrection, or of His ascension, or of any of His wonderful works, or "later glories." But of Him falling under His cross, or struck and buffetted, and crucified, in other words, of the "scandal of the cross," you cannot visit the glorious amphitheatre of Titus * without evidence that *this* people is not ashamed.

But is that stranger-nation, which wanders through its streets in search of whatever is beautiful in its completeness, or majestic in its ruin, not so ashamed? Were a Hindoo or a Mahommedan to spend days in London, would he meet one object, beyond the bare symbol on the towers of churches, which speaks not to his sense, or mind, that would teach him that its inhabitants honoured and loved their Lord, the head of their religion, on account of His abjection, His ignominy, His pains and torments, and His death? And, even here, do not too many of our fellow-countrymen express abhorrence of the visible proofs to which I have alluded, of honour and devotion towards our benign Saviour in His passion?

But, dear brethren, I am dwelling on the lowest standard of honour for Him. How bold and how practical are these two sayings of St. Paul :—First. " God forbid that I should glory, save only in the cross of our Lord Jesus Christ." (Gal. vi. 14.) Second. " Willingly, therefore, will I glory in my infirmities, that the power of Christ may dwell within me." (2 Cor. xii. 9.)

* The Colisseum, round which are painted the Stations of the Cross.

N

Astonishing words, and to the sense of man scarcely
reconcilable ! For the apostle saith, that he will glory
in his own weaknesses, while he has solemnly deprecated
the thought of glorying in anything save the cross of our
Lord Jesus Christ. Are then our infirmities of body and
soul so unified, incorporated, identified with the cross of
Christ, that to glory in them, is to glory in this ? Most
certainly, my brethren, these texts combined can convey
to us no other meaning. Nay, the second of them says it
all: St. Paul declares that he will " glory in his infirmities,
that the power of Christ might dwell in him." And what
is " the power of Christ" ? Nothing, surely, else but what
he calls by that name—that cross which was to the Jews
" a stumbling-block," but to us " the power of God." St.
Paul then clearly believed, that affliction, penury, losses,
calumnies, persecutions, and unjust death received a consecration from the cross of Christ, which united them so
intimately with His sufferings, that they were honourable,
and glorifying, as if His own.

Now, is this the feeling or thought of modern Christianity ? Patience and resignation to God's will, we preach
and poorly practice ; but who dares say to the rich sufferer :
"Glory; rejoice in your pains ; because through them the
power of Christ's cross dwelleth in you. Call your sores
' the mercies of God,' as did St. John of the Cross." Who
will venture to preach in the hospital, to the sick, the
maimed, the crippled, that their's is a place for rejoicing
and exulting ; for there Christ reigns, with the magnificent sceptre of His glorious cross : and where He reigns,
there should be gladness, and even bliss ? Even where
the " angel of Satan buffetteth" through " the sting of the

flesh," and the apostle prays that it may depart from him, our Lord refuses : because His grace sufficeth, and power is shown forth more perfectly in weakness. (2 Cor. xii. 7.)

No, indeed, we are far from reaching the standard of the Gospel, on this moving subject. We do not wish to be too much like our divine Saviour. We would gladly resemble Him in His virtues and graces, in His gentleness and meekness, in His kindness and tenderness, in His wisdom and prudence—in a word, in whatever is noble, amiable, pleasing before men ; but certainly not in His homelessness and dereliction, in His destitution and hunger, in His persecution by tongue and arm ; in what would have made Him but little popular, little loved in the modern world.

Truth, indeed, compels me to say it : we shrink from too close a resemblance to our heavenly Master in all that regards His most peculiar distinctives. We do not wish, nor do we like, to be as " a leper, a man of sorrows, as one struck by God, and humbled; as one in whom there is no comeliness or beauty ; as a stunted shrub, trodden under foot and despised." (Is. liii.) The cross *is* a stumbling-block to us as to the Jews; we do not glory in *His* cross, or in our own infirmities.

Thank God, however, in His Church there has ever been that love of Jesus Christ in His abjection and suffering, and the desire to resemble Him, kept vivid and verdant through a long line of saints. After the age of the martyrs, who best resemble Him, there germinated, as if from the foot of the cross, that succession of holy religious, who, after resigning rank, even regal, entered the monastic life, to swell that glorious army of the cross which, in

poverty and obedience, has, from age to age, fought against
the world, and vanquished it.

Such was holy St. Francis, who had no love and no
desire but to show forth, in his very body, Christ, and
Him crucified; in cold, in hunger, in nakedness, and in
solitude and meditation ; till God gave him a still more
singular conformity with the very wounds of his crucified
Lord.

Such was the blessed and dear St. Elizabeth, who
honoured poverty and sores so tenderly, as to place a poor
leper in the royal bed, which, when her indignant lord
uncovered, he found there the Lord of lords, whom that
poor outcast symbolised better than he did, thorn-crowned
and wounded. And after his death, she showed how she
could glory in her own suffering, under every trial and
mortifying humiliation.

Such, finally, to come nearer to our own times, was
the venerable Benedict Joseph Labre, whom the Church
will, probably, one day raise to the honours of canoniza-
tion, though some yet remember him in this city (Rome)
a poor mendicant, begging his bread, and imitating
voluntarily the poverty of his divine Master.

A celebrated modern writer, not distinguished by any
strong Christian feelings, has observed, that the most
daring and wonderful characteristic of Christianity, was
its casting a veil of holiness over all that the world and
human nature recoil from, and exalting it above what
they love and covet.

And it is so, my brethren ; paganism never exhibited
the least respect for poverty, or the least affection for
suffering, apart from personal ties. No hospitals, no

nursing of the sick, no love for widows or orphans, no care for the poor, except to press them into the service of the state. Scorn, contempt, severity, cruelty—such were the natural portion of the destitute. Next to crime, perhaps on a level with it, was misfortune.

After the priest of the Capitol, the Levite of the Temple passed, almost equally unheeding. The Jewish law, the law of God, inculcated kindness, charity, love. Alms were a duty; the cause of the widow and the orphan were put under divine protection ; the poor mendicant was not to be passed by, nor the naked left unclothed, nor the hungry unfed. But there was no brightness shed on the countenance of the poor, no songs of angels cheered his lonely couch.

Then came at last, Jesus of Nazareth, an infant laid on straw, and lodged in a stable. Poverty and affliction are the first welcomes He receives on earth. These precede the Magi's presents. Yes, He is poor ; His mother is poor ; His reputed father is poor. And afterwards His apostles are poor, and His disciples, and His chosen associates. Then He boldly preaches poverty, and denounces riches : bids His rich followers sell their property if they wished to enter His kingdom ; and bids His chosen ones rejoice when they want all things, and when the world hates them.

Such are the three stages through which afflicted humanity has had to pass. In the first, scorned and unpitied ; in the second, tolerated and compassionated ; in the third, loved and exalted. Yes, loved upon earth by the Son of God from Bethlehem to Calvary, from the manger to the cross; loved in retirement, loved in public

life; loved amidst publicans and sinners, loved among
Pharisees and Rulers ; loved when urged to become king,
loved when proclaimed one, naked on the cross ; and so
borne upwards, and enthroned with Him, at the right
hand of His Father.

And there surely may He well say : " Blessed is he
who is not scandalized in me !"—not scandalized in the
weakness of a human body, transcending in glory the
brightest spirit in the angelic choir : wounds and rents
in a Man's flesh more radiant than the very stars in
Mary's crown ! Who will, or can, be scandalized at
these ? And yet that flesh is of earth, and those wounds
were inflicted upon earth, " in the house of them that
loved Him." (Zac. xiii. 6.)

No ; we are scandalized or shocked at nothing that is
bright, or glorious—not even at those forms, or scars of
humanity, in which, when bare, and mocked at, and bleeding on earth, we dare not glory. Yet, my brethren, what
bore up so high that hunger-worn and extenuated form,
with its bleeding and pleading gashes ? Not the pomp
of this world, nor its honours, nor its affluence, nor its
own perfect comeliness. They were the buffet and the
scourge, the nails and the lance, the shroud and the cross,
beyond all, which were as wings to raise that blessed
Humanity above Principalities and Powers ; they formed
the fiery chariot of His triumph to the eternal heaven of
heavens.

And how, dear brethren ? You have heard it from St.
Paul, when he told you that " Christ crucified, the stumbling-block of the Jews, is *the power* of God." (1 Cor. i.
23.) For it is in Him crucified that are all the might

of our faith and the firmness of our hopes. He redeemed us on Calvary, and not on Thabor. He sendeth forth His apostles to travel over the whole earth without even a staff; to build thousands of churches without a purse; to fight and conquer an empire, never before, or since, equalled in power, matched with it as sheep are with wolves.

Reverse for a moment this order of things, as is done in our times. It is no satire, no, nor envious parallel that I am going to place before you. Let us imagine some missionary going out from some society in our country, to preach the Gospel to the benighted inhabitants of interior Africa, or of some coral reef in the ocean. It is far from improbable that such a one, who may not have become poorer by relinquishing his paternal nets, would be addressed in terms not unlike these :—

" You are about to carry the Gospel light to nations sitting in darkness. But while you will bear in one hand the torch of truth, you will carry in the other the lamp of civilization; and the two flames will mingle into one—the light of wisdom. The people, supremely ignorant of all things, without science, or even an alphabet, will soon acquire a respect for you, so much better instructed, so much more highly cultivated; they will listen to your words with docility; they will accept your assurance for what they do not see or comprehend, on the warranty of that knowledge which you will exhibit concerning visible and common things. They are indeed jealous, savage, and inhuman, but fear not. The British name is known there, and is a shield and a charm among

the most barbarous nations; you will land under the
shadow of its protecting standard, flashing above the
huge vessel, which will overawe any attempt at violence,
and yet, by its wonderful mechanism, subdue the intellect
of the savage, and prove your claims to a superior condition in the scale of human nature, and your right to
be heard."*

Such a charge would not seem extravagant. Yet, how
we must invert the Scriptures to give it weight. How
must St. Paul be read, to support it ? Thus—" The
wise things of this world hath God chosen, that He may
confound the foolish; and the strong things, that He may
confound the weak; and the things that are, that He may
confound those that are not."

But Jesus Christ spake not, and did not, thus. Let
us, on the other hand, imagine St. Peter and St. Paul,
with, perhaps, Aquila and Prisca, and Linus and Clement,
standing at the gate of this city, the fisherman and the
tent-maker, in their outlandish uncouth garbs, looking
through the lines of the ferocious guards, into its hard
ungenial heart. Patricians and ladies of highest rank;
corrupted citizens, steeped in idleness and luxury; philosophers and sophists, orators and poets, with an imperial
court uniting every element of man's highest powers and
attainments : such are the inhabitants ; while every

* A few years ago, a dignitary of the English Establishment, lec-
turing in a great manufacturing town, endeavoured to show that
miracles were no longer needed by the missionary to savage countries;
because science and mechanism, as possessed by us, were sufficient to
establish the teacher's claim to be heard, as bearer of his high message. He mentioned the steam-engine as thus having taken the place
of healing, or other miraculous evidences of a divine mission.

material object exhibits grandeur or beauty, whatever can excite admiration, or inspire attachment to things of this earth. It is to these men that they are sent, to induce them to uproot and cast off all these feelings.

Is it on a fool's errand that they are come ? Shall they turn back, or, like Jonas, enter in and boldly preach penance, or the wrath to come ?

If their steps faltered for a moment, and they required encouragement, we may easily imagine such words as these to have come down from heaven ; or rather the remembrance of them to have echoed in their hearts :— " Fear not, little flock, for it hath well pleased your Father to give you a kingdom." (Luke, xii. 32.)

Yea, *this* kingdom; this empire at whose gate ye stand. Go on, and fear not, little flock. This city is wise, and you are foolish ; it is strong, and you weak ; it great, you little ; it rich, you poor ; it noble, you abject. But remember, again, this city, and the empire which it commands, is as the huge mass, inert and helpless ; you the small handful of leaven to be thrown into it, and ferment it. It is as a corrupting and perishing provision for the grave ; you are the few grains of salt that will refreshen it. In both, it is the lesser that overcomes and transmutes the greater.

Thank God, my brethren, that it was so then ; or the world would never have been converted. For the little flock walked on ; that loathsome heap of pagan corruption was salted ; that mass of lifeless learning was fermented ; and Christian civilization, and Christian wisdom, sprang from the quickened re-animated decay.

And " the kingdom" became Peter's, and this city, as

its capital. But it was from a cross that he ruled over it. He bore to the end the scandal of that cross, which his good Master told him, too truly, would at first make him fly. Instead of its being his stumbling-block, it became, and remained, his strength; and he bequeathed to imperial Rome, for ever, the two-fold legacy of the Wisdom of God, and the Power of God, which are in Jesus Christ, and Him crucified. Blessed is he who is not scandalized in either.

SERMON X.

Triumphs of the Cross.*

GAL. vi. 14.

" God forbid that I should glory, save only in the cross of our
Lord Jesus Christ."

To those, dear brethren, who were witnesses of the scenes
which the Church is now about to commemorate, there
must have appeared a strange and almost unnatural
contrast, between the triumphal entry our blessed Saviour
made this day into Jerusalem, and the sad close of His
agonizing sufferings upon Calvary.   How many may have
been tempted in their folly to say, when they saw Him
stretched as a victim on the cross : " How little, on the
first day of the week, did He expect to meet so ignominious an end !"   How would they be able to reconcile
in their minds, with foreknowledge of His subsequent death
upon that cross, His entry into Jerusalem upon the first
day of that eventful week, when the garments of men
were strewn upon His path, when palms of triumph were
waved around Him, and hosannas of welcome echoed
through the air ! Oh how little indeed could any one have
anticipated that it would all come to this desolate close !
But any one endowed with Christian foresight, any

---

* Delivered at St. George's Cathedral, on Palm Sunday, 1849.

one who contemplated these scenes in the spirit of St. Paul, expressed in the words of my text, would indeed have well comprehended, that it was but one mystery from first to last ; that He, who was this day riding into Jerusalem amid the congratulations of the people, knew full well that those same voices, that were that day raised in rejoicing, would in five days more swell the outcry that raised Him to the cross. Even we, my brethren, well know that in the course of a few days our heads will be bowed down in grief and sympathy for our blessed Redeemer's sufferings ; we foresee full well that we shall cast ourselves in sad and naked sorrow upon the pavement of this church, and weep with the daughters of Jerusalem for Him, treasure of our heart's love, scorned, persecuted, and bruised, the object of hatred and contempt, proceeding with faint and weary steps to complete His sacrifice on Calvary. And yet, though foreseeing and knowing all this, we cannot resist raising our heads in triumph this day, and hailing with holy joy our blessed Redeemer, not merely by words, but by acts of solemn worship, imitative as far as possible of the piety of those who then surrounded Him, and welcomed Him, as the King of Sion and the Lord of Israel. Yes, because we know what St. Paul knew, what the true believer must then have known, that this only triumph which Jesus permitted Himself on earth, was in truth but the first of one unbroken chain of conquests, the first step in a great work, that was to be completely crowned with victory. And even as He came into Jerusalem, meekly riding on an ass, so in the course of time, and through successive ages, entered He into royal and imperial cities, and successfully claimed them for His own, until He took unto Himself the rule of the kingdoms of this world. That triumph, too, was but the type of another and greater, when He is to appear glorious among the choirs of angels ; and the sign of the Son of Man is to be seen triumphant in the heavens. Yes, the triumph of this day is the triumph of the cross. It is the triumph of Christ crucified ; it is the triumph, indeed, of the law of humiliation ; but, at the same time, it is the triumph of the New Law of God. Oh, then, on this day, God forbid that I should glory in aught save the cross of our Lord Jesus Christ, or that I should speak to you on this the first evening of a solemn period, commemorative of our Saviour's Passion, of anything else than of that which should absorb our thoughts, which should engross our affections, throughout this holy season !

Yes, my brethren, this is the day on which the cross of Christ is to be contemplated triumphant; as on Friday next we shall have to dwell on its humiliation and pain. I will speak to you, therefore, of the triumph of the cross of Christ : and show you how from this day, on which it began, it has endured in the Church of God until our own time, as it will continue to the end. I will show you how the cross of Christ was a cross of triumph in this world ; and how, although it was the instrument of His sufferings, and the altar of His sacrifice, it has literally conquered the world, nay, become its very pride and glory—conquering it materially, conquering it morally, conquering it spiritually.

The word of God has given us in an early page (Jud. ix.) a beautiful allegory, in which the trees of the forest are represented as debating one with the other who should be their king ; and we might almost, without a figure, make ourselves conceive that there was some such contest in the days of our Redeemer. I would rather, however, place the thought before you in a more simple and natural form. No doubt, my brethren, there were in the forests of Judea, at the time of our blessed Saviour, many fair and stately trees. There was the lofty and beautifully tapering pine, that rose above its fellows, and seemed with its topmost branches to woo for itself the purer atmosphere of heaven. There was the royal cedar, that spread itself forth on every side, and covered with its shadow a vast extent of land. We may imagine the proud possessor of this noble growth of the forest come, and, looking with complacency on the riches which he held, give orders as to how their worth should be realized into wealth. He says to his forester, " See that elegant and towering tree, which has now reached the maturity of its growth, how nobly will it rise above the splendid galley, and bear itself, in the fell fury of the wind, without breaking or bending, and carry the riches of the earth from one flourishing port to another. Cut it down, and destine it for this noble work. And this magnificent cedar, overcasting all around it with the solemnity of its shade, worthy to have been built by Solomon into the temple of God, such that David might have sung its praises on his inspired lyre ; let it be carefully and brilliantly polished, and embarked to send to the imperial city, there to adorn those magnificent halls, in which all the splendour of Rome is gathered ; and there, richly gilded and adorned, it shall be an object of admiration for ages to come." " It is well, my Lord," replies his servant,

" but this strange, this worthless tree, which seems presumptuously to spring up, beneath the shadow of those
splendid shafts, what shall we do with it? for what shall
it be destined? it is fitted for no great, no noble work."—
" Cut it down, and if of no other use—why, it will make
a cross for the first malefactor !"   Oh, strange counsels of
men ! That soaring pine, perhaps, after a few years, dashed
the freight that it bore against the rocks, and rolled, the
worthless fragment of a wreck, upon the beach ; and that
noble cedar which witnessed the revels of imperial Rome,
fell by the earthquake beneath the arm of avenging justice, or in the fire that the barbarian kindled in those
splendid halls, fell charred into their heap of ruins, and
the winds of heaven wafted its ashes over the land.

But that ignoble tree, that despised trunk, which
men spurned as of no value save to be put to the most
ignominious of uses,—oh ! that tree, that cross which
upon Calvary bore the price of the world's redemption,
that tree has been gathered up and treasured and enshrined, as though its every fragment was worth more
than gold ; yea, so far beyond it, that it would be as the
sin of Simon the magician to offer all the world's treasure
for one of its smallest portions.   And thus has this cross,
this contemptible tree, risen above all that the world
is worth, in value to the Christian heart ; and not only
now, but in every age, has it been considered worth all
that the world doats and sets its heart on.   For that
wood, that material wood of the cross of Christ, an
empress crossed the seas, and searched among the silent
tombs of the dead.   For that which was thought a vile
and contemptible thing, was built a magnificent church

on Mount Sion. For that wood, the Emperor Heraclius made war against the King of Persia; and when he had recovered it, bore it, as his Master had before, barefoot, and in an humble garb, to Calvary. For that tree, Constantine, the great emperor, built a most venerable church, yet standing among the ruins of the palaces of Rome, and brought the very earth from our Saviour's own land; as though none other were worthy to be there, save that upon which the precious fruit of redemption had first fallen, in the life-giving blood of our blessed Redeemer.

And from that time His Church has considered this relic as one of the greatest treasures entrusted to her keeping, and all in it have been ambitious of possessing but a small fragment thereof. Our own country, too, saw some of its noblest fabrics dedicated to religion, rise to the honour and the glory of that holy rood of Christ. When thus we see what was but a fragment of the tree of ignominy so valued, that gold and precious stones, and whatsoever the world most prizes, are deemed but worthy to form its shrine and outward vesture, and noble temples piled up with the richest materials and the noblest productions of art, thought fit only to house and to shelter it; may we not truly say, that the very wood of Christ's cross has achieved a triumph over the world, trampling under it, and rendering subject and subservient to itself, what forms the boast, and pomp, and pride of that world? And what was our Saviour's honourable entry into Jerusalem, but the first step in this triumphal progress of His cross over all the globe, showing that it derived from Him a value beyond all that earth can possess? And thus, even materially, has the cross of Christ triumphed over the world.

But what is this, my brethren, compared with the great moral triumph which the cross of Christ has achieved? Let us cast our eyes over the world immediately after our blessed Saviour's glorious ascension to heaven. We see going forth from the land of Judea a few rude and illiterate men, without fortune, without station, without reputation, without estimation before the world. I see one, like Bartholomew, go undaunted into the frozen regions of the north; another, like Thomas, penetrating amidst the effeminate people of the south. I see James wandering through the barbarian lands of the extreme west; and Peter and Paul, anxious and thoughtful, no doubt, but still calm and confident, proceeding on the apparently hopeless mission entrusted to them, and entering on foot the imperial city, there about to commence the work, of converting that immense and corrupt population. They have been sent forth without scrip or staff; they are poor in every way; they bring with them no books of hidden lore; they employ no wonderful flights of poetry or of eloquence, by which to convince or to allure. Yet I see each of them surrounded by a multitude eager to listen to his teaching, and no less eager to practise what is taught. I see in those fastnesses of Armenia the royal princess kneel before the poor emissary of Galilee, and stretch out her tresses to be cut off, that she may thus renounce every love but for One that was not of earth. I see the learned men of those southern regions, wedded, by ages of solemn speculation, to the religious traditions of their country, give them up willingly, desirous no longer to bathe in their sacred rivers, but to be washed in the laver of salvation, by the word of God's minister. And in Rome I see, not

o

merely the learned philosophers anxious to become
acquainted with this new religious system; not only the
virtuous household of a Pudens, or other senator, wherein
purity and morality already prevailed, interested about
the new doctrine; but I see Nero himself, trembling upon
his throne, at the prospect of success which already shows
itself, in the simple teaching of these men. And what
is the lure, what is the bait, whereby they draw thus
about them, and lead in willing captivity, these subject
nations? Has the lyre of the fabulous Orpheus been put
into the possession of him who has travelled into Scythia,
so as to charm around him its grim and savage tribes ? or
has he who hath gone into the south borne with him the
sword of Alexander, to subdue its effeminate population ?
or have they who penetrated the imperial city polished
their tongues, and prepared themselves well to catch the
ear of a voluptuous race, with a soft and flattering
philosophy ? No, my brethren, each and all, however
different his mission, goes forth with but one charm, one
instrument of conquest, with but one augury of success.

Each takes in his hand the cross of Christ, and
preaches, not the perverse words of human wisdom, but
Him, and Him crucified, alone. He raises aloft that
cross, which is the symbol of patience and resignation,
which sanctifies humility and self-abasement, which con-
secrates poverty, and elevates into more than a stoical
endurance a renunciation of the things of the world.
With this, and this alone, they were able to subdue the
savage in the north, and the soft half-civilized Brahmin in
the south, and the luxurious, haughty and self-sufficient
Roman ;—with one single weapon, by the power of the

cross, bringing them all into subjection to Christ's law, making of them but one kingdom, but one empire, but one people, but one Church, but one body, closely united to Him, its crucified Head. Thus, by degrees, in spite of every opposition of the world to Christ's conquests, the day soon comes when the glory of that cross covers the earth, as the water covers the sea.

But a new generation thinks it necessary to unsheath the sword and light up the faggot, in order to quench at once this rising, as they deem it, superstition. Yet in vain : that cross which a few years before was the badge of ignominy, that cross which the Roman was not allowed even to speak of,—the very name of which was a word excluded from polished conversation,—that cross, upon which none but the slave was doomed to die in the imperial city, becomes the very crowning summit of the diadem of the Cæsars. But, in effecting this, in making this change through the whole earth, in bringing all nations into this subjection, what a variety of triumphs were necessary ; in how many ways was the world, in its affections, to be mortified, to be annihilated, before it would wear that badge of disgrace. Behold in mind the Christian of those days brought before the tribunal of the emperor. See him asked, with a haughty glance, a look, a tone, and gesture that strike terror into the satellites around that tribunal, " Who art thou, and what art thou?" And the questioned answers not in words, but, as we frequently read in the simple and genuine records of the ancient martyrs, raising his hand, signs his forehead or his entire body with the sign of the cross : and he who sits on the judgment-seat well understands its meaning. It seems to say to him at once, " I am a worshipper, I am a lover of Him who suffered upon the cross, and died on it, to purchase for me infinitely more than thou canst do for me. I spurn the honour, wealth, and station that thou profferest, and I confidently and lovingly cling to this sacred symbol, emblematic though it be, of what you call foolishness, of that which you despise. It assures me that by virtue of the cross I shall be shielded from evil, that I shall be able to do battle against the world in its most fearful shapes, to conquer it not only when it is alluring and tempting, but when it crushes and destroys. It tells me that I may mock at your boiling cauldrons, at your heated gridirons, your ingenious racks, your pointed swords, your sharpened hatchets, and the thousand other instruments of death that you have prepared. I scorn all, and over all of them I will ride triumphant to the heavenly Sion, because Christ my Saviour hath triumphed before me: nay I welcome these dreadful forms of death, because they will bring me to Him who redeemed me on the cross." Yes, in that sign of the cross was the profession of faith; in that sign of the cross was expression of hope; in that sign of the cross was charity symbolised the most perfect. For this the Christian martyr of old suffered and endured all, because he saw in angels' embrace the cross of Christ shining in the heavens, shedding forth rays into his very heart, which warmed, and kindled, and strengthened unto martyrdom, and made him despise the torments of this world, because Christ had first been crucified and had died upon that cross.

This, too, was the strength of those, whom the terrors of persecution drove forth from the haunts of men. Go into those trackless deserts of Africa, through which, in passing, a conquering army would soon faint and lose strength, and drop piecemeal and dissolve amid the burning sands,—those sands which, before or since, the industry of man never made to produce a single blade of grass ; and see hundreds and thousands of men either gathered together and living in common, or each alone, in his silent cell, by some brackish fountain, or beneath the shade of some solitary palm.   See them there, not for a few years, but through a long life of seventy or eighty years, like Anthony or Hilarion.   No splendid temples are there to excite their devotion, no well-furnished library of books whence to draw or improve their ascetic lore ; nay, scarcely have many the power even to turn over the sacred volume, and learn from its pages the heroic virtues that they practise.   But God gives them strength for this severe and apparently unnatural seclusion.   And what is its source ?   Two broken reeds fastened together, and rudely fashioned into a cross, stand upon the fragment of rock, before which the anchorite sits at his daily labour. Or go in, and you will find the same sacred symbol roughly cut in the rock of his cell.   Before this he kneels, before this he prays, before this he meditates ; there he fills himself with the spirit of Christ crucified, and strength and courage for forty or fifty years of a life of solitude, and of complete separation from the world. He has trampled on that world, he has triumphed over all its temptations, nourished only and strengthened by that cross of Christ, which has been the food of his pious thoughts, and a heavenly manna in the wilderness, to his soul.

And, my brethren, thus might we proceed for age after age, in contemplating the lives of those eminent Saints of God, who astonish us by the brilliancy of their virtues. In every one we shall find that the cross was deeply engraven on their hearts ; that that alone was their comfort in af-fliction, their consolation in hidden sorrow, their strength in weakness and temptation. It was at the foot of the crucifix, that the depths of Christian philosophy were explored, that the purest light of Christian theology was sought and obtained; and they who have thus studied, not in themselves but in Christ crucified, have owned, like the great angelic doctor of the Church, that from the crucifix, rather than from the illumination of their own minds, they drew their knowledge. And such have ever been rewarded by the approving words, addressed to them from the rood, " Thou hast written well of Me ; what shall be thy reward ?"

But, my brethren, in every rank of life we see this cross achieving new triumphs, accomplishing new wonders ; not only in the wilds of heathendom, but in the deep recesses of the civilized heart, forming thus the spiritual triumph of the cross of Christ. There have been kings great and powerful, surrounded by all that could make even a throne more valuable ; not in days such as these when a crown is but a painful bauble and easily cast aside, but when a crown was, indeed, a noble thing, and when kings were great and honoured ; yet even in those days kings would come to the foot of the altar, and would there lay down their diadems, and assume in its stead the religious cowl; and joining the ranks of an austere community, would praise God with those their poor brethren, and devote themselves to His service for the rest of their lives. And what was this, my brethren, but a triumph of the cross, what but an acknowledgment that it was better to be like the King of heaven than a king of earth, better to be a worshipper at the cross of Christ, than one of the noble and illustrious of earth? There have been, my brethren, in every rank of life,—and this, in a Catholic pulpit, may be considered as almost a common-place,—there have been amongst those brought up in luxury and everything that could wed them to the world, whether by the gentleness of their sex or the tenderness of their education, many who have fled from that world and its flowery fascinations, and have chosen rather to tread the rough, and thorny, and narrow path. And why? because upon the summit of that sacred mount to which it leads, there was planted that cross of Christ towards which their looks ever turned; nor were they able to see around them aught that won their affections like this. And therefore towards it they directed their steps, in the lowly garb of religion, serving God in humi- lity and holy contemplation, or devoting themselves for their lives to the service of the poor and sick, even as did their great model, the Man of sorrows, who expired on Calvary.

It would be an endless task, my dearly beloved brethren, to enumerate the multitude of ways in which the cross of Christ has triumphed in the hearts of men, triumphed over their weakness and their strength, over the violence of their passions, and over the feebleness of their natural dispositions. But strange, indeed, would it be if the holy Catholic Church did not, in a multitude of ways, prize and honour by holy ceremonies this sacred emblem, which is

to her not merely a badge or ornament to crown the outward pinnacle of the material temple, but an emblem
engraven on the heart, a staff to be grasped by the dying
man on his last journey, as a weapon whereby he is to
beat back his spiritual foes. And what wonder that,
where the cross of Christ has become only a name, but is
no longer a thing, where it is never brought before the
minds or senses of the people, there religion should have
lost all feeling, all idea of what is symbolized by the cross
of Christ ; that it should no longer know anything of inward mortification, or external penance ; that it should
not understand the meaning of control or subjection, or
desired humiliation ; that it should have destroyed all
traces of that inward and outward affection for the cross,
which shows itself in a thousand different devotions in the
Holy Catholic Church ; such, for instance, as that which
I rejoice to see has been lately introduced into your
Church, and is followed with so much devotion, the Stations,
or Way of the Cross ; that the cross should have ceased
to be clasped in the hands, with the image of Christ crucified pressed to the lips and the fluttering heart of the
expiring Christian. And what wonder that a religion like
this never should have brought forth a generous and
noble youth like St. Aloysius, who renounced his patri-
mony, his principality, his family alliances, to attend the
sick in the hospital, and to die in the flower of his youth,
of contagion, caught by ministering to the infected ?
What wonder that such a system should never have
produced one man like St. Vincent of Paul, who could
spend his whole life in serving the least ones of Christ,
gathering up in the cold winter mornings these nurslings

of charity, outcasts from maternal affection, thus becoming
to them at once father and mother, and educating them as
if his own children? What wonder it never produced a
man like St John of God, whose whole life was given to
the most splendid and heroic works of charity, who became
as a fool for Christ, shut himself up day and night with
the sick, braved the flames to save them, and died poor
himself, because he sought no other reward than that
which is given to His servants by their crucified Master?

No, dear brethren, it is not wonderful, indeed, that this
should be the case; but the Catholic Church, from the
beginning, has set a value on the cross of Christ, has
treasured it up even in its very material substance, as
more valuable than all earthly treasure, as that whereby
she has conquered the nations of the world, and brought
forth so many great, heroic, and splendid specimens of
charity and virtue. Oh! it would, indeed, be strange, if
this Church did not, when the time for the commemoration
of our Saviour's passion had come round, show in a
thousand loving ways, even in exterior forms, how her
heart is entirely in sympathy with her blessed Redeemer,
and the cross upon which He died. Hence, in the offices
for this week, there is a softened tone of joy and triumph,
in the Church's commemoration of the sufferings of her
Redeemer. While indeed she weeps and puts on her garments of mourning, and speaks in soft and tender words
to her children, still in the gentle music of her sweet
tones, in the simple magnificence of her worship, even
in those impressive and solemn rites which form the service of Friday, there is a mixture of gladness, subdued,
indeed, and as it were steeped in grief; there is a smile

that will fain break through the tears that she sheds; at thinking that after all He who is thus humbled, He who is thus crushed beneath the weight of contempt, persecution, and suffering, will break the chains of death and hell, and will again be seated triumphantly upon His throne ; and will, by means of this very ignominy, conquer His assailants, and make friends of His foes. She rejoices in His sufferings, because they are the sufferings of redemption. Her heart beats tenderly for His afflictions, because they are the afflictions of love ; and she looks not merely with awe, but with complacency and soft affection, upon the blood that flows from His manifold wounds, because they are the streams of life which fill the cup of her salvation.

Truly, beloved brethren, these days are days of solemn and tender, but of real, triumph to the spouse of Christ. Oh ! come then to these holy offices with spirits properly attuned to those deep and solemn mysteries which we are about to commemorate, and ready to beat in harmony with them. Come with a desire to learn and to improve, and you will indeed rejoice in spirit ; when, having purged yourselves during these days of affliction from sin and all that is displeasing to God, you will be able to join in the triumphs and rejoicing of your divine Redeemer, as He rises victorious over death, and opens to you the gates of life. But, even in the midst of that exultation and triumph, the cross shall not be forgotten ; for as the Church during paschal time suppresses all other com- memorations in her daily offices, retaining that of the cross alone, so when our blessed Redeemer shows himself risen again to His apostles, He desires to be recognised as their Lord and their God, not by the splendour which

invests Him,—not by the subtle energy wherewith His
glorified body can penetrate the closed doors,—but by the
marks of the nails in His hands and feet, and by the
precious wound in His side: thus to show that, in His
very glory, He wishes to be loved even as on Calvary.

Oh! blessed Jesus, may the image of these sacred
wounds, as expressed by the cross, never depart from
my thoughts. As it is a badge and privilege of the
exalted office, to which, most unworthy, I have been
raised, to wear ever upon my breast the figure of that
cross, and in it, as in a holy shrine, a fragment of that
blessed tree whereon Thou didst hang on Golgotha, so
much more let the lively image of Thee crucified dwell
within my bosom, and be the source from which shall
proceed every thought, and word, and action of my
ministry! Let me preach Thee, and Thee crucified, not
the plausible doctrines of worldly virtue and human
philosophy. In prayer and meditation let me ever have
before me Thy likeness, as Thou stretchest forth Thine
arms to invite us to seek mercy and to draw us into
Thine embrace. Let my Thabor be on Calvary; there
it is best for me to dwell. There, Thou hast prepared
three tabernacles ; one for such as, like Magdalen, have
offended much, but love to weep at Thy blessed feet ; one
for those who, like John, have wavered in steadfastness
for a moment, but long again to rest their head upon Thy
bosom ; and one whereinto only she may enter, whose
love burns without a reproach, whose heart, always
one with Thine, finds its home in the centre of Thine,
fibre intertwined with fibre, till both are melted into one,
in that furnace of sympathetic love. With these favour-

ites of the cross, let me ever, blessed Saviour, remain in meditation and prayer, and loving affection for Thy holy rood. I will venerate its very substance, whenever presented to me, with deep and solemn reverence. I will honour its image, wherever offered to me, with lowly and respectful homage. But still more I will hallow and love its spirit and inward form, impressed on the heart, and shown forth in the holiness of life. And oh! divine Redeemer, from Thy cross, Thy true mercy-seat, look down in compassion upon this, Thy people. Pour forth thence abundantly the streams of blessing, which flow from Thy sacred wounds. Accomplish within them, during this week of forgiveness, the work which holy men have so well begun,* that all may worthily partake of Thy Paschal Feast. Plant Thy cross in every heart; may each one embrace it in life, may it embrace him in death; and may it be a beacon of salvation to his departing soul, a crown of glory to his immortal spirit! Amen.

* Alluding to the Mission just closed by the Fathers of the Institute of Charity.

SERMON XI.

Meditation on the Passion.

PHILIP. ii. 8.

" He humbled Himself, becoming obedient unto death, even
the death of the cross."

THE very name, my brethren, which this Sunday bears
in the Calendar of the Catholic Church, prescribes to
us the solemn matter which should occupy our thoughts,
and will not allow us to seek around us for other subjects
of instruction. For it hath its name from the dolorous
Passion of our dear Lord and Saviour Christ Jesus ; and
no other topic can be found worthy to associate in our
minds with the contemplation of His dying hour. This
is the house of mourning into which it is better for us to
enter than into the house of feasting. From this day,
till the celebration of His glorious resurrection summon
us to joy, our hearts and affections must dwell with His,
in the desolation of Olivet, in the injustice and cruelty
of Jerusalem, and in the ignominy of Calvary. Yes,
farewell for the time to Horeb and its miracles; to
Sinai and the terrors of its law ; to Thabor and its magnificent visions; and let " the mountains of myrrh," of
bitterness and sorrow, be the place of our abode. Oh !
there will be a rich variety of grief, a plentiful diversity
of afflictions for us all, and enough to prevent weariness

in any. There shall be sympathy for the virtuous, and contrition for the sinful ; consolation for the afflicted, and mild reproof for the light of heart ; soothing encourage- ment for the persecuted of men, and utter confusion to the proud and unjust. There shall be tears that will drown all human sorrow; and thorns that shall prick to compunction the hardest heart; and sighs that as balm will heal the bruised spirit, and blood that will wash clean the deepest stains of sin !

Come then, my dear brethren, and let us enter with willing, if not with cheerful, heart, upon this way of life to us, though of death to Jesus. And, as I trust you will make the thought of His sufferings paramount in your minds, in the days that shall ensue, and will often turn your affections towards one or other of His many sorrows, I will offer myself this day, with becoming diffidence, to be your guide, by simply suggesting to you a few of the many reflections, that may occupy your thoughts upon the different parts of your dear Redeemer's Passion.

First you will follow Him into the garden of Olives, where you will see Him leave His apostles at some dis- tance, taking along with Him His three more chosen ones, from whom, however, He further retires. While they, oppressed by nature, sleep, He enters upon the most mysterious portion of His Passion. This the Scripture describes by words which imply, as we shall see, a fright- ful mental suffering. He prays to His Father to remove from Him the cup which He is about to drink; He falls upon the ground in anguish, and requires an angel as His comforter. Such is a brief outline of this stage of our Saviour's Passion; and you will, perhaps, ask yourselves, wherefore was it endured: and an easy answer will present itself.

Suppose then, that wicked Judas, when he rushed out of the supper-hall, had brought in the satellites of the priests, and had seized Jesus in the midst of His apostles, there would have been something unbecoming the majesty of His sufferings to be thus surprised, as though unprepared, amidst the calm enjoyment of society with those He loved. The whole Passion would have appeared to us a deed of violence ; and that spontaneous assumption of pain and death, which is its leading characteristic, would have hardly appeared. It was right, therefore, that a separation from the rest of mankind should take place, that Jesus should calmly and deliberately prepare Himself for all that was to follow, and give Himself up to His sufferings, as chosen by Himself. Hence, when His enemies came to seize Him, He is pleased first to throw them thrice upon the ground, before He surrendered Himself to their power. He showed in His agony and in His prayer, that He foresaw what was to ensue, and submitted to it all.

But, moreover, it was unbecoming that men should strike the first blow upon the Victim of sin; for, whatever they inflicted was but in consequence of a just and stern decree. It was the Eternal Father who must first lift His hand upon this His Isaac, and by investing Him with the character of the universal oblation, give Him up to the cruelty of man for the consummation of the mysterious sacrifice. And here, indeed, He laid His hands upon His head, as did the High Priest upon that of the emissary goat, laying upon Him the iniquities of us all, and hold-

ing Him responsible for their enormity. During the rest
of His Passion our thoughts are distracted by the harrowing spectacle of bodily torments, and by the detestation
inspired by the conduct of His enemies. Here we are exclusively occupied with the consideration of inward grief;
we see Jesus alone with His own personal sorrows, and
come to consider those as so essential a part of His sufferings, so deep, so overwhelming, as that whatever he afterwards endured in the body shall seem but as an addition
and appendage to them.

For observe diligently the awful expression of the
sacred text: " And being in an agony, He prayed the
longer;" (Luke, xxii. 43) and His own words : " My
soul is sorrowful even unto death." These expressions
suggest to us the only comparison that will illustrate the
anguish of His spirit—the last struggle between life and
death, when in ordinary men the latter conquers. They
represent to us the convulsions of exhausted Nature,
resisting in vain the wrestling of a superior destroying
power, that gripes it closer and closer, and presses out by
degrees its vital energy, till it sinks crushed and hopeless
within its iron embrace. They give us an idea of the
heart smothered in its fitful throbs, by the slow ebbing of
its thickening streams; of the chest rising against a
leaden weight that oppresses it ; of the limbs stiffening
and dragging one down like icy lumps; of the brain
swimming and reeling in sickening confusion. But
then, when we stand by such a spectacle on the bed
of a dying friend, awful and painful as it is to our
feelings, we have the consolation to know, or to believe,
that the feebleness of nature which causes it is a

security against its severity, that the sense is already
dulled, and the mind brought down almost to the verge of
unconsciousness. But here is one in the very prime of
youth, in the vigour of health, without a stroke from man,
or a visitation of evil fortune, or a domestic bereavement,
so seized upon in one instant by inward sorrow, as to be
cast into this death struggle, through its intensity. Oh
who can imagine the fearfulness of the conflict ! To be
assailed by such grief as is capable of causing death, and
to have to grapple with it, and resist it so as to prevent
by endurance its fatal effects ; to feel death, in the very
pride and fulness of life, attempt usurpation, by strong
and armed hand, against the wakeful and resisting powers
of vitality ! And to wrestle through the dark hours of
night, as Jacob did with the angel, unaided, unsupported,
alone ! Good God, what a conflict, and what a victory !
When you stand by one reduced to his last struggle, you
see with compassion how the cold sweat settles upon his
brow; you see in it the last symptom of the intensity of his
pain; and, if he were your bitterest enemy, you would not
refuse to wipe it gently away. Look then at the agony
of your Saviour, and see how, in it, that sweat is blood !
yea, and blood so profusely shed, without wound or stroke,
as to flow upon the ground !

There are plants in the luxurious East, my dearly
beloved brethren, which men gash and cut, that from
them may distil the precious balsams they contain ; but
that is ever the most sought and valued which, issuing
forth of its own accord, pure and unmixed, trickles down
like tears upon the parent tree. And so it seems to me,
we may without disparagement speak of the precious

P

streams of our dear Redeemer's blood. When forced from
His side, in abundant flow, it came mixed with another
mysterious fluid ; when shed by the cruel inflictions of
His enemies, by their nails, their thorns, and scourges,
there is a painful association with the brutal instruments
that drew it, as though in some way their defilement
could attaint it. But here we have the first yield of that
saving and life-giving heart, gushing forth spontaneously,
pure and untouched by the unclean hand of man, dropping
as dew upon the ground. It is the first juice of the
precious vine ; before the wine-press hath bruised its
grapes, richer and sweeter to the loving and sympathizing
soul, than what is afterwards pressed out. It is every
drop of it ours ; and alas, how painfully so ! For here no
lash, no impious palm, no pricking thorn hath called it
forth; but our sins, yes our sins, the executioners not of
the flesh, but of the heart of Jesus, have driven it all out,
thence to water that garden of sorrows ! Oh is it not
dear to us ; is it not gathered up by our affections, with
far more reverence and love than by virgins of old was
the blood of martyrs, to be placed for ever in the very
sanctuary, yea, within the very altar of our hearts !

But we shall have a very faint idea of our Saviour's
sufferings, upon this occasion, if we learn it not from His
prayer. All that our imagination could feign would not
give us an estimate equal to that contained in those few
words : " Father if it be possible, let this chalice pass
away from me." For, consider how low indeed must
His strength have been reduced, how fearfully must
the repugnances of the afflicted man have been allowed
to prevail, against the earnest love, and longing

desires that engaged Him to the accomplishment of our salvation, to make Him even for a moment flinch before the sufferings that awaited Him, and hesitate whether or no He should draw back from the painful undertaking, in which He had already taken so many steps ! Oh, how the cause of us poor creatures trembled for a moment in the scale; while on one side, weighed that reverence in which He was held, so as to make all His petitions effectual ; and on the other, His love for man, and for each of us in particular ! How may Heaven be supposed for a moment to have stood in suspense, to see which should prevail ! But no, blessed be Thou, my loving Jesus, for that little clause which Thou insertest in Thy prayer: " if it can be done." Yes, I well understand its meaning, pregnant as it is with the fate of my salvation. " If the cup," it seems to say, " can be removed, yet so as man shall be saved, if it can be put aside, consistent with my determination and pledge, to offer a full and sufficient ransom for sinners ; then, and only then, let this nau-seous draught be taken from before me. If this may not so be, then welcome its bitterness, that lost man may be saved." Yes, well had He taken care to enter a caution in heaven against His prayer being received, when wrung from Him in the anguish and agony of His soul, and well did He clog it with such a condition, as would prevent its being received, to the interruption of our redemption.

But do you wonder, my brethren, that He should either have recoiled from drinking this cup, or that He should have afterwards cheerfully drunk it to the dregs ? What was there in that cup ? Our sins and the punishment due to them.   And what was to be gained by His drinking it ?   Our   salvation.   And is not the mystery solved ? Do you wonder either that the Lamb of God, pure and un- defiled, should have shuddered at the very thought of invest- ing Himself with your transgressions, which even to your own minds are now so hateful; or can you wonder that your dear Saviour should have loved you so much, as to master this repugnance, and swallow that poisonous potion, so that His death might be thy life ?

Oh ! then, whenever you offend God by sin, think that your offence was an additional drop of bitterness in that draught, another pang in the heart of Jesus, which you might easily have spared Him.   When you have over- come temptation, rejoice to think that, here at least, you have refrained from swelling the already too full measure of sorrow, which He accepted for your sake.

But when you have meditated, with an affectionate heart, upon the first stage of your Saviour's sufferings, you will turn to Him with various feelings, according to the reflections you have made.   Sometimes, seeing Him aban- doned by His disciples, you will address Him as if you were present, and had it in your power to attend Him, and comfort Him.   " Drink," you will say to Him, " my good and loving Saviour, drink, I entreat Thee, this bitter cup, that so I may be saved.   It is true I have helped to mingle in it the gall of dragons, by the bitterness of my ingratitude to Thee ; but still I know Thou lovest me to that excess, that Thou wilt endure it all, rather than that I should be lost as I deserve.   But oh ! let me add to it one more ingredient, which will make it less hateful to Thee—the tears of a sincere repentance.   Be comforted some little with the thought, that of those who helped to prepare for Thee this loathsome potion, one at least shall not be ungrateful, for the boundless love which prompted Thee to drink it."

Or, perhaps, prompted by a feeling of more generous ardour, you will desire to share in your Redeemer's sufferings. You will imagine Him asking you, as He did the sons of Zebedee, if you are willing to drink of the cup whereof He should drink? And you will say to yourself: "Oh, who could resist such a question, or hesitate to answer, yes? Who would decline to drink from the same chalice, however bitter its draught, which His blessed lips had consecrated and sweetened? Welcome, then, my dear Saviour, my portion in Thy cup, as in Thy cross. I will drink of it resignedly in all trials, and afflictions, studying to bear them in the spirit of Olivet. I will drink of it penitently, in sorrow and contrition, weeping often here in Thy company, and grieving that I should have so cruelly agonized Thy tender heart. I will drink of it lovingly on Thy altar, when in holy communion I partake of Thy precious body and blood. And, in the end, grant, my dear Jesus, that I may blissfully drink it, new with Thee, in the kingdom of Thy Father, there face to face to thank Thee, for Thy sorrows and Thy pains."

After our blessed Lord has been seized by His enemies, upon receiving the traitor's kiss, and has been led into the city, the scenes of the bitter tragedy succeed one another so closely, and present such a variety of feeling subjects for meditation, that it is impossible for us at present even to touch upon a small portion of them. First, then, we have Him presented to the high priests, and their confederates, who prepare the preliminaries for His trial next day. It is an instructive and consoling occupation to follow these wily and unprincipled enemies in their course of cunning injustice ; for they seek to save their characters, while they condemn the Lord of glory. Hence they suborn a number of witnesses, whose testimony Jesus confounds, by simply remaining silent. Nothing can be more completely triumphant for His character than the result of this most partial investigation.

But there is one incident in this stage of the Passion, that particularly rivets our attention—the denial of Peter. Jesus, from the beginning, had been abandoned by His apostles, after the first rash effort, made by Peter to rescue Him. He stood without a friend amidst the ruffianly servants and guards of the chief priests, who had let loose their cruelty upon Him, and were loading Him with every indignity. At length, this ever boldest and most zealous of His friends draws nigh, and ventures into the crowd. Surely he is come to give his dear Master some comfort, and assure Him that all His chosen ones remain faithful to Him, and sympathize in His sufferings. He must be ready, if necessary, to die with Him ! Alas ! he is come on a very different errand, and Jesus who has foretold it to him, well knows it ; he is come only to disown and foreswear his Lord, and perjure his soul most frightfully and treacherously, that he knows not the man ! It would seem as if this special trial had been permitted, expressly to break down every comfort, which the suffering humanity of Jesus otherwise might have felt. What a wreck of the toils, the lessons, the warnings and examples of three years ! In vain has He been labouring to teach him that the Son of man must be

MEDITATION ON THE PASSION.

delivered into the hands of sinners, and be mocked, and
scourged, and so put to death. Peter, after them all, does
not know the man! And who, can He then hope, ever will?
Yes, and there is the solid foundation of His Church, the
rock on which it was to be built, melted away like wax,
before that fatal fire in the priest's hall! There is all the
work of years in forming His apostle's character, dissolved
like frost-work, at the breath of a foolish servant girl!
Oh what a painful sight to Jesus in the midst of His
other torments! How more grievous a stroke than the
blows He was receiving on His cheek! How much blacker
an insult than the spitting in His face!

But, on the other hand, observe His conduct. Peter
was no longer worthy of His notice, much less of His
affection. He had treated Him most disloyally, and most
ungratefully. Jesus might have justly abandoned him for
ever. At least He surely had enough to think of for Himself, and might leave him until after His resurrection.
But no; He would not delay one moment to touch his heart;
He would not die unreconciled to him. He heeds not the
thick crowd of tormentors around Him, but turns to
Peter. Oh, what a glance must that have been! a look,
never to be effaced, so long as he lived, from the heart
and memory of that apostle. His features are scarcely
discernible, through the disfiguring effects of the outrageous treatment He has received ; but His eye, unclouded
in its mild majesty, darts a beam, which not only passes
far beyond His insulters, through the gloom of night,
and reaches the outer hall, but finds its way into the very
recesses of the apostle's heart, breaks the spell of forgetfulness that binds him, softens once more those finer feelings,

which fear had benumbed and frozen, and brings them out in a flood of tears. And who of us will not feel that look as bent no less upon us? We have again and again disowned and abjured our Saviour; perhaps before men by cowardly timidity in His service; often certainly before the face of His angels, by the apostacy of sin. And often have outward warnings been lost upon us; as the crowing of the cock was upon Peter. But one look of Jesus, in His sufferings, must surely be irresistible to our hearts; an expostulation from Him so mildly spoken, so lovingly urged, so winningly softened by His proffer of pardon, from Him whom not other men, but we whom He so treats, are cruelly ill-using, cannot be rejected by the hardest heart, by the most unfeeling transgressor.

I pass over, my brethren, the brutal inflictions of that night of sorrows, in which, as in every other part of His Passion, the meekness and patience of the Son of God shine brightly, in proportion to the black and hateful behaviour of others towards Him. I pass over the first accusations at Pilate's tribunal, the outcries for His blood, the mockery of Herod, the silence of Christ,—all rich themes for meditation; because I will rather pause on the more striking events of that eventful day.

And first, Jesus is scourged. Notice how Pilate proposes this insult. "I, having examined Him, find no cause in this man; I will chastise Him therefore, and let Him go." (Luke xxiii. 14, 16.) What an impious blasphemous idea! To chastise or correct Him, who is the eternal wisdom of the Father, purity, innocence, holiness and all perfection! And who is it that undertakes to chastise Him? One of the lewdest, most tyrannical, most hateful

of heathens.   He proposes to chastise the spotless Lamb
of God, to correct His faults, and send Him back to the
world an amended man !   And how is this correction to
be effected ? By the scourge ! By the punishment of slaves,
of the vilest of mankind ! See, then, how Pilate proceeds,
without remorse, to put his offer in execution, fancying
that he is thereby actually doing a favour to Jesus !
Contemplate well the scene which ensues, when He is
delivered over, for this purpose, to the rabid soldiery.

He is placed in the hands of probably the most hardened class of men on earth; men inured to carnage, each
one of them ready, when commanded, to be an executioner,
an office reserved in later times for one who is deemed
an outcast ; men who hated the stranger and the conquered, and who ever bore a particular antipathy to the
Jewish nation.   Now to the absolute power of these men,
Jesus is abandoned.   They see given up to them, not a
hardened rough criminal, one like themselves, with whom
they would probably have sympathized, or whom they
would have thought it but an every-day occupation to
torture ; but one whose first appearance shows Him to
be of the noblest descent, and of the tenderest frame ; one
whose modesty and bashfulness can but poorly stand
the disgraceful exposure to nakedness and ignominious
punishment ; one whose meek and calm demeanour, so at
variance with their brutality, stimulates their cruel appetite ; still more, one whose alleged crime is the desire
and attempt to drive them and their whole race out of
Palestine, and overthrow the empire, which gives them
for their bread the plunder of the world.

What wonder that the scourging inflicted by those

pitiless wretches should have been ever represented
as one of the cruelest parts of our blessed Redeemer's
Passion ?   What wonder that He Himself should have
almost always alluded to it, when He spoke of His
crucifixion ?   For, if to any man it was so disgraceful
an infliction, that St. Paul himself pleaded his right as
a Roman citizen in bar of its execution, what must it
have been in this afflicting case ?

Well, now, see the innocent Lamb of God, surrounded
by this ruffianly mob, the subject of their coarse jests and
gross ribaldry, those men whom St. Ignatius Martyr later
characterised by the name of *leopards*.   See how they
strip Him, with rude hands ! how they tightly bind His
wrists, and tie Him to the pillar.   Gracious God ! is it
possible that Thou wilt allow His virginal flesh to be
touched by a scourge ; is it possible that Thou wilt permit
the ignominious lash to tear and disfigure that most comely
and holy of bodies, formed by Thine own immediate
agency in the pure womb of Mary, the most precious
work of Thy hands since the creation of the world !
Angels of God ! can you withhold your indignation,
and refrain from rushing upon this mad soldiery and
overthrowing (as ye did Heliodorus) those who are
about to treat your Master, your happiness and joy, as a
vile malefactor, as the lowest of slaves, and will instantly
proceed to tear and bruise His adorable body, and
sprinkle His blood over that profane floor ?

But, no ; there seems to be no mercy, no pity for Jesus,
either on earth or in heaven ; He is abandoned to the
anger of God and the fury of man.   The executioners
surround Him with savage delight, and shower on Him

their cruel blows, till He is covered with blood, and gashed, and swollen, over all His sacred body !

See now, how the brutal executioners proceed to the task of inflicting cruel torment upon your dear Redeemer. Having bound Him to the pillar, they deal their furious blows upon His sacred shoulders, back, chest, and arms. First His tender flesh swells and inflames, then the skin is gradually torn, and the blood oozes through ; gashes begin to be formed, and wider streams pour down in profusion. At length every part is covered by one continuous bruise ; gash has run into gash, wide rents meet in every direction, and the flesh is torn in flakes from the bones. One wretch succeeds another in the cruel work, till they are tired, and their patience, though not that of their Victim, is exhausted.

What a piteous spectacle does our dear Jesus now present ! What a contrast with what He was but the day before, when seated at His table of love with His twelve, and John reposing on His bosom. If that disciple sees Him now, what a tender sorrow must he not feel, and how bitterly must he deplore the sad change which this ruthless infliction had made ! And ought I not to feel as much as John for my dear Saviour's sufferings ? Was He not as much my Saviour as his ?   This sorrowful act in the sacred tragedy now ended, our Lord is untied from the column, and left, as best He may, to shift for Himself. There is no friend near to help Him : His disciples are all out of the way, and the unfeeling soldiery are not likely to render Him any assistance. Every limb is sore, stiff, and benumbed with pain, so as to be almost powerless ; yet, He must again put on His rough woollen clothes upon His mangled limbs, to grate, and fret them, and increase their smart.

But now, consider the change which has taken place in His situation before His people. He is now a disgraced degraded being. The base lash has touched, nay, cruelly torn Him. He stands in their presence as a tried and condemned criminal, as a public malefactor. They will not believe that their priests could have gone to such extremities, as deliver a descendant of David to the heathen's scourge, without good and solid reasons. But, be He as innocent as possible, He cannot again hold up His head among the children of His people. One who has been scourged can never hope to head even a party among them. He must give up all pretensions to be their Messias. Who will now own Him? Oh! how many, upon seeing Him thus treated, denied Him like Peter? How many not only swore that they never had known the man, but inwardly regretted that they had ever followed or believed in Him? How many are ashamed, at this first step in the scandal of the cross?

And after you have afflicted your heart with this sorrowful spectacle, will you not break into a loving expostulation with the Saviour of your soul, and say to Him: "O my good and ever-gracious Jesus, this was really too much for Thee to endure, for such a sinful wretch as I have been; it was too much goodness, too much affection, to submit to such degrading, such savage treatment for my sake. It is a spectacle too distressing for even my flinty heart to contemplate; oh would it had been spared Thee! But Thy love knows not the phrase too much; it is insatiable, it will devour every igno-

miny and every torment, to save and to win us to itself.
Oh let me then never know that word, in gratitude and
requiting love.   And yet I address Thee, as though I had
had no hand in this barbarous infliction ; as though my
sins had not been Thy true persecutors and executioners,
that laid the lash upon Thy sacred body.   Let shame and
sorrow, but ever loving sorrow, overwhelm me, when I
think upon what they have made Thee undergo !"

But another scene of extraordinary barbarity yet awaits
us.   The soldiers have exhausted the power which the
law put into their hands; but their fierce desires are not
exhausted.   They know that Jesus is charged with declaring Himself King of the Jews, and they proceed to make
this just claim the ground of a strange mockery.   They
prepare for Him a new unheard-of diadem woven of hard
sharp thorns, and place it upon His sacred head.   Then
they press it down on every side, till its points pierce the
skin and penetrate His flesh.   Now behold your Saviour still
further disfigured, and dishonoured.   Before, His body had
been torn, but even the scourge had respected His venerable head.   But now this is assailed by this invention of
ingenious cruelty, which, under the repeated strokes of the
reed given Him for a sceptre, and taken from His hand,
changes its position, and inflicts at every blow a new or a
deeper wound.   His hair is all entangled in the knotty
wreath, and clotted with His sacred blood.   His fair
temples and noble forehead are strained and pressed down
by it ; while it shoots its points into them, and opens so
many fountains of life, waters of salvation, springing warm
from His affectionate heart.   See how they trickle down
first slowly, then in faster and thicker streams, till His

sacred face and neck are streaked with blood, which running down over His body, mingles with that flowing from the gashes of the scourge. " Go forth, ye daughters of Sion, and see king Solomon, in the diadem with which His mother crowned Him, in the day of His espousals, and in the day of the joy of His heart." (Cant. iii. 11.) Yes, His own nation, whose Son He was, and in that day when He stretches forth His hand for a pledge of love, from the souls of all He has redeemed. And who will not answer His call the more lovingly for seeing Him reduced to such a state ? What would the diadem of Solomon, or that which David his father made of the spoils of his foes, have added of grace or glory to the brow of the Son of God ? What dignity or majesty would gold or precious stones have bestowed on that Divine head ? But wreath it with thorns for my sake, and enrich it with blood poured out to save me, and I recognize, not the world's diadem, but the bridal crown of that Spouse of blood, who would gain our souls at the price of His life.

" I will extol Thee, O God my King, and I will bless Thy name for ever." (Ps. cxliv. 1.) " He, who of old, had conquered at the games, preferred a myrtle crown to one of gold; he who had vanquished enemies in battle, a laurel wreath; and he who had saved a citizen, one of oak. And I will ever love beyond them all that which Thou hast chosen for Thyself, a crown of thorns. Thou shalt place it on my heart, and it shall be at once a goad to my love, and a prick to my remorse ; and I will love Thee sorrowing, for the ignominy and pain to which Thou hast stooped on my account."

After you shall have duly taken a view of the remaining portion of this stage of the Passion, of the manner, in particular, in which Barabbas is preferred to Christ, of the awful cry with which the wretched Jews call down His blood upon their heads, and the miserable spectacle of Jesus carrying His cross, you will hasten on to Calvary, to witness the consummation of the solemn tragedy.

Consider now the cruel torments which our dear Jesus must have endured during His three hours remaining on the cross. His body was stretched out upon this hard knotty trunk ; for certainly they who prepared it studied but little how to make it soft or easy to His limbs. Every sinew and muscle of His body must have been in a state of unnatural tension, both from the situation in which He was placed, and from the effort which Nature would make to diminish the pressure upon the wounds of the nails. We find it weary enough lying for a few hours in one position upon a soft bed, and cannot bear being long without turning, upon a hard board ; what, then, must it have been to hang in the air extended upon this rough tree, especially in the state of our blessed Saviour's body ? From head to foot He is one wound ; His head, if it press against the cross, is gored by the points of the thorns, which are thus driven deep into it. Truly now are verified, in their truest and saddest sense, His plaintive words : "The Son of man hath not where to rest His head." His shoulders and back, which are pressed necessarily against it, are flayed, and torn with the inhuman stripes, which have been inflicted upon Him. Against these open wounds does this cruel bed press, so that any change

of posture, so far from relieving Him, only increases His
sufferings, by grating upon, and rending wider, the blisters
and gashes with which He is covered.   But let us not
lose sight of those four terrible, but most precious, wounds,
whereby He is fastened on the cross.   Each of His hands,
each of His feet, is transfixed by a long black nail, driven
into it with violence, and every moment, by the natural
gravitation of His body, tearing wider and wider the
rent it has made.   Oh! what a smarting, torturing
pain—what an unceasing suffering during three hours of
crucifixion!   Who, dear Jesus, shall be able to recount
all that Thou sufferedst for me, in that short space!

But, beyond these sufferings, immediately inflicted by
the act of crucifixion itself, there were others no less
severe, which resulted from it.   The uneasy and unnatural position it produced, caused a disturbance in all the
nobler functions of life.   The lungs, surcharged with
blood, panted with labour and anxiety, in consequence of
the compression of the chest : the heart, from the same
cause, beat heavily and painfully, clogged in its motions
by the impeded circulation : the blood, unable to return
from the head, by reason of the veins being compressed,
must have caused a tingling apoplectic pain.   The same
causes would produce a distressing heat and irritation all
over the surface of the face, neck, and chest, which He
had no hand to relieve, and which, consequently, must
have been torturing in the extreme.   To these sufferings
we must add, exposure to heat and air, with a body
already wounded in every part, and covered with sores,
inflicted by the torments of the preceding night and that
very morning ; so that not only those parts of the body

which pressed upon the cross, but every other, must have been painfully sensitive, and subject to grievous sufferings.

Truly, my Jesus was the king of martyrs, the severest sufferer the world ever saw, for the sake of others !

Add to all these torments the many other accessories to the tortures of crucifixion, which our beloved Saviour endured for you. He, the most modest and purest of beings, is exposed unclothed before the multitude. He is an object not of their compassion, but of their absolute derision. He sees before Him an immense crowd, all animated, or rather possessed, by one evil spirit of hatred and scorn of Him; every word that reaches Him is a word of bitter insult and mockery. Nearer Him, indeed, is a smaller group of faithful and sympathizing followers, but so far from His receiving comfort from these, they stand in need of it from Him, and cheerfully He gives it. Peter and His other companions, apostles, and disciples, the many who had followed Him from place to place, have disappeared, and hidden themselves from the sight of men. All that He possessed on earth, His few clothes, even to His seamless garment, are unfeelingly divided, or diced for, between the soldiers who have executed Him. He is thus alone in the world, without one smallest link with it, save His love for man, and His earnest desire to accomplish his salvation. In fine, He suffers a racking thirst; His parched lips can no longer endure the dryness which afflicts them, and call out for relief. And the barbarians who surround Him, present Him with gall and vinegar to drink. Can outrage go beyond this ? Could brutality be carried to a higher excess ? Now, surely, we may say that all is accomplished, and that the anger of the just God has no more dregs left in the chalice of suffering which He had mingled for His Son, as the world's Redeemer. Now, be His name praised for ever, nothing more remains but that death come and put an end to so much suffering.

But how complete it was determined, by the inexorable justice of God, that the abandonment of His Son should be, how filled to the brim the chalice of His bitter sorrows, when even His dear and blessed mother, instead of being any longer to Him what she had ever before been, a source of comfort and happiness, was destined to aggravate His sufferings, and render His last hour more desolate! If there could be one tie between Him and earth which His heart might continue to cherish, it was His love for her who had borne Him, and had loved Him as child and as man, far beyond any other created being. If all the world had abandoned Him, she at least had not; if most that stood near Him sympathized but little, or even rejoiced in His sufferings, she partook of them with a mother's sensibility, and alone endured more than all earth else, Himself alone excepted. If few would feel His loss, to her it would be irreparable. Her then He sees at the foot of His cross, overwhelmed with anguish, and unspeakable woe. He knows how she is revolving in her mind, whither she shall go when she has lost Him; not from any selfishness or self-seeking, but from the utter worthlessness of all earth, when He should withdraw from it. What an additional pang to His sacred heart, to witness her inconsolable grief, and irremediable distress! What an accumulation of sorrow to His overwhelmed soul, to have no power to comfort her, to be obliged to give her up, to abandon her, to have not a good or cheering word to utter! How did their looks and their hearts meet at that hour! How were all the affections of both, if possible, renewed, and how did they melt into one loving thought, in the fierce furnace of their common sufferings! How did Mary remember the happy days when He was an infant in her bosom, and when she heard His Godlike words, sitting at their homely but cheerful meal: and how did Jesus remember the cherishing love with which this tenderest of mothers had nursed and caressed Him! Here was, indeed, depth calling upon depth, grief superhuman upon grief such as none had felt before. Still Jesus cannot leave this earth without making some provision for the future welfare of His loving parent, who had taken care of Him for thirty years. Gladly would He take her with Him into His glory, and bear her as the first present of earth to heaven. But this comfort is denied Him: for if granted, He would have died with one pain less, with one consolation more, and this was incompatible with the stern decrees of justice. No, He must have the pain of knowing, as He expires, that He is leaving her, whom He loves beyond all other persons and things, to misery and poverty, and to the charity, however secure, of strangers. He looks about Him for some protector for the remainder of her days, and finds the only apostle faithful to Him in His hour of sorrow.

Consider the blessed words which Jesus spoke; for thou hast a deep interest therein. First, looking down, with His sweetest expression, on Mary, He said, referring to John: "Woman, behold thy son;" then to John: "Son,

behold thy mother." Here was a new relationship
established, wherein it was intended that we should all
have a part. For, as the Church of God has always
believed, in John we were all represented; and so Mary
was made our mother, and we were made her children.
But as this relationship may form, in due season, matter
for its own meditations, let us keep our attention to what
Jesus here did. How did He feel the distressing nature
of the exchange He was proposing, in offering to the
affectionate and already crushed heart of Mary, John for
Himself! But if to her He was thus necessarily hard,
see, on the other hand, how lovingly He thought of us
the while, and how, even in the depth of His afflictions,
He devised new blessings for us, and appointed new aids
to salvation. He bestowed on us this mother—this
tender, loving mother—this compassionate and merciful
mother—while suffering the most excruciating torments
for our sins and ingratitudes! His death was approaching; He had given us Himself; He was just about to
seal the donation by expiring, but He bethought Him of
another bequest—nothing, indeed, in comparison with
Himself, but still better, nobler, more valuable than
anything else. He had adopted us as His brethren in
regard of His eternal Father; He had made us co-heirs
with Him of the kingdom of heaven; yet, He wished
our relationship to be even closer still, and us to be
His brethren in respect to His dear mother—one family
with Him, where our feelings can most easily be engaged
in favour of our kindred. At the same time, who can
refrain from admiring the steadiness and wonderful
strength of the heart of Jesus, thus discharging His duty

as a son, in the midst of the most frightful torments of
body, when exhausted by His wounds, and when oppressed in mind by an unspeakable weight of woe. How
amiable, how perfect is every line in the character of
this our dear Master and Saviour, whether in life or
in death.

Let us then exclaim : " How shall we ever sufficiently
thank Thee, dear Jesus, for having thus made Thine own
sacrifice, no less than Thy loving mother's loss, our gain ?
What a motive for gratitude to Thee and to her, to have
found a place at such a moment in both your hearts—
to have been considered worth mention upon Calvary,
amidst the sympathizing sorrows of Son and mother !
And here, surely, all the gain was mine; for she but
acquired in me a froward and undutiful, and often rebellious, child; whereas, I obtained a tender and most watchful parent, who through life has been my patroness and
kindest friend, ever making intercession for me most
effectually with Thee. But let me never forget what
this adoption cost Thee. For I see that to establish it,
Thou wast pleased to bring Mary to the foot of Thy cross,
piercing her soul with a sharp sword of grief, which went
back to Thine own, wounding deeply Thy filial heart ;
that for three hours Thou allowedst Thy bitter passion
to be aggravated by the sight of her inexpressible
wretchedness ; that so she might conceive us in sorrow
and pain, and have a stronger maternal interest in our
salvation. Blessed be ye both for so much love ! Blessed
above all Thou, my dear Jesus, for whom no suffering
seemed too much, which could give us any further
blessing !"

But to these many sufferings must be added a deeper
and more mysterious woe : the desolation of His soul,
from the abandonment of His eternal Father. " My God,
My God," He exclaims, "why hast thou abandoned me?"
Had the world alone deserted Him, it would have been to
Him no loss.   But to see Himself now an object of the
indignation of God, in whom His love and being were
centred, oh this was the true consumnation of His wretchedness ! This is the only sun which to His eyes is
darkened, the only brightness that is dimmed.   All joy is
extinguished in His heart, His soul is drowned in
unutterable anguish ; and, uttering a loud cry, expressive
of His desolation, He gives up the ghost.

• Oh sit down and ponder, what the world lost at that
moment, and what it gained.

   What important changes did that instant produce upon
this globe !   The richest treasure it had ever possessed is
gone : an eclipse as complete in the moral splendour of earth
took place to the eye of heaven, as had three hours before
in its visible brightness.   What was the world without
Him, but a wilderness and desolation ?   The fulness of
His grace, the perfection of His virtues, the majesty of His
presence, the effulgence of His divinity, all were fled; and
the earth which, to the sight of angels, had been as a part
of heaven, during His sojourn on it, returned to its
unmitigated aspect of sin and of sorrow.   But to man,
had his eye been opened by faith, a brighter vision would
have appeared.   The veil was rent from top to bottom not
only in the Temple of Jerusalem, but in the sanctuary of
heaven ; and only waited for the third day to be drawn
aside, and the glories within put into man's possession.

The handwriting against him was at that instant effaced, the shackles had fallen from his feet, his birthright was reclaimed ; and the evil spirits, that had urged on the furious people, to accomplish the death of Jesus, stood aghast, and trembled, and gnawed their hearts in rage, to see the ruin they had brought upon themselves. The bolts spring back from the gates of the prison, in which the saints of old were confined, its doors fly open, a bright and shining splendour breaks into it, and the soul of the blessed Jesus descends to their embraces, amidst hosannas of triumph.

Such is the Passion, such the death of Jesus ! And now that I have hastily led you to it, I feel so completely how unequal I have been to my undertaking, that I fear lest I should have rather weakened, than directed or assisted, the emotions which your own affections would have awakened. For it is one of those topics on which our hearts can be more eloquent than our tongues, and whisper those things, which these may not have the courage, even if they have the power, to utter. We began these our instructions in the name of our infant Jesus, we close them this day at the foot of His cross. There should they ever part, who desire to meet again in Paradise. Whatever I may have laboured, whatever I may have striven, useless servant as I am, I leave in confidence on that sacred spot, asking no reward save that some few drops of the life-giving streams that there flow, may fall upon it, and make it spring up in your souls, unto your eternal profit. Whoever ye are that have not disdained so humble a ministry, I commend you to that blessed company that stands around, and still more to

Him that hangs upon, the tree of life ; to those under whose roof we have so often met, whose united names have been called upon this holy place, to Jesus and to Mary.* Though from one another we now separate in the body, yet may we, through the spirit, be in their society united.   There shall we find peace and joy, assurance and hope : and the scandal of the cross, here below loved by us in our silent meditation, shall be the theme of our loud and grateful praises in life everlasting.   Amen.

* The church of *Gesù e Maria*, in Rome, where this sermon was preached.

SERMON XII.

On being of Christ's side.

St. Luke, xi. 23.

" He that is not with me is against me, and he that gathereth
not with me, scattereth."

ALBEIT in ordinary times, when things are regular and
peaceful, a virtuous citizen will seek to escape from the
excitement of party-contention, and confine himself to the
unpretending discharge of his domestic and particular
duties, yet are there times of public danger and disquiet,
when it is a crime to prefer our proper ease to the tur-
moil of a more stirring life. For when factions rise high,
and wicked men stalk abroad, and principles of turbulence and disorder fill the heads of the ignorant, or
proud usurpations disgrace the hands of the powerful,
or vice is openly countenanced, and all things become
perplexed and confused, then if the wise and virtuous,
the lovers of men's souls and of men's happiness, stand
aloof, leaving all to the evil to destroy and to corrupt,
and do not rather come forward, and openly and fearlessly
declare themselves for the side of justice, and throw into
its scale the weight of their influence and good counsels,
they shall prove themselves to be so cruelly indifferent

to their country's weal, as to be rightly accounted among its enemies. And hence Plato, in his Republic, considers those citizens as wicked, and to be punished with death, who, in times of public disorder and confusion, refuse to take a side, and declare themselves of one party.

It is in some such sort that our Divine Redeemer declares, in the words of my text, how He would have us act. For again and again He speaks of Himself as having come on earth as the leader of a party at open and deadly war with a hateful faction, that hath the advantage in numbers, in rank, in wealth, and in every worldly prominence. He came down to bring not peace but the sword; (Mat. x. 34) He came not merely to enlighten the world, but to set it on fire. (Luke xii. 49.) He declared and waged war against the leagued powers of darkness and of earth ; and for this purpose He gathered together His little band of followers, to whom He has committed its conduct, whom He has charged to continue the warfare even unto death. But then He will have no dastards in His army; He will have no faint-hearted, cold, indifferent followers, who will slink away when the sound of the trumpet is heard. Like Gideon, neither those that prefer their homes and families to His camp, nor those who lay them down at full length by the torrent to take deep draughts of earthly refreshment, will He acknowledge as His partizans, or fit to be mustered in His ranks. A few will do for Him, for He is come forth to conquer; but those few must be His, hand and heart, body and soul. At the same time, woe to those who have shrunk from the danger when it came, or have been ashamed of His cause when it seemed poor and depressed; for on all such He hath pronounced sentence in the words of my text, saying that they shall be accounted not merely as indifferent, but as hostile to Him. " He who is not with me is against me ; and he that gathereth not with me, scattereth."

Two things, it should seem, are here worthy of consideration: first, what signs may we have, or what test will Christ use, to determine whether we be with Him or no; secondly, what will be the consequence of our not openly declaring on His side.

Had our blessed Saviour contented Himself with the first portion of His sentence, we might have found place for doubt, or flattering uncertainty, regarding its application. We might have said, each one to himself : " Oh ! I surely am with Christ, for I believe in His doctrine, and I hope in His mercies, and I abstain from whatever His law forbids. I wish well to His cause, and my heart is ever with those that forward it." But the comment upon the first phrase in the second part of the sentence will not allow us to reason thus. " He that gathereth not with me, scattereth." The service whereon Jesus is engaged is one of active exertion, and we must join Him in it. We are not to be lookers on, idle admirers of His or another's efforts, but workmen as well as they. If it be a harvest which He is gathering of precious grain, that is of souls most dear to Him, you might as well be helping the storm to scatter the ears away from His hand so that they perish, as be a mere spectator, refusing to share His labour. If it be His followers that He is gathering together for some great work which requires the co-operation of all, you are in secret league with His

enemy to disperse His force, if you refuse Him your
active aid, not only by yourselves coming, but by moreover bringing others, to the standard. It is, then, an
active stirring interest in His cause that He exacts from
all that wish to be accounted of His side, and not their
good wishes and silent adhesion.

But upon what grounds is this claimed, or how shall
we ascertain its measure? Why I will first say it is
demanded on the lowest possible grounds, and the
standard of its measure that I will propose is the
simplest and the nearest that I can find. What do
men in general expect you to do, when you profess with
earnestness or zeal to belong to any school or party?
Surely Christ may ask as much, and with as good
reason. Let us, then, examine how He may judge us
by these tests.

First, He will see how men act who give themselves
up to the opinions of a particular school. They read
and meditate, day and night, on the works of its principal masters ; they discuss unceasingly their difficulties,
till they fancy they are all explained ; they admire their
doctrines and their persons with such enthusiasm, as
sometimes to declare that they would rather be in error
with those wise men, than think aright in company with
the rest of mankind. They seek proselytes to their
sect with unwearying ardour; they combat strenuously all
contradictions to its professed principles; they rise in zeal
and often in anger to rebut every imputation upon its
honour; they wear openly badges of their belonging to it;
they boast of its maxims being the rule of their conduct, and in work they show it. Such were of old the

disciples of Plato and Aristotle; such Christ saw were in
His own times, the Pharisees and Sadducees; such have
continued to our days the partizans of philosophical systems. Can He reasonably expect less from His disciples ?
can He in very decency propose a lower test for Him or
for us to judge by, whether we belong to His side ?   Try
yourselves, therefore, by it.   It is simple in its application.
It requires no great diving into the hidden mysteries of
your hearts, no unravelling of its complicated feelings, it
is a test by outward and palpable manifestations.   Do
you then show but a hundredth part of a similar attachment
to the law and doctrines of Christ, as these scholars have
done to the dark conjectures and uncertain theories of
fallible men ?   Do you love them so as to exert your abilities in propagating, defending, and illustrating them ?
Or do you content yourselves with silent approval, and
inactive concurrence ?   And are ye then the partizans,
the avowed followers of Christ Jesus ?   Are ye with
Him, even as men are with one another ?   He will look at
men's conduct, when they place themselves decidedly on
one side, in times of political excitement.   How they will
sacrifice their own opinions on particular points to the
views and aims of their party !   How they will inveigh
against their opponents, and study to baffle all their arts !
How they will rejoice in every triumph of their friends,
and in every defeat of their adversaries, as though some
personal advantage had befallen them !   How they crowd
to the standard of their leaders, when their active exertions are demanded, and open their coffers when their
wealth is needed !   And shall the Son of God, in reason,
be content with less ?   Shall He see men willing to be

cozened, cajoled, wrought up into enthusiasm, or even lashed into fury by the zeal of worldly partizanship, and when His cause is treated, when His interests are to be defended, think they shall be considered His partizans, because they have not joined the opposite ranks, or because, forsooth, they have honoured His part with tacit approbation ?   Is He alone to be put off with cold fellowship, and wavering fidelity, and call those friends who proffer it, while they themselves shall scout at such professions in the paltry concerns of earth ?

But, moreover, He will see the hearty devotion and fervent worship which each of us pays to the idols of his own heart, and wonder how only on His behalf we think so little quite enough.   Did He find that the follower of ambition, or the gatherer of wealth, or the lover of praise, strove onward in the pursuit of his particular object, with some of that lukewarmness and indifference wherewith we all espouse and pretend to love His cause; nay, did He perceive that the wretched slave of luxury, that the bondsman of passion, hugged his chains with even the same half love which we His servants and ministers put forth in His behoof, then, perhaps, might He conclude that His cause was not treated at least worse than others, however degrading the comparison, and consider the coldness of His side as only resulting from some common and universal influence.

But, good God ! how can He fail to observe, on the contrary, that to the enemy's partizans this reproach cannot be made : for see how they sleep not, and slumber not, and relax not in their efforts for the mastery.   See how they recruit their forces on every side, and now by deceit, and now by violence, strengthen their host. They have entered upon their cause with heart and soul, and it is no other than to set up this world in rivalry and opposition to the Lord Jesus. First they have built it up with marvellous contrivance, till its breadth and height seem greater far than those of His Temple here below. Every passion has contributed some alluring ornament to decorate it ; every science has laboured, with its peculiar powers, to recommend it ; its courts are filled with sounds of joy, its walls are made to echo with shouts of defiance ; its precincts are crowded with the young and the old, the rich and the poor, the honoured and the ignoble. They have drunk of its charred pleasures till they are intoxicated unto frenzy, and they sally forth from time to time to assail the host of the God of Israel, and to disperse His camp. Their march is steady and systematic, their assaults skilfully directed, their blows are nervous and well aimed, their efforts unwearied and persevering. The men of learning, who have espoused their side, bring the weight of their various studies to demolish our outworks ; the sprightly and witty sharpen the arrows of their satires, to bring down their defenders ; the dissipated and vicious sap the foundations of our moral truths ; and the open scoffer and blasphemer attempts to storm the strongholds of faith. And when the Lord of Hosts looks round for his adherents, alas ! where are they ? True that He needeth not our aid, that He knoweth well how to tread the wine-press alone, as when He said : " I looked about, and there was none to help. I sought, and there was none to give aid ; and mine own arm hath saved for me, and my indignation itself hath helped me." (Is. lxiii. ˙

5.)   True it is that, with but a whip of small cords, the Son of God could in one instant drive back all that attempt to bring dishonour upon Him and His holy place.   But no less true it is that He has some right to expect those that call themselves His friends, as zealous, at least, in His cause, as His enemies are against it.   Surely it is but reasonable that He should find those who affect to love Him, as ready to protect His interests on earth, to avenge His honour, to kindle His love, and to promote His glory, as evil men, that love him not, are to impugn, to disparage, and to offend Him.

And yet is it so ?   Will the activity of the two even admit of a comparison ?   Is not vice rampant and ambitious of display, and is not virtue skulking and obscure ?   Is not incredulity boastful, and is not sincere belief retiring and silent ?   Is not the love of the world a living stirring principle, and is not the love of God buried in our hearts as in a sepulchre?   Do I then call upon you to do your works openly that they may be seen by man ?   God forbid.   Fast in secret, that your Father, who seeth in secret, may reward you; pray in secret that He may hear you in secret; give your alms so that your left hand know not what your right hand doeth.   But believe in the face of men, and profess and avow that belief; honour Him openly before the world ; let it be seen that you are not ashamed of the Gospel.   Let your light shine before them, that they may be brought to glorify your Father who is in heaven.   Nay, I will say more.   Leave not the vindication of His honour, and the exaltation of His name, to His priests, as though they were bound by office to relieve you of all responsibility.   You are to be saved as much as we, and this you will not be, if you be not with Christ, if you gather not with Him. It is not a cross hidden beneath your cloaks, but one engraved on your foreheads, that will make you be acknowledged by Jesus before His angels, as one of His. Whoever has taken upon himself this His badge, hath thereby become His sworn knight, His champion ever harnessed to do battle in His quarrel, against any that shall presume to oppose or contradict Him.

Surely, such criterions as these are sufficiently obvious in their application, and of a standard almost disparaging to the cause whereto they are applied. But, thanks be to God, His cause has not been insulted, by such alone being proposed. There have been those who have shown forth in their lives what it is to be with Christ, to our shame as to their glory. The saints in every age, they who have taken up their cross and followed Him, have taught us in their conduct the estimate they made of this obligation. I will not alarm you, nor attempt to confound you, by turning your minds to the conflicts and torments of martyrs, or to the glorious labours of apostles, or to the austerities of penitents in the wilderness. I will not remind you of those who watched entire nights in prayer, or who fasted for years in expiation of one sin, or who clothed themselves in sackcloth under royal robes. Yet even of all these, I might ask you was there one who thought he was doing more than was necessary for him to be avowed as one of Christ's side, as exerting himself more than any zealous follower and lover of his Saviour holds himself obliged. But rather I would ask you to look at the devotion of heart wherewith each of the saints

R

gave himself unrestrictedly to God, and to His service, to the advancement of His glory, and the diffusion of His love. See how with them the zeal for God's truth, and for His honour, had become an affection of their souls ; how some of them have so loved His law, as to have swooned away upon hearing mention of an offence against Him ; how others have wept in the bitterness of their hearts, when they have seen His commandments violated; how any one of them would have given his life, and thought it well bestowed, to prevent a single sin !

And if this estimate of our duty appear to us exorbitant, and far beyond our reach, what shall we say if our Saviour should choose, in rigour, to measure it by that of His own example ? For if He call upon us to be with Him, it was that He was first with us, and He gathered us up first, before He asked us to gather with Him. Was His an indolent or a cold-hearted interest in us ? Did He hand over our interests to others, or leave our cause to be pleaded even by His angels ? Can a fowler use more art to surprise and ensnare the bird, than He did to take us captives to His sweet law, watching every opportunity to seize upon our affections ? Can the enthusiast pursue the object of his researches with half the devotedness, earnestness, and perseverance, wherewith He pressed on, with untiring eagerness, to the possession of our souls ? Can a mother with greater love watch over a sickly child, and care for its recovery, than He hath felt over us in misery and sin, and when striving to save us from perdition ? Will He not, then, justly upbraid us when He contrasts our service with that which the world receives from its votaries, viewed in comparison with what each side has received from its leader. "They," He will justly say, "laboured so much and so earnestly to serve it, and yet it suffered nothing for them, it felt nothing for them. Not one of the objects of their applause and flattery would, they well knew, scorch a hair of his head to assist them; not one of their false and hollow idols would have put his finger into the flame to save them! And yet, even without love, they were devoted in their slavery and frantic in their zeal. And I, who have stood by you to assist you at my own proper cost, who have spared neither pains nor labour to make you mine, neither sweat nor blood to purchase you, neither happiness nor life to save you—shall I not ask in return some proportion of fervour and zeal, of earnestness and love? Or shall it be said that ye are more easily won to thraldom and stripes, by contempt and ingratitude, than to favour and honour by kindness and affection?"

Such, my brethren, would be a just estimate of what our blessed Saviour has a right to expect from every one of us, that we may be able to say that we are with Him in some measure, as He may say He has been with us. But if we neglect His admonition, and be content to stand neuter in the daily conflicts between Him and His adversaries, what must ensue? He Himself has told us, "He that is not with me is against me."

I might here, my brethren, place before you the frightful consideration of what God hath in store in the treasures of His wrath, for those that hate Him. I might trace for you the picture of His judgments denounced in the Old Law against His enemies and His people's; the

awful imagery of plagues and scourges, defeats and captivity, under which He has veiled the vengeance wherewith He will pursue His rivals in dominion. I might
take you, in imagination, to the contemplation of that
final consummate woe, wherein such as have been against
God in life must be under Him for eternity. But such
topics as these would be abhorrent from my present discourse, and lead us too far astray from its more practical
though less striking subject. Suffice it, then, to say,
that we shall be considered by Christ as enlisted on the
opposite side, and as contending against Him.

When in ordinary contests men elect their side, whatever other motive they may have, they must be greatly
influenced by the hope of ultimate victory. They will
seldom choose to support a cause which they already know
to be desperate. Even the most furious faction will not
long persevere in its course, without some hope that in the
end, however remote, success will crown its efforts. But
in the two sides engaged in the spiritual conflict, no such
ambiguity of issue can exist. Christ, the conqueror over
death and the grave, must necessarily triumph over all
His enemies. Every one that hath risen up against Him
will, in the end, be beaten down, overthrown, and irre-
coverably destroyed. See, then, I will not say the risk,
but the certain fate, that you incur, if you once allow
yourself to be numbered among those who stand against
the Son of God. There is no escape, no hope ; your loss
is certain. Will you, then, expose yourself to be placed
among those foes of God, by your negligence and indifference ?

But such a lot would be not only fearful, but most

pitifully incurred. For even here on earth you would experience the fate of all faint-hearted persons, who have not sufficient resolution to adopt a decided course. You will not be trusted by the zealous friends of God, afraid that your timidity would betray them, and bring scandal and reproach upon His cause, should it, in your person, be exposed to trial by the cuffs or opposition of the world. Your own convictions and conscience will not allow you ever to join with heart the counsels of the wicked ; and so will you go on, lukewarm and negligent, halting between good and evil, virtue and vice, God and His enemies, unclaimed, unvalued, unloved by either.

But, speaking humanly, even the abjectest slave of his passions has at least what seems to him some equivalent for the heavenly gifts which he throws away. He has a tumultuous joy around him, and some intoxication within him, to shut out the whispers of conscience; and he gives way to the impulse of passion with a willingness that, for the time, assumes the appearance of a pleasure. But the Christian who, too weak to resist the current of example, yet too well convinced to yield without remorse, is necessarily carried away from time to time by the torrent into transgression, with all the consciousness of his guilt, and without even the miserable compensation of deadness to its sting. And even if he escape this more decided incurrence of offence and punishment, he will find himself, at the end of his course, neither hot nor cold, neither fit for heaven, nor, in his own estimation, worthy of hell, but to God's sense most loathsome, and utterly unworthy to be ranked among His friends. (Rev. iii. 16.)

But, my brethren, I have said that when the conflict

is finished between the Son of God and His enemy, His victory is certain; and that victory shall be graced by a triumph worthy of its cause. It will be on that glorious day when, surrounded by His angels, with His banner displayed, He shall come to judge the world. And in that triumph we must all find some place. Now, when anciently such pageants were performed, they who attended on them were of two, and only two, classes. For first there came, rejoicing in their leader's glory, and feeling part therein, they who had fought with him his well-earned fields, and helped to procure him so much honour; their countenances were cheerful, their step bold, their helmets were wreathed with laurels, and they shouted forth their cry of victory. But behind the car would come a sorrowful spectacle, of many with weeping eyes, and downcast looks, and hair dishevelled, and torn garments of mourning. Of these there were some, who boldly with arms in their hands, had fought and been overcome; but there were not a few who had handled no weapon, and struck no blow, but who, without courage to abandon the cause of those that surrounded them, had neglected to join that of the conqueror, and had remained at home in neutral repose, till swept away, as enemies, into perpetual captivity. Now, had one of these sought to avert this fate, and to escape being numbered among more active enemies, who had deserved a heroic doom, he must needs have pleaded a right to pass into the other class, to stand among those who had fought with the victorious host. It would not have sufficed him to plead that he had not measured weapons with them in actual battle; he must show that he had combatted in their ranks. He would have justly been asked to state in what conflicts he had been engaged, under what special banner he had fought, at whose side he had stood. He would have been interrogated what scars or wounds he had to exhibit, such as none but the enemy's weapons could have inflicted. Could he but give such proofs, he would have been received with open arms into the society of the victor and his followers ; if not, he must remain among those who have deserved no mercy at their hands.

And even so it will be at the triumph of Him who "vanquisheth the world." Beneath His cross His battles have been fought; and none have fought in them, and none must triumph for them, save they who have fearlessly upheld and defended it, against the scorn and the reproach of its enemies. By Him who hung upon it hath the warfare been conducted : and none have partaken in it, and none must be crowned for it, who hath not heard from His lips its watchword, and obeyed His commands. For Him who died on it have its fierce blows been struck, and its wounds received ; and none have felt them, and none can claim reward for them, who hath not willingly and joyfully endured pain and all suffering for His dear sake. For mark, how strongly He was pleased, under a fearful emblem even on that cross, to declare that there was near it no standing place for the cold and indifferent; that two classes alone might surround it—of friends or of foes. I will not ask you to look upon the crowd, and see on one side Mary and John, and on the other the brutal soldiery dicing for the seamless vest of Jesus ; nor looking further off, to see how only two parties appear,

of such as with the priests and elders mock and insult
Him, and such as with the centurion and others beat
their breasts and own Him for the Son of God; nor
again, to see how there is no intermediate order between
the pious women who openly weep after Him, and buy
spices to embalm His body, or Joseph of Arimathea, who
boldly goes in to Pilate to beg it, and the cruel wretches
who offer Him to drink, gall and vinegar.   No; I will
rather tell you to look upon those three crosses on the
summit of Calvary, for an exemplification of the awful
doctrine of my text.   It would have seemed that in such
an hour, in such a state, there could have been but one
feeling in the hearts of the three who hung on them; that
common calamity would have made all friends, or that if
selfishness excluded in the two earthly sufferers all interest
in their companion's fate, it would, at most, have produced a quiet and passive indifference regarding it.   But
no ; even there no such a state was allowed ; and God,
in His inscrutable judgments, permitted that while the
one should declare himself the partizan of Jesus, and
openly worship Him, and acknowledge Him in the face of
an insulting outrageous mob, the other should forget
his own sufferings to join in their scoffs, and die blaspheming Him !

And in this way, methinks, the hour of death will
decide for us all, and range us necessarily in one or
other of these two unmodified irreconcileable classes.   The
measure, then, of what we deserve will be that which we
have done.   Whatever we have done or suffered for
Christ's sake, will then seem to us as so much solid gain.
To have done nothing against Him will be a burthen the

less upon our conscience, but it will be no assurance to our hopes. And then too, all those foolish motives for reserve, all that false prudence and bashfulness which made us hide our principles from the world, and afraid of its censures if we declared that we loved and served God, will appear so bare and so disgraceful, that we shall be confounded at the thought of the opportunities of good they have caused us to let slip. We shall see what an honourable thing it would have been to appear before Jesus with some marks of tribulation upon us endured for His sake, with some token of battle, or some scar of stripes inflicted by His enemies and ours, from decided hostility waged in His name. But still more glorious will appear, could we come into His presence loaded with a nobler spoil, a booty of souls, snatched by our zeal, from the jaws of the lion, and from the mouth of the pit, to have the testimony of many whom we leave on earth, that but for our active and loving exertions they might have been lost; to have the crowns of some already in bliss cast by them upon our heads, as we stand before the judgment-seat, as gained through our zealous efforts in Christ's cause. Yes, they who shall then gather up such laurels, shall be truly allowed to have gathered with Him, and shall in their turn be gathered as good wheat into the granary of His eternal Father.

Encouraged by this hope, let us not be discouraged by the difficulties we may have to encounter, any more than is the husbandman by the heat and toil of his harvest, or the humbler gleaner by the slow labour of his gathering. Each looks forward to the long enjoyment of what a few days' labour will procure him. Let us enrol ourselves in the army of God, let us be of the number of His soldiers by whom He opposes, and overcomes the world. Let our voices be heard in every protest against its errors and corruptions; let our example be a living contradiction of its baneful maxims. Let us fight with Christ here below, that we may reign with Him hereafter in heaven.

SERMON XIII.

On Temptation.

MAT. iv. 1.

" Then Jesus was led by the Spirit into the desert, to be
tempted by the devil."

I KNOW not, my brethren, how the word of God could have
declared more strongly the perfect holiness of our blessed
Saviour's character, than by the passage of His life commemorated in this day's gospel.   It records the efforts of
the wily tempter to draw from Him one proof of frailty,
or to stain at least the purity of His mind, by the passage
of some evil thought.   But see, in what strange and powerful ways this was attempted ; see what a gigantic effort
of wicked might was necessary even to make the trial !
We need not be led forth into a desert, to wrestle alone,
and face to face, with our adversary.   Whatever we see,
whatever we touch, and feel, is to us matter of danger; the
very breath of the world is a fuel to our lusts, the very
contact with mankind is to us contagion : and had the
evil one in like manner been allowed to chose for the
holiest anchorites of the desert, a place for temptation,
he would have transported *them* from their caverns, and
their date-trees, and their trickling fountains, on to the
embroidered couches of Damascus; (Os. iii. 12) or, as St.

Jerome tells us, he was in imagination carried, into the
golden chambers and festal assemblies of the Imperial
City.   But He was not like unto us, on whom the world
had exerted in vain its tainting influence ; the tempter
had seen with jealousy its example powerless, and its
maxims contemptible, when tried on Him, and could not
flatter himself into hope of success, save by an unwonted
trial, in a lonely wilderness, apart from every sympathy,
and every support.

Yet, did not even this suffice.   We require not much
allurement to make us trespass in the gratification of our
desires ; the ordinary daily claims of life are our incentives
to excess ; we are intemperate in satisfying Nature's wants,
we are dissipated in the enjoyment of necessary recreation.
What a lofty idea of our Lord's superiority over the rest
of men, must the observation of His life during its thirty
years have suggested to the evil one, to make him wait
for the hunger produced by a forty days' fast, before he
would venture to whisper to Him a thought of intemperate desire, or suggest the use of His own lawful power, to
shorten the period of probation Himself had chosen!

We want no unusual splendours to tempt our ambition;
crowns or sceptres need not be hung before us, to stir up
the restless strivings of our inordinate wishes ; the gilded
toys of fashion, which a touch may break, the gaudy
trappings of any nominal dignity, which are but the livery
of the public slave, are quite enough to make us break our
peace of mind, and our eternal welfare upon Ambition's
wheel.   How supremely raised above every range of this
towering and rapacious passion, must His soul have
seemed to the king of pride, when he thought it necessary,

that he might give his power a fair trial, to raise Him on a lofty mountain, and unroll before Him the mimic represen-tation of all the earth's dominions, with their mighty cities, and their huge armies, and their costly merchandise, and their sumptuous buildings ; and, having seduced the first Adam, in all the power of innocence and primeval righteous-ness, with a tempting fruit, and its unseen prerogatives, attempt to conquer the second, whom, as yet, he deemed but a simple, and consequently a fallen and frail, man, by offering Him the visible and tangible empire of the world !

But, in one short word, it is not to solitary conflict with this arch-foe, that the Spirit of God would send us forth, as Saul sent David to his single combat with Goliah, thereby to accomplish the certain discomfiture of the evil host. What, then, must He have been who was chosen as the champion of God, the sure avenger of man's early frailty, the crusher of the wily serpent's head, and the destroyer of his pernicious might !

Yes, it is in this glorious light that we should view the victory achieved by our Redeemer, over His tempter in the desert, as the accomplishment, in a great part, of that first prophecy, as the fulfilment of the type which man's first parent presented, of a second and better Adam ; in a word, as the solution, in contest, and in victory, of the great momentous mystery of temptation.

I have called temptation "a mystery," as forming part of what the apostle so well calls, " the mystery of iniquity," (2 Thess. ii. 7) and being, in fact, the principal instrument whereby it " worketh" evil. To it is to be traced, as to a root, all the present condition of man, his strangely com-pounded nature, and the providential workings of God in

his behalf.   Upon its issue hung, for one fearful moment
of suspense to creation, the weal and woe of every generation of our race; their immortality, or their death; their
adoption, or their banishment ; their innocence, or their
sinfulness ; their friendship, or their enmity with God.
And, when that issue was painfully decided against us,
what a long train of evil consequences did the one side of
these alternatives produce, through the physical derange-
ment, and the moral degradation, of man!   Had our first
father proved victorious, that one temptation would have
been the only test of our fidelity, and the free will of our
entire kind would have been fixed in a rootedness of
purpose for good, in an inflexibility of tendency towards
the divine will, which would have defied and prevented
every repetition of the trial.   It was the great struggle,
whether the power given to the evil one to tempt, or that
bestowed upon man to resist, should become perpetual ;
whether evil should have an active principle in creation ;
or virtue, and moral perfection, be its exclusive law. The
seducer triumphed, man was vanquished ; and the former
gained the power for which he had wrestled, that of ever
disturbing the moral order of things, by his suggestions ;
of ever holding the iron sceptre of an antagonist's influence
in the working out of our destinies ; and of keeping up an
eternal conflict, between his darkness and the light of
God, between death and life, evil and good.

Every religion, every philosophy, had been aware of this
strange conflict, of the unaccountable disturbance which
seemed to have occurred in the nature of man ; of the
torn disjointed appearance which faculties nearly connected
present, as though riven insunder by a sudden convulsion,

and of the medley of precious ore, and vile dross, which some unnatural revolution had produced in his constitution. Every attempt to solve the anomalous problem led to error ; the philosophy of the east imagined an evil co-ordinate power which divided sovereignty with the better deity, and thus, at once, circumscribed the infinity, and destroyed the perfection, of God. The Indian invented a still more fearful representative of this power, in a sanguinary Godhead, crowned and begirt with serpents and human skulls, and armed in his many hands with weapons of destruction, beneath which the human race is crushed, and driven into the flames ; while at his side a goddess of milder aspect, receiving their supplication, represents the redeeming or regenerating power, which yet remains after the great catastrophe.* Others, in fine, recurred to an eternal inflexible destiny, which ruled over gods themselves, thwarted their benevolent intentions, and thus made evil paramount to the very attributes of the Deity.

But there was another aspect, still more solemn, wherein this problem presented itself to the individual solution of each mind, and appeared involved in still more irreconcilable conditions. The soul of each is to its possessor the scene of conflicts which he cannot compose. He seems to find in himself a two-fold being, a diversity of wills and desires, whereof one side ever seems opposed to his happiness, and hardly to belong to himself. He is conscious of evil suggestions, proposed with a suddenness and an inconsequence, that make them seem to come

* Sive and Parvati. See " Creutzer, by Guigneaut," Plates, fig. 24.

from without,—of envious or malicious whisperings,
which no inward reflection seem to have raised, of
proud emotions which spring up with a startling newness,
for which his familiar sentiments may in nowise account.
And he feels that he loaths and fears these unsought
ideas ; and he turns him from them, yet they haunt him
as phantasies which disappear not, when the eyelids
are closed : and he adjures them by every name that
is most powerful, but they laugh at his spell, as though
raised not by him ; and he grapples with them manfully,
but they resist, and wrestle with him, as though having
in them an energy and life distinct from his, and if he
persevere and conquer, he seems to notice the sullenness
of the retiring foe, who, ever and anon, looks round again
and wishes to renew the skirmish, and keeps him for some
space armed and upon his guard, till once more he feels
himself alone.   In his solemn musings upon the holiest
things, he experiences, at whiles, an impertinent intrusion
on the part of discordant and uncalled-for recollections ;
in his secretest communion with his own spirit upon the
surest truths, the voice no less secret of a scoffing
adversary seems to be heard, proposing ill-timed and
jarring objections, which even suppressed, cast a gloom
over his consoling occupation, and spread a mysterious cloud
over the blessed visions, which his eye had caught.   The
purest soul seems to itself, at times, defiled by the presence
of monstrous imaginings, before which it cowers down in
shrinking horror; the aspirations of the most perfect after
a union with God, are checked and arrested by the interposition of a shifting adversary who seems ever to come
before them ; and the blessedness whereof man is capable,

and which should be summed up in virtue, is alloyed and disturbed by the interference of another power, mischievous, as unhappy, with every effort for its consummation.

This complication of moral phenomena, forms that mystery of temptation, which the revelation of God hath alone sufficiently explained, and which the gospel of this day has abundantly set forth.

For, in the first place, we here learn that, as in the first trial of man's fidelity, the evil spirit actively and perseverently strives to bring us into the commission of sin, which at once explains that instigation to wickedness which, in spite of our desires, and our repugnance, obstinately pursues us. Difficult as it is, to account for this powerful energy opposed to our wishes and endeavours, though apparently springing from faculties under the mind's control, we should have attributed it simply to our now inborn corruption, had not God's holy word taught us to view the conflict in a more solemn light. " For our wrestling" says St. Paul, " is not against flesh and blood, but against principalities and powers ; against the rulers of the world of this darkness, against the spirits of wickedness in high places." (Ephes. vi. 12.) Hence, we see that the evil power is active indeed, though so only permissively, and subordinately to a wisely-counselling and well-directing power of good. We learn, that the tempter is, in fact, a spirit that having an existence distinct from ours, can yet communicate inscrutably with our minds ; and thus without debasing, like them of old, the supreme Godhead into a contest with a rival power, or still more, into a submission to a constraining destiny, the warfare is transferred to a lower stage, while man is

s

elevated into the champion against an order originally higher than his own, but than his more fallen; and the justice and goodness of God in this permission, to harrass and annoy, is amply vindicated in the triumphs of His might, through such feeble instruments as we, in the splendour of reward which crowns the victories of His conquerors, and in the unspeakable grandeur of redemption which could not have been without the existence of this rampant energy of evil.

All this is, in fact, displayed most practically in the gospel I am expounding. In it, we see the spotless Son of God, whose thoughts were united ever with the all-perfect mind of God, even Him on whom no taint of man's spiritual mortality had been breathed, subjected to the same trial, and the same engagement with the spirit of wickedness. And, shall the justest, then, amongst us repine, if he con-tinue, in spite of every effort, to be assailed ? Or, shall the purest of us complain, if thoughts which make him shudder, disturb the serenity of his holy meditations ? Who shall be exempt from inward tribulation, when Jesus, after forty days' fast, is tempted to sensuality ? Who shall be safe from the world's dangers, when on the summit of a rocky mountain, in a desert, *He* was allured towards ambition.   No : here, indeed, the just may learn that, even their very holiness shall be to them matter of danger in the wily enemy's hand ; for they shall be drawn through it into peril of presumptuous pride, and be incited to fancy that they are secure against a fall, because "God hath given His angels a charge over them, to bear them up in their hands." (Matt. iv. 6.)   What greater comfort could we, who are imperfect and sinful, have in the humiliation of our constant incitements to transgress, than thus to see how He, who was undefiled from birth, should have been assailed with untiring obstinacy, and unchecked effrontery, in this, His three-fold temptation ?

But our courage will surely be much increased by the consideration of how here is exemplified another part in the mysterious action of this wicked power, its dependence on a divine permission. St. Paul has beautifully expressed this assurance, when he tells the Corinthians, that " God is faithful, who will not suffer us to be tempted above that which we are able, but will make also with temptation issue (or means of escape), that we may be able to bear." (1 Cor. x. 13.) This matter is amply set out in the touching history of Job, wherein the tempter is represented as obtaining a leave to assay that faithful servant, under conditions, and limitations which God held in His hand. And when the first strokes, heavy indeed, and to mortal endurance terrible, had but confirmed His virtue, and hardened Him for a weightier calamity, those limits were further enlarged, and the reins of permission somewhat relaxed, that so, his virtue might be perfected and re-warded, through the infirmity of the flesh. (2 Cor. xiii. 9.) Even so do we find in our gospel. Thirty years Jesus had lived, quiet and undisturbed by the attempts of the wicked one ; but when, at length, it was time for the manifestation of His splendid virtues before the world, and when it was decreed fitting by His almighty Father, that He should give glory to Him through His prowess against the foe, the Holy Spirit leads Him by the hand into the lists, for that purpose prepared, and the infernal dragon is unchained, to feel his cunning baffled, his venomous gall crushed out, and his might trampled under foot, by one in the human form whereat he had ever mocked.

Thus we see that, even where danger was sure of failure, yet a disposing order of Providence chose the time, and place, and outward circumstances of the conflict : and how much more will that watchfulness, jealous of our welfare, as of its own honour, be exercised, when the frail and the feeble are summoned to engage? Yea, so anxious was our beloved Saviour for our advantage and instruction, that He submitted even in the more essential circumstances of His temptations, to a likeness, so far as consistent with His undefiled nature, with those which we may suffer. For three-fold, as you have been taught, is the battle-front of our warfare, and three-fold was the form of His temptation. Inasmuch as we have been called to make a triple renunciation of the world, the flesh, and the devil, He, on His part, received the attacks of these very three forms under which the evil principle presents itself.

For, as to the world and its gaudy pomps, it assaulted Him when on the mountain, in that exhibition of the kingdoms of earth, which were offered Him, on the unworthy condition, of doing homage, as too many have done, to the wicked one, whose slaves they became to gain pre-eminence. Then, as touching the flesh, it could not indeed urge and prick Him, as the rest of men, with unholy desires ; but, it strove to persuade Him to a premature miracle for the gratification of its wants, and the satisfaction of a craving appetite, sharpened by so long a fast. And then the devil, in his more proper shape, appeared as Lucifer the king of pride, instigating Him to confide presumptuously in His great holiness, and acceptance by God, and, in haughtiness of heart, throw Himself headlong into the arms of guardian-spirits, who waited on Him to keep Him from a fall.

Thus it was that He determined to show Himself as the apostle has described Him, " tempted in all things like as we are, yet without sin." (Heb. iv. 15.) Ah! yes, my dear brethren, here is the great difference between us ; here, unhappily, the resemblance terminates. He went through His trial unscathed : we too often come away crippled and sadly hurt, if not positively overcome. But let us not therefore repine. Let us rather rejoice, that He, our champion and head, did, by the completeness of His victory, fully avenge the overthrow of our first parent, in our first temptation ; and in our flesh, win again the crown which our father, in the flesh, had forfeited. And hence, we see a certain proportion kept between their two temptations, yet, so that the contest wherein the enemy was to be baffled, should be such, as to give him every apparent chance of victory. The first sinner was allured by a fruit tempting to the eye, amidst a paradise overgrown by all that man's appetite could require or desire, to be gathered at will ; the second Adam was solicited to the allaying of actual hunger, by simple bread, in a howling wilderness, where none could relieve His wants. Our first parents were seduced by the vain, and impossible, offer of becoming like unto God : our Regenerator was assayed by the feasible promise of becoming an earthly sovereign. For as in the first respect, the greatness of the urgency, so in the second, the smallness of the reward—great in itself, but

still within compass—must have made our Lord's temptation the more formidable.   And yet He conquered, where
the others were overcome : so to make the enemy of man
not a little to rue his early success, in the mortification
of this great discomfiture, which opened a new unending
series of victories to be achieved by regenerated followers,
who thus were taught to conquer, through His example
and in His name.

For, after all, my brethren, the great resolution of the
mystery here given by Him, so far as we are concerned,
consists in His justifying to us the mercies of God in
His permission of this work of evil ; by showing how
necessary it is unto our crown, and how easily it may be
turned to our advantage.   Yes ; the shortest demonstration
of any solution is in the success of its application.   Easily
will that general meet the question of a discontented host,
" wherefore have we been brought into this danger ?" who
can but delay his reply, till on the yielded battle-field he
may point at the enemy's spoil, and merely say ; " to
conquer."   This it was that, above all other things, Jesus
had in view when He submitted to temptation, to encourage us by showing how easy this victory is ; nor will it
be difficult, by running over the chiefest circumstances to
be noted in our gospel, to discover how He brought us to
this knowledge.

And first we see, how to each temptation he opposed a
fitting resistance, which, as by a sudden blow, at once dis-
concerted and baffled His cunning enemy.   For when He
was asked to change stones into bread, He turned His
thoughts to the contemplation of better things than such as
satisfy the body.   He compared things spiritual, to things

temporal; weighed the pure delight of the former, against the emptiness and disappointments of the latter. He thought of the far greater importance of nourishing the soul in virtue, and strengthening it unto perfection, and summed up the momentous conclusion of His thoughts in that expressive saying, that not on bread alone, not on the meat that perisheth, doth man live, but upon the word of his God, its sweet hopes and its unfailing promises. And such, too, should be our preparation for the daily assaults of worldly solicitude, and the cravings of insatiable humanity; to make the will of our Father our daily food, to prefer like the Jewish crowd many days of Jesus's company in a desert, fasting, to the care of the body, and so disentangle our hearts from the bondage of the flesh, till our conversation is all in heaven. And thus shall we be well prepared for every assault which our unruly appetites or vain desires may attempt.

We cannot indeed doubt, but that so simple an enunciation as our Saviour on each occasion employed, was in this manner but the expression of many and complicated feelings. For when the arch-deceiver bore Him up into the lofty mountain, and showed Him all the kingdoms of earth, with all their bravery and all their strength, little did he consider how different from what he desired was the look to Him he tempted. The one pointed out the rich and varied prospect, fair as the valley of Jordan before the Lord overthrew Sodom, and Gomorrah, or as Egypt to them that came down from Emath: while the other was busy counting the venomous serpents that trailed among its flowers, and the crested aspics that coiled on every path. The tempter bid Him mark the sumptuous

palaces of princes, and hearken to the din of wassail that
sounded from them; and He saw through their walls into
the unwholesome banquet-room, and studied the wasteful
riot which, like the drunkard, of Ephraim, treads under-
foot a crown of glory, (Is. xxxviii. 3) and the dull
brutalized countenances of the revellers, and the gloomy
recklessness of the spendthrift host, with the lamb from
the poor man's bosom upon his table, and the unpitied
Lazarus at his door.   The deceiver would show Him His
future armies squadroned for victory under their flaunting
banners, and in glittering array.   But on every hand He
sees a stain of innocent blood, and on every shoulder a
load of spoil that crieth to heaven for vengeance, on behalf
of the widow and orphan.   Then would he point out the
crowded cities throbbing with life through every avenue
as men paced to and fro, all busy and intent on their
various pursuits.   But the other not only sees but knows
them all : the one is the prowling thief that goes about to
snatch his prey, and the other the assassin that is tracking
his victim; this is the adulterer that is watching his hour
to enter, that the fiend's own ally, the seducer of innocence.
In fine, he will, perhaps, direct our blessed Saviour's eye
to this imperial city, and amidst the gorgeous piles of
magnificent edifices open to Him one, where the crowned
despot sits upon the world's throne, dooming its inhabitants
as his slaves, and dictating laws to prostrate princes.
"This," he tells Him, " shall be your place, these shall be
your honours, all the world can give."   But He whom he
addresses hears him not ; His eye hath pierced through the
double folds of the purple robe, and searched a heart
wherein every black passion seethes and foams in fearful

agitation ; He hath raised the wreath from His brow, and found that its bay-leaves cut more deeply, and strain more cruelly, than shall His own thorns on Calvary. And, in all this, what temptation could there be, save to disgust and abhorrence, rather than to jealousy or ambition? And thus shall we, too, conquer, if, not content with the surface and outside show of things that tempt us, we endeavour to penetrate within. For then shall we discover them to be hollow and naught, and hold them for despicable rather than to be desired. And in this manner, too, we shall be brought justly to estimate the base condition whereon they are to be purchased : that of falling down and worshipping the monster who tempts us, in the hideous form of that vice or passion which he solicits us to gratify. And, in conclusion, we shall learn how God alone is great, and how He alone is worthy to be adored and served, as our true and loving Master.

But why, my brethren, did our Redeemer choose to be tempted in a desert ? Doubtless, that He might better show how, even in the solitude of our thoughts, we should resist and repel the suggestions of evil. When the tempter's offers were made, there was no ear to witness them. Had He yielded and obtained the world's mastery—I suppose an impossibility for the better illustration of the matter—none would have known but that He had honourably acquired it ; He would, in fact, have gained it as well as did many who held it. But even in that loneliness, He wished to show that the brightness of God shone no less than in His temple ; and we must resist to the last, from regard not to man or his opinions, but to God and His judgments. Nor even

defeat ? The field of war is your proper element. Your armour of proof must never be unbuckled, the shield of faith must ever hang over your head. Be faithful to the end, and ye shall have the crown of life. But do any of you complain that you have fought your good fight, and have not proved braggarts, but have vanquished in the name of your God, the Lord of Hosts, yet that still a sting of the flesh is left you, an angel of Satan who buffetteth you ? The grace of God still sufficeth for your complete victory. These are trials no longer of your fidelity, but steps towards your perfection ; opportunities for new merit, and for gaining brighter rewards. For when the lord of the vineyard wishes to shake from its flowers a sweeter odour, or to display its colours in a brighter splendour, he must needs command a ruder breeze to ruffle it, and disturb its repose. Whenever he is tempted, the Christian is treading in the footsteps of his Lord, and whoso with Him conquer, with Him and by Him shall be crowned.

SERMON XIV.

The Kingdom of Christ.

ISAIAS, ii. 2, 3.

" In the last days, the mountain of the house of the Lord shall be prepared on the top of mountains, and it shall be exalted above the hills, and all nations shall flow unto it. And many people shall go and say : Come, let us go up to the mountain of the Lord."

FROM the circumstances under which our Blessed Redeemer first manifested Himself in the flesh, it is no wonder, my brethren, that His advent should have been so little noticed by the people whom He came to save. When the emperor's edict went forth, enjoining a general enrolment, and commanding that, for this object, every family should repair to its ancestral city, we can easily conceive the universal movement which it would produce, and the various interests which it would awaken ; and these, alone, would sufficiently occupy the minds of men, to leave them neither inclination nor leisure to observe this momentous arrival.

For it was natural that each one should be anxious to trace his origin to the most noble stock; and if he could establish such a claim, to display an appearance suited to his asserted rank. It is, however, easy to imagine how proud and happy, beyond all, they must have felt, who, descended from the royal lineage of David, had now an opportunity of supporting their pretensions in the face of the whole nation, and receiving an official and authoritative confirmation of their claims. Doubtless, no sacrifice would be spared which could enable them to support their assumed distinction ; any expense would be cheerfully incurred to travel with a train, and appear with a splendour, becoming the members of a royal house—of a house now expecting the restoration of its rights, in its head—the coming Messiah.

It is amidst all this parade, and all this pride, that a little group is seen to advance slowly towards Bethlehem, the royal city, from the mean and obscure village of Nazareth. A poor artizan guides the wearied steps of the humble beast of burthen, whereon is borne a tender lady, apparently unfit, from her condition, for so long and toilsome a journey. To their straitened circumstances in life, obedience to the imperial edict is a serious inconvenience ; to their poverty, their royal lineage is rather a reproach and a burthen than an honor. Humble, meek, and unpretending, they are passed on the road by the crowds, who hasten forward, with a feeling of contempt, and almost of shame, that their noble blood should be disgraced by so ignoble an alliance. They creep where others run : and so, when they arrive at their journey's end, no friendly greeting cheers them, no claim of kindred salutes them. Every place of lodging has been occupied, until, to that tender maid and mother, no shelter is left but a stable, and no cradle but its manger.

And yet, my brethren, not even the Ark of the Covenant, when it went forth to victory over the enemies of

God, escorted by squadrons of Levites, and greeted by the shouts of the whole people—not even it, moved forward with half that interest to heaven, or half that promise to earth, with which this humble Virgin, bearing within her, in silence and neglect, the richest work which Almighty God had yet created. More than the Old Ark—true Ark of the New Covenant—she bears its lawgiver, not its sculptured laws. Upon this little household angels attend with tender care, more than for the ordinary just, lest they should dash their foot against a stone. For in it are centred all the counsels of Heaven, since the creation of man ; on its safety depends the fulfilment of prophecy, the consummation of the law, and the redemption of the world.

How true it is, my brethren, that the kingdom of heaven came "without observation"! (Luke xvii. 20.) And yet, though existing from that day to this, how often it is overlooked with negligence far more unpardonable than was that of the Jewish people! For its characteristics have now been clearly defined, and rendered most conspicuous. Hence, while the Church, during the seven days before Christmas, directs part of her offices* to proclaim the titles and honours attributed by the ancient prophets to the Son of God, she hardly passes over one day, without repeating this noblest prerogative of being King over all the Faithful. For there can be none more glorious to Himself nor more honourable to her, than this universal dominion by His religion, which His Father bestowed upon Him at His

---

* Antiphons O, at the *Magnificat.*

own special request, and of which she forms at once the
object and the depositor. It is, therefore, to this high
and most important prerogative enjoyed upon earth by
the new-born King, that I wish to turn your attention ;
and to trace rapidly to your view the prophecies which
describe it, and their subsequent fulfilment will be the
object of a few remarks.

The future kingdom of the Messias was the very soul
of Jewish prophecy. The humble character of His birth
and life, His labours, His sufferings, and His death were
indeed contemplated and described by the venerable messengers of God. But it is only in an occasional and
rapid sketch that these painful scenes are represented.
Each comes like a gloomy cloud, overcasting the mind of
the seer, on which are decidedly, but evanescently, traced
the outlines of his Redeemer's life and death ; but which
always breaks into a flood of light and glory, like that
which canopied the apostles on Thabor, when He discoursed with Moses and Elias. (Luc. ix. 31.)

If to David, His great ancestor, He is exhibited in
excess of agony, with His hands and feet pierced, His
garments divided among His unrelenting and insulting
persecutors, and crying for help to God, who appeared to
have abandoned Him, it is only that he may be more
gladdened by the conclusion of the same prophecy ; that
in consequence of these sufferings "all the ends of the
earth shall remember and shall be converted to the Lord,
and all the kindreds of the Gentiles shall adore in His
sight. For the *kingdom is the Lord's*, and he shall have
dominion over the nations." (Ps. xxii. 28, 29.) Hence, no
sooner is this theme touched in any of the inspired

writings, than the prophetic vision glows in all its splendour, the most brilliant imagery is employed to detail its promises, and the most animated phraseology to express its hopes. As the course of ages flowed on towards its completion, new traits were added which, without effacing the preceding, more strikingly defined their object ; that was more minutely described which before had been only generally expressed, and the future kingdom of the Son of David is distinctly foreshown in its plan and its constitution, and characterized by marks which might lead the ages of its fulfilment to recognise, to acknowledge, and to obey it.

When David saw himself seated on the throne of Israel, the master of a wider extent of country than his nation had ever hoped to possess, surrounded by wealth such as no contemporary monarch had amassed, only one more thought on earth was capable of causing him pain or uneasiness. Saul had, like himself, 'been chosen and anointed monarch of God's people, and yet his race had been rejected from the succession. Might not the same lot await his progeny ? It was to allay this anxiety in His faithful servant that God sent the prophet Nathan. (2 Kings, vii. 16.) He passed His solemn word that after him a descendant should rise, the duration of whose reign, and the extent of whose dominion, should far surpass his most visionary hopes. "I will set," He exclaims, "his hand in the sea, and his right hand in the rivers . . . and I will make him my first-born, high above the kings of the earth. I will keep my mercy for him for ever and my covenant faithful to him. And I will make his seed to endure for evermore, and his throne as the days of heaven." (Ps. lxxxviii. 26-30.) It is after receiving this divine

T

communication that we may suppose the Royal Prophet to
have been elevated in spirit to the contemplation of this
glorious period, when he heard this future descendant of
his, already existing in a superior state, exclaim, " The
Lord hath said to me : Thou art my son, this day have I
begotten thee : ask of me, and I will give thee the Gentiles
for thy inheritance, and the bounds of the earth for thy
possession ;" (Ps. ii. 8) or, when anticipating the enrap-
turing vision of Stephen, he saw the heavens open and
his Lord, yet his son, invited to sit at the right hand of
God until all His enemies had been bowed before his
footstool.

Such, my brethren, was the glorious prospect which
opened itself to this early prophet ; a kingdom to be
established by his great descendant, which should hold
undivided dominion over the most distant parts of the
earth, unbounded and unchecked by any of those political
or natural limits, which distinguish the monarchies of the
earth, or the species of the human race, and permanent as
the laws that regulate the heavens.

If so splendid a prospect was unfolded to allay the
domestic anxieties of one prince, we may easily imagine
what additional clearness and beauty it received when
used as the instrument of consolation to a whole suffering
people. If it was exhibited with such solemn asseverations
when all things augured long prosperity, to the house of
David, how much stronger must have been necessary when
its utter downfall and extinction appeared to be consum-
mated. In fact no sooner did idolatry and immorality bring
on the final dissolution of the Jewish monarchy and religion,
than the prophecies of this new kingdom became more

marked, and appeared with ten-fold lustre amidst the surrounding gloom.

When Jeremias sat upon the ruins of Jerusalem, and
wept over the mingled ashes of its palace and its temple,
he still considered them only as the funeral pile of a
degenerate dynasty and a corrupted worship, from which,
after a few years, should arise, like the phœnix, a faithful
monarch to restore and perpetuate the kingdom and the
priesthood. " Behold, the days come," he exclaimed by
command of God, "and I will raise up to David a just
branch : and a king shall reign and shall be wise : and
this is the name that they shall call him : The Lord our
just one." (xxiii. 5, 6.) Even though sent to announce
that if Jechonias, the last king of Juda, were a signet on
God's right hand, yet He would pluck him thence, (Jer.
xxii. 24) and that there should not be a man of his seed
to sit on the throne of David ; " (30) yet is he ordered to
proclaim in the name of the same God : " Thus, saith the
Lord : If my covenant with the day can be made void
and my covenant with the night, that there should not
be day and night in their season : *then* may, also, my
covenant with David, my servant, be made void : that he
should not have a son to reign upon his throne, and with
the Levites and priests my ministers." (xxxiii. 21.)

But at this period the prophecies regarding this future
kingdom undergo a striking modification, or rather
receive an additional feature of the greatest importance.
The reign of the Messias now becomes identified with the
formation and propagation of a new religion, and all those
characteristics of unity, of government, of universality of
dominion, and of perpetuity of duration, which, in the

earlier prophecy, distinguished the reign of the descendant of David, are transferred to that religious system, which it is shown to have denoted. " And it shall come to pass in that day," says Zacharias, " that living waters shall go out from Jerusalem" to the four quarters of the globe, "and the Lord (God) *shall be king over all the earth: in that day there shall be one Lord, and his name shall be one . . . . And all they that shall be left of all nations shall go up to adore the King, the Lord of Hosts,"* and to keep the feast of tabernacles. (Zachar. xiv. 8, 9, 16.) Here, then, is the obedience of all nations to this future king, manifestly identified with their all worshipping the same God and practising the same religion.

But it is in the evangelical prophet Isaias that this connection is most strongly marked : " There shall come forth," he exclaims, " a rod out of the root of Jesse, and a flower shall rise out of his root ; . . . . therefore, the earth is filled with the knowledge of the Lord, as the covering waters of the sea. In that day shall be the root of Jesse, who standeth for an ensign of people, him the Gentiles shall beseech. And he shall set up a standard to the nations, and shall assemble the fugitives of Israel." (xi.) Hence, also, it appears that this new institution has not only to extend to the farthest bounds of the earth, but, in every part where it shall reach it, has to be a conspicuous rallying-point to all. It is compared by one prophet to the cedar which, first planted as a tender sapling on a mountain high and eminent, on the high mountains of Israel, shoots forth its branches, and bears fruit, and becomes a great cedar, so that all birds shall dwell under it, and every fowl shall make its nest under

the shadow of the branches thereof. (Ezec. xvii. 22, 23.)
It is compared in the words of my text, and in the prophet
Micheas, to the mountain of the Lord's house, elevated upon
the highest pinnacles of mountains, and exalted above all
other hills, towards which all nations shall flow, to learn
the ways of God, and how to walk in His paths.

The mysterious veil is now at length thrown off: no
longer disguised under the figures of the earthly monarchy, though still invested with similar qualities, this
conspicuous and magnificent institution is depicted in the
most alluring colours, and guarded with the most splendid promises: within its pale, harmony, security, and
abundance of peace shall reside; its interests shall be
watched over and nursed by kings and by princes;
and, constantly increasing in numbers,—" because the
Lord will lift up His hand to the Gentiles, and will set
up His standard to the people,"—it shall, day after day,
enlarge the cords of its tabernacle, and push further back
the landmarks of its inheritance, without any more fear
that the mercy of God will depart from it, and the covenant of His peace be moved, than that His oath to Noe
shall be made void, and the waters of the deluge be
brought back upon the earth. (Is. xi. xlix. liv.) Only
one point now remains to complete these prophecies, that
the period when their fulfilment was to commence should
be clearly pointed out. This is done by Daniel, who
closes the prophetic annals upon the subject, adding, at
the same time, such characteristic marks as should render
his predictions the epilogue and abridgment of the preceding. He tells us, therefore, that when the fourth great
empire shall be falling into decay, that of God shall come

like a stone cut without hands ; and, filling up the space occupied by the foregoing monarchies, swell gradually into a mountain that should fill the whole earth. " The God of heaven shall set up a kingdom that shall never be destroyed ; and His kingdom shall not be delivered up to another people ; and itself shall stand for ever." (Dan. ii. 44.) " All people," he says, " tribes, and tongues shall serve him : his power is an everlasting power that shall not be taken away, and his kingdom that shall not be destroyed." (vii. 14.)

After having thus cursorily reviewed the history of prophecy upon this interesting point, it will not, I think, my brethren, be difficult to collect from its scattered elements a complete and simple idea of the plan and characteristics of this kingdom of the Messias. It was to consist, manifestly, of a religious system widely spread over the whole earth, the most extreme points of which must, however, be connected and related by such principles of unity and subordination, as can entitle the whole to be considered as forming one only body or empire. This system which has to endure, according to the words of Scripture, " until the sun and moon be taken away," will, at every moment of its existence, be eminently conspicuous, and distinguished by its constant tendency to expand.

If, therefore, there is any truth in the Divine promises, and if the spirit of prophecy be not a spirit of falsehood and deceit, we must feel convinced that in this instance they have been fulfilled to the letter ; so that in every age there must have existed a body satisfying these conditions, and a body not only having a clear, defined, and sensible existence, that others may be able to join it, but rendered eminent and distinguished, so as to attract the eye, and win the attention, of those who were not united to its standard. And such, my brethren, has really been the case. No sooner did the apostles receive the Divine commission to teach *all nations*, and to be the witnesses of Christ's doctrine "even to the uttermost parts of the earth," (Acts, i. 8) than they prepared to lay the foundation of this vast structure. Their jealousy of receiving the Gentiles into their communion was soon removed by a declaration from heaven; (Acts, x.) and no other barrier remained to check their zeal. To men, only twelve in number and less confident of the Divine support, the project might have appeared chimerical, of founding a religious community, whereof the whole Roman empire was only to form a part. They would have preferred to concentrate their power and abilities upon one point, and trust to time and opportunity to spread gradually on every side. But, supported by the promises of God, they feared not to weaken their strength by separation; they dispersed immediately in opposite directions, and Spain and India, Scythia and Africa, saw rising at the same moment the distant, but harmonising, parts of the vast system. The same doctrines, the same government, the same constitution, the same form of worship, linked together into a whole the most distinct points; nor was it ever imagined that the vicissitudes of states, or the formation of new political boundaries, would ever be authorised, or able, to break the bonds which united them into a common empire.

It was not long before the formation of this stupendous system attracted the notice of the whole known world. It

soon became a city built upon a mountain which could not
be concealed ; it soon became a beacon towards which all
directed their course who valued the doctrine of salvation;
and even the wrath of those who could not bear its light,
only rendered it more marked and conspicuous.   The
flame of persecution only added splendour to its lustre ;
the blood of its martyred followers fell like a fruitful seed
upon the earth, and the decree for its extermination went
forth as a warrant for its propagation.   In the midst of
all their sufferings, the most distant churches consoled one
another, and corresponded with all the sympathy of members of the same body.   The Sovereign Pontiffs, in the
concealments of the catacombs, received the reports of
distant provinces, regulated their affairs, or convened
synods for more weighty consultations.   Clement thus
ordered the disturbed church of Corinth by his letters ;
Victor called to account the practice and discipline of the
Asiatic churches, founded by St. John ; Stephen pronounced sentence upon the disputes of the African bishops.

Thus was this new kingdom, within a few years, extended
over the whole world, still preserving that unity of plan
and of government, which is so essential to constitute one
kingdom ; every day becoming more conspicuous, till, at
length, its splendour overcame the obstinacy of the Roman
emperors, and it planted the badge of its Divine Founder
upon the diadem of the world.

Now approached the trying period, when it was to be
seen whether this vast system, like all *human* institutions,
contained in it the principles of dissolution, and whether,
like the overgrown empires of the earth, it would crumble
into pieces by its own weight. But it was soon discovered

that, although the Roman dominion, with which it was more than commensurate, could become the prey of anarchy, or devastation, this had a principle of vitality, proper to itself, which made it independent of earthly support. Whatever revolutions agitated the globe, the Church of God alone remained unmoved : and as all the changes which take place in the vast system of creation, occur within the being and immensity of her Founder, without communicating to Him the slightest variation, so numerous and portentous vicissitudes daily occurred within her precincts without modifying her government, her doctrines, or her rites.

In vain did the north open its flood-gates of desolation, and pour its deluge of barbarians over the rich provinces of the south. No sooner did the torrent stagnate, than it received the care of this universal benefactor ; the scene of its former devastation, and the wilderness which it had created, soon began, in fulfilment of prophecy, " to rejoice and flourish like the lily, to bud forth and blossom, and rejoice with joy and praise." (Is. xxxv. 1.) Often, even in the career of victory, their arm was arrested by its meek interposition ; the sword of the conqueror was charmed into its sheath by the mild doctrines of Christianity, and the proud head of the despot hung abashed before the rebuke of its ministers. But they were not content with subduing the obstinate hearts of their invaders ; they pushed their spiritual conquests into the territories of their enemies.

For never did the kingdom of Christ receive such triumphant increase as during those ages, commonly denoted the dark times of ignorance and superstition.

In the fifth age, St. Palladius and St. Patrick, both
commissioned by Pope Celestine, preached the faith : the
former to the Scots, the second to the Irish. In the
sixth, St. Augustin opened his mission among our Anglo-
Saxon ancestors, under the auspices of the holy Pontiff
St. Gregory. The following century saw the Nether-
lands added to the Church, through the ministry of St.
Willibrord, sent by Pope Sergius. During the eighth,
St. Boniface, under the direction of the second Gregory,
gained the title of the Apostle of Germany. In the
ninth, Sweden ; in the tenth, Denmark was illumined by
the light of the Gospel ; the Hungarians—the Livonians,
parts of Tartary, and Lithuania, were the conquests of
the following centuries ; and when the field for new conversions seemed thus exhausted, new worlds in the east
and west were thrown open, in order that the prerogative
of the Church, to be ever extending, might not want
space whereon to be exerted.

   Nor, my brethren, was this ever-expanding kingdom
of the Lord lost in obscurity or sunk into insignificance
during this period of darkness and confusion. It became,
on the contrary, more and more conspicuous and distinguished. Conspicuous, from the almost exclusive learning of its rulers and dignitaries, and from their successful
care to preserve that spark of literature and science, from
the ashes of antiquity, which could alone have lighted up
the way to modern improvement ; conspicuous, by its
care, to smoothen the rudeness of the times, to soften the
asperity of manners, to improve the condition of the poor,
and plant the basis of all those wise institutions which
we now cherish and admire ; conspicuous still more in

the holiness and beauty of character of so many who devoted themselves to its service ; conspicuous, above all, by being the common link between distant or discordant nations, the common object of awe to all the evil, and of consolation to all the good, the common country to which all belonged, the common altar round which all would rally. Honoured and protected, it never altered its constitution nor broke its succession : its voice silenced every murmur that rose to disturb its harmony ; and its sentence paralyzed every movement made to break its unity. Of the hundred sects which rose before the fifteenth century, only one, (the Vaudois) and that an obscure and lingering remnant, yet survives in Europe, the blight of its anathema.

My brethren, at this epoch let us take our stand. We have seen what sort of a system was required, by the ancient prophecies, to fill the character of God's kingdom upon earth ; and you are assured that such a one must have existed, and must exist for ever, if they were true. What alone could boast these qualities when the apostles established the Church, no one can doubt. For fifteen centuries after that epoch I find only one religious system universally diffused, which could be said to wear the features attributed to this spiritual empire ; one alone conspicuous and distinguished, for till then, it had not even a rival; one community accused of bearing too much the form of an organized kingdom ; one ever spreading the light of religion, and alone diffusing Christianity to the benighted regions of the earth; one alone, in short, from which its more recent separatists boast that they receive their mission and ordination, which would be void and useless if it was not, at least till then, the true and only inheritance of these prophecies and the continuation of their fulfilment. I find, too, that retrograding from the period mentioned, it is connected from age to age by the constant succession of pastors and supreme rulers, by a series of councils, canons, and constitutions, framed for its government, by a train of writers in its defence or instruction, by all those links, in fine, which can give historical identity to a moral and continued body. If, then, the promises of God were fulfilled, it could be in this body alone; and till that century when the rise of rival claims to be the true Church of God involved the case in controversy, it must be acknowledged that no doubt could possibly exist that the great, the magnificent kingdom of the Messias was wholly identified with the only religious system which was widely disseminated, was eminently conspicuous, or which spread on every side the doctrines of Christianity.

It is true, my brethren, that we have often heard and read of foul corruptions in practice, which had crept into the Church, of shocking immoralities which disgraced its ministers, of gross perversions of God's word in its doctrines, during this period. But upon this point we may ask one obvious question. Were these such as to obliterate from this Church the characteristics of being the kingdom of God founded by the apostles? If you answer in the affirmative, then I ask what became of His promises that His kingdom was a kingdom of all ages, which should never be destroyed; for as there was no other institution yet in existence to receive its reversion, if it it ceased to remain there, it ceased equally to exist.

But if these supposed stains only sullied its purity yet did not void its title, then it follows that at the period when the great separation of religion took place, the body from which they separated was in as full possession of its claims, to be the true kingdom of the Messias, as it was at the commencement of Christianity. What power or what title could then or since transfer this Kingdom to another people, contrary to God's holy promise ? Not the accusation of corruptions, for it is proved that they could not have been sufficient before, to deprive it of its rights. Not any authority of man, for its title deeds had been signed and sealed by the spirit of prophecy. Nothing, then, can since have despoiled us of those rights which we possessed at that time ; and, indeed, when I look around at the present moment, I find still existing all these characteristics which were foreshown by the Divine word.

When, from this centre of our religion, I cast my view in any direction, I behold an unbounded prospect, independent of any natural or political horizon. Under every climate, under every form of government, I discover myriads who daily recite the same act of faith, and perform the same worship, as myself ; who look at the same objects and institutions with reverence, and acknowledge the same supreme power, under whose more immediate authority I now address you. I see, in every part, the missionaries of religion advancing each day farther into unconquered territories, treading the dark forests of the Western Hemisphere, or disguising themselves in the populous cities of the ends of the East,—in both directions daily adding new subjects to the kingdom of the Lord. I see this vast and extended, yet compact and

coherent, society everywhere a conspicuous and distinguished body, the boast of many powerful monarchs, the
pride of learned and eminent persons, and even where
existing in a more humble and depressed state, still the
object of universal attention and curiosity, from the
splendour of its worship, the uniformity of its doctrines,
and the constant increase of its numbers.

But if, instead of directing my looks abroad for these
characterizing marks, I cast an eye upon the ground on
which I tread, I find still more speaking evidence of their
existence here.   When I trace back, through every age,
the ecclesiastical monuments which surround me, and find
them carry me back to the earliest period of Christian
history,—when I see myself kneeling before the very altars
which a Sylvester anointed, and where a Constantine
adored; above all, when, standing in the proudest temple
which the hands or imaginations of man ever raised to
the Divinity, I behold myself placed between the tomb of
the Prince of the Apostles and the throne of his present
successor, in a direct lineal descent, and can trace almost
every link which unites these two extremes, through the
ashes that repose in the tombs, or beneath the altars that
surround me, oh! will any one ask why I cling with a
feeling of pride and of affection to that body which car-
ries me back to the foundation of the Church, and unites
in unbroken connection, through ages of fulfilment and of
prophecy, the creed which I profess, with the inspired
visions of earlier dispensations!

If then, my brethren, you feel in these considerations
joy and satisfaction, greet with holy rejoicing the birth of
your infant King, who comes to purchase you these bless-

THE KINGDOM OF CHRIST.

ings. " For *now* a child is born to us, and a son is given
to us, and the government is upon his shoulder, . . . his
empire shall be multiplied, and there shall be no end of
peace." (Is. ix. 6, 7.) Go in, like the Magi, and acknowledge Him your king ; and if His humble guise and His
poor appearance shock your pride, oh ! remember that it
was for you that He put them on. Yes, and remember
that, whatever He may appear outwardly to suffer, it is
nothing compared to the agony of His tender mind.

My brethren, the outline which I have traced has been
but imperfectly filled up. I might have added much to
confirm the truths which I have placed before your minds
for your consolation, or your serious consideration. But
there are characteristics and qualities attributed to God's
kingdom on earth which can be felt rather than described,
and which are intended more to attach "the children of
the kingdom," than to attract the stranger to it. For
while the signal grandeur, extent, and durability of the
Church, as clearly foretold in prophecy, form powerful,
and really incontestible evidence to those without, the
fulfilment of those predictions which promise to it abundance of peace, unity, internal tranquillity, and security
can only be recognized, or rather felt, by those who live
within, as in their own house. (Ps. lxvii. 7.)

These alone can enjoy the peace of conviction, through
the consistency, firmness, and unchangeableness of their
grounds of faith, qualities communicated to every doctrine
they profess : the peace of unanimity ; for all who bear
the name of Catholic believe the same truths without
dissension or doubt, especially in the bosom of the family ;
a peace of direction, from the feeling of confidence in the

divine guidance granted by the Holy Spirit to the Church
and to its ministers, and through them to the individual
conscience ; a peace of reconciliation, after transgressions
and amidst frailties, from the thorough assurance that
God has lodged in the hands of His priesthood the power
to forgive sins, and to restore to grace; a peace of assured
confidence, arising from the abundance of cherished graces
in so many sacraments and other helps to salvation, in
the power of holy indulgences, in the community of
merits throughout the Church, in the intercession of
angels and saints in heaven, and the sublime patronage
of Mary ever pure, in life and death, and in the suffrages
of the living after our departure : finally, a peace of
sweetest charity, affection, and closest union with God,
in that unspeakable mystery of grace and love, in which
Jesus Christ gives us Himself.

Who can worthily speak, to those who have not experienced them, of those treasures of goodness and mercy
which make the inmates of God's house cling to it with
a joyful fidelity, an unshaken security, that is inconceivable to those who are still outside of it ?   Let this our
own enjoyment of such internal evidences, and such
manifold blessings, be generous, in our wish to see every
one partake in them.   Stretch out your hands, O all ye
sons and daughters of God, not merely to offer bread to
those who hunger for it, but to draw in each weary
pilgrim, who faints on his way, that with you he may
find rest, peace, shelter, and food !   So will you deserve
to stand one day at the right hand, which rewards fully
every spiritual, as every corporal, work of mercy.

SERMON XV.

Devotion to the Blessed Virgin.

CANTICLE OF CANTICLES, viii. 5.

" Who is this that cometh up from the desert flowing with
delight, leaning upon her beloved?"

ARE these words, of the most difficult and most mystical
book of Scripture, supposed to be spoken on earth or in
heaven ?

If on earth, then, my brethren, I can only imagine to
myself one who, like Simeon of old, gifted with the knowledge of the future, and in saintliness of life, was looking
out from the inward temple of his own holiness, or from
the visible temple in which he habitually dwelt on earth,
to catch the first glimpse of God's salvation coming to man,
and seeing the earth around him appear as but a desert,
wayless and waterless, in which as yet there has been no
path traced out for the sure guidance of man's steps, in
which no well has been dug at which his soul may be refreshed ; the whole land covered with the darkness of
death, with a night, to its greatest extent, of idolatry and
crime, and more immediately round him with the dimness
of a formal and carnal religion.   And yet he knows that
in the course of but a few short years at most, there will
arise that Sun of justice who will steep and gladden with

U

brightness the whole of that desert region, and will make
it glowing and glorious before God and men. But does
it seem to him that He will arise suddenly, without a har-
binger to announce His coming ?   Will He start up in
the fulness and brilliancy of His majesty ?   Will there be
before His rising no dawn to shine first on the earth,
and dispel some portion of the darkness resting on its
face ?   Will he not rather be able to say, "Who is she
that cometh as the rising dawn," (Cant. vi. 9) whose
light, falling tenderly and softly, is not a mere reflection
of the sun's beams, such as may be gathered by the
mountain's tops, but is a sweet emanation from it—a
part of that radiance softened, but still the same as He
is coming to shed over the earth ?

If such thoughts ever entered into his mind, if even
they clothed themselves before him in living and speaking imagery, what must not have been the fulfilment to
his mind of that which he had before fancied, on that
day when his wishes had to be accomplished, and when
he saw that mother filled with grace, overflowing with
maternal joy and with virginal comeliness, entering from
the wild desert of this worl intod the temple of God ;
bearing in her hands that very Sun that had to brighten
the whole earth.   Yet not bearing Him so much as leaning on Him, her beloved—leaning on Him as her only stay,
her only strength, her only joy ; leaning on Him, as St.
Augustin, speaking of that venerable old man himself,
says, that "while he seemed to bear Him in his arms, in
reality, he was supported by that child."

But were these words of my text perhaps recorded in
that sacred book, not as words spoken on earth, but as

belonging to a nobler mystery and a higher place ? Then, looking through what we may know, from glimpses granted us, of the heavenly Jerusalem, of scenes that may have occurred there, when could those words have been more perfectly fulfilled than on that day, when that same bright creature ascended thither; when she came up from that which to angels' eyes must be but a desert and place of banishment; when she came not as other saints must have come, but so as to force a new burst of exultation from the lips of blessed spirits; when she came as a new star may break suddenly into the firmament—a fresh and precious addition of joy to that unspeakable bliss.

We may imagine how, then, the whole of heaven was moved at seeing her approach, and how the angels and saints may indeed have said : " Who is this so wonderfully favoured, now coming up from that desert below, flowing with delights, flowing with graces, with majesty and beauty ?" If to others have been granted these gifts to the fulness of the cup, her fulness is that of the fountain overflowing ever, and yet ever at the full. And she is introduced not as others might be, led by guardian angel or patron saint through the opening ranks of that celestial host to the throne of God, and there kneeling before the faithful Rewarder of His servants, hear those words spoken : " Well done, thou good and faithful servant ;" but from the door of heaven, leaning, in the full confidence of love, on her beloved, as a bride on her bridegroom, as a mother may lean on her son.

Then, my brethren, do not these words, so wonderful and beautiful, seem naturally to apply themselves to the two entrances, when born first into this world of trial, and then into that country of bliss ; and may we not justly consider them as belonging to her especially, even though partially they may be applied to others? These words come naturally before my thoughts, because the Church, in the course of this week, will celebrate one of these first appearances of this chosen saint, of the most blessed Virgin Mary, the mother of the Incarnate Word of God.   For in the course of this week occurs the festival of her Conception, which the Church, even before it had defined it as of faith, believed to be immaculate ; that is, without sin, without spot or stain ; a mystery wonderful in itself, but, except by Catholics, little under-stood.   I have, therefore, thought that I could not better prepare the thoughts and feelings of my hearers for the celebration, with peculiar solemnity, of this festival, than by explaining the meaning of it, and the manner in which it is understood and felt by Catholics ; not by proving it, not by entering into arguments which involve long quota-tions and discussions, but only by putting it before you in its simplicity, and endeavouring to make you feel how natural this belief is, and how obvious it must be to Christian feelings.

But allow me to begin somewhat remotely, because a groundwork must be laid for my argument.   Allow me, at first, in a simple and obvious mode, to bring before you the grounds on which Catholics celebrate, at all, the festivals of the saints, and what they mean by it ; and thus led step by step, you will see how natural it is that this festival should be to us one of the greatest consolation and joy.

There is not a single class of Christians that does

not possess what is well known by the name of its
calendar. Let it be a common almanac, such as is
published by authority in our country, or let it be that
which is printed uniformly at the beginning of every
prayer-book that contains the service of the Church of
England. That calendar has probably been looked at
again and again by every one; yet it is possible that
some of its most striking features may not have been
sufficiently observed. It will be found that, in addition
to certain greater feasts, there are marked on particular
days the names of persons long ago deceased; the
names of persons with whom individually we can have
no sympathy; the names of persons who have not any
special relation to our national ideas, or any connection
with our history, but still whose names are there; and
it is not difficult at once to see that they are there
because they have been men distinguished for virtue, for
holiness of life, for what they have done or suffered for
Christ. There are Saints Peter and Paul, St. Luke, St.
Matthew, St. Austin, St. Elphege, with other names
scattered over the pages, recorded, no doubt, for some
particular purpose. Is it a practical purpose—one which
is brought ordinarily into action, in connection with
the thoughts or feelings of the day? With hundreds
and thousands most likely it is not. But it is more
than probable that many persons, if asked why the
names of those who are called saints are recorded there,
would reply, because they were there many years ago,
when a practice existed of devotion to the saints, though
perhaps it might have been better had they been withdrawn; while there are some who consider this a part of

what has been saved from the plundered treasures of the ancient Church ; who think that the record of those saints is a constant protest against forgetfulness of devotion which should be paid to them, and that they are mentioned to excite the faithful to a communion of some sort, even with those whose names are not handed down.

But to explain the meaning, according to Catholic thought and feeling, of this record of names, I will for a moment put that book aside. We will close the prayer-book, and turn to the old family Bible, where we find a calendar at the beginning containing names, and those names marked with particular dates. To pass over more sorrowful events, there has been registered the day on which each child of the family was born, and that day is noted as a sacred one in family feeling and family usages. It is true that among those names there occur those of some who for a long time have not been seen.

Perhaps there was one child who, from early years, manifesting a manly and independent spirit, went forth to the regions of the west, bearing with him what the family had been able to give him as his portion, and there, by industry, and honesty, and steadiness of life, he is known to have amassed considerable wealth, and to have acquired for himself a high position, so as to be well spoken of and honoured, by all who know him. There was another who, in his opening youth, filled with courage and ardour, went to the east to fight his country's battles ; who has gained victories on the sultry plains of India; till at length his brow is overshadowed with laurels, and his name is chronicled in the history of his country ; and he has gained not only honour but glory among men.

But, distant as they may be, far away as they sojourn in the east or the west, that record in the family calendar is the bond that unites them. Does the mother forget the returning birth-day of these her absent and renowned children ? Does she not make preparation beforehand — does she not invite the friends and relations of her children to join with her in commemorating that day, because it gave life to one who is yet both honoured and loved ? And the feast is prepared, and all are seated round its table, and all hearts are most joyful ; younger children are there that have never seen their elder brethren, who had departed from home before they were even born ; and yet they feel they have a right to be proud of them as brothers, and they feel a love towards them, and they know them, and on that day they speak of nothing else. And the parent loves to record incidents of the early days of the one who is commemorated, incidents that gave foreshowings of his future wisdom or greatness ; a thousand anecdotes are preserved of his words and of his actions, and they are repeated again and again, year after year, to ears willing to listen and to hearts filled with love. And now suppose that just at that moment, when the father is opening his lips to speak in benediction of that child that has given honour to his grey hairs, and when every eye is glistening with joy, and every ear intent to hear the repetition of his homely and dearest thoughts, suppose that at that moment some one with scornful eye and bitter words were to say: " What folly ! what delusion ! Know you not that the affections of home cling not to a man when he has attained the object of his life ? Think you that they who are now at ease in a distant land, who have

the fulness of their desires given them, who are now
surrounded by new friends and connexions more properly
their own, think you that they care any more for mother
or brethren left behind in the toils and struggles of home ?
No; it is folly to recall the memory of such ; they are gone
from you for ever." Will the hearts of those sitting round
sympathize with these words or not ? No; they sympathize
with the tears of sorrow, or more of indignation which burst
from the mother's eyes. Is it not the pride and joy of her
heart to think that on that same day, at that same hour, the
absent ones are recalling to mind what is being said at
their dear home, about them; that this is a bond of sympathy with the younger ones who have still to win their
reward ; and that each one is wishing and praying for
happiness and joy on those whom, though distant, he
loves? Is not this the natural feeling which any of you
will entertain of the affections of this life ? What, then,
have I to say when similar words are spoken of those
who have been ours, who are ours, and who still love us ?

Return now to that other record in which are those
of whom I first spoke. Your Mother the Church will
tell you : These are my children, this is the birth-day to
life, to true and eternal life, of a brother of yours, a child
of mine, nursed in the same bosom that bore you, fed
with the same milk which has given vigour to you, taught
by the same mouth from which you have learned ; this
was a child of mine, to whom his Lord and Father gave
five talents and sent away to a distant region from Himself, or rather He withdrew Himself from him, and those
talents by his trading he has doubled in the sight of his
Lord ; he has been a merchant, and has laid up for him-

self treasures in heaven, where the moth consumes not, and the rust destroyeth not. It is a St. Francis, who gave up all for Christ, that he might the more completely win and embrace Christ; it is a St. Vincent of Paul, who, whatever were the riches which the great ones of the world poured into his open arms, lavished them again with no less open hands on the poor of Christ, and for all that he cast away, laid up ten times the amount in heaven: this is the child far away from us, whose birth-day we commemorate. And the other—this was Laurence, or Stephen, a child full of ardour, and zeal, and the love of God, who went forth to fight His battles, who fought, who conquered and triumphed; and he now reigns glorious in heaven, and his name is a very benediction in the mouths of all. And you come and tell me that it is folly to think more of them, that they are dead, and for ever gone, whose bones are crumbled to dust, whose souls have forgotten men. And I ask in return, Is it your opinion that heaven is a place in which, whatever is honourable to man, whatever is most precious to his soul, whatever is most beautiful in his nature, after the corruption of sin has defiled it—that love, in short, which is the very nature of God, is a thing not only unknown there, but banished thence, and never to be admitted? Tell me, then, that you consider heaven to be a place in which the soul is to be employed for eternity, in looking or diving into the unfathomable abyss of love which God is, and seeing that that love is a love not merely sleeping and inactive, but exercising itself in ten thousand ways, with all the resources of infinite power; and yet believe that in that ocean you must not love what God loves.

Tell me that you believe heaven to be a looking into the face of Christ, and there wondering for ever at the infinite love, and tenderness, and mercy, and compassion, and affection beaming from it, and those wounds received that men might be redeemed at such a price—tell me that it consists in the happiness of loving your Saviour for what He has done for man, and endeavouring as much as possible to be like to Him; and that yet you must contrive not to love that which is the very spring of all which you admire in Him, and endeavour not to be like Him in that in which He is most amiable to us.   For there He is interesting Himself for men, showing His wounds, and pleading still by them with His heavenly Father: and we are to understand that we must not join in such an office, and must not take delight therein.   Tell me how you understand heaven to be the association of holy souls, united by a bond of the strictest mutual love forming their very life; and yet when one who has been dear to you on earth comes into that same happy region in which you enjoy bliss, it is to be understood that you will receive him as a stranger, you will know nothing of him, and it will be a glory to you that your heart is unfettered by the ties of duty, gratitude, or love.   Tell me, have you accepted heaven from God on these conditions? have you insisted that when your soul has been called forth from this earth, and you are to ascend to heaven, that instant, that moment, it is your intention, for if it is God's will it ought to be, to forget child and wife, and parents, and to care no more for them?   Oh, if the precept of renouncing father and mother, and whatever we love on earth, for Christ's sake,

be not truly the price, of which we obtain a hundred-fold
enjoyment hereafter, hard indeed would be the condition,
were it thus made the terms, not for obtaining more, but
for losing even that for ever !

And now, my brethren, returning to the point from
which I started, you will understand that there must be
a scale of love ; that if in heaven saints have different
prerogatives, that if, when united together, there will be
some who have a right to pray with a more powerful
intercession, some who have peculiar claims to a greater
love from us on earth, who have still greater right to
love us themselves, there must be some rule whereby
this hierarchy of saints is regulated. And the rule is
one simple and obvious enough, to all who have ever
considered the prerogatives of God's saints. We honour
them, we esteem them, we love them, we believe them
to have influence, in proportion as they are nearer to
God. The martyr who has done the utmost that man
can do, who, by giving his life for Christ, has shown
the greatest love that man can bear, must be placed
far above those who have not attained this privilege,
and who consequently plead not that same intensity of
love. The apostles, who were the immediate followers
and companions of the Son of God in life, whom He
chose to be with Him in His trials, to whom He committed His full power on earth, who, in addition to
martyrdom like others, had also the glory of being
His messengers over the whole world—they are naturally placed in a higher sphere nearer the throne of
God, more closely approaching Him, more vividly be-
holding Him, enjoying greater familiarity and more

intimate union with the affections of their divine Master.

Then what shall we say of her whom God chose to adhere in every time and place to the Redeemer of the world, His own Word incarnate; so that never for a moment was she allowed to be willingly separated from Him; who alone saw Him born and saw Him die, who alone heard His first infant cry, and heard also His last agonizing commendation of His soul to His eternal Father; who nursed Him through infancy, and attended Him in His last hours; who may be said to have shared with Him all His sorrows, all His tribulations; who went with Him to Egypt, flying from the wrath of Herod; who nourished Him in His childhood, who hungered with Him, who bore poverty with Him in His youth at Nazareth, who followed Him weeping from city to city, and sought Him through calumny and reproach, even to the persecutions which threatened His life? If the closeness with which any one was privileged to stand by our Lord on earth, is the criterion of the place occupied in heaven, and of the prerogatives there granted, who can doubt that she, the most blessed Virgin Mary, has a place in the court of her Son such as is granted to none other? Who can doubt for a moment that when she was introduced in heaven into the royal and divine presence of that Son, that same scene took place which is described as occurring when Solomon's mother was announced: " The king arose to meet her, and bowed to her; and a throne was set for the king's mother, and she sat on his right hand"? (3 Kings, ii. 19.)

For, after all, when we speak of her close connexion

with the Son of God, as associated with Him through the whole of His painful life, all this is a consequence of something higher still; it is because she had an interest in Him, a claim on Him, which no other human being could ever establish, and a claim which of all others was on His heart, and, through His heart, on all redeemed mankind. It was because she gave to Him all that He had, of that human nature, with which, as an instrument, His Divinity worked on earth; those feet, that went forth bearing glad tidings to Jerusalem; those powerful hands, which dropped healing on the sick and the infirm, and restored life to the dead; those ears, that were open to every sigh for compassion, every cry for help; those eyes, that ever beamed with mercy and forgiveness on the distressed and the sinner; those lips, that never spoke but in words full, as the honeycomb, with wisdom and sweetness·; that heart, into which she transfused her own blood, and which He poured out again to the last drop for man, as the price of his redemption; that breath, that life, which He gave in expiation for sin, and for the redemption of us all. To have given all this to the Son of God, to have made a present to mankind of it all, surely established in the eternal counsels of God, first a link between Him and her, and then between her and us —a link which cannot be shared by angel or by saint. And therefore does the Church of God place her incomparably above all created beings; and therefore do the hearts of the Church's children yearn towards her, knowing that her Son as she loved Him must have loved her.

But we have given her prerogatives enough when we make her enjoy such privileges as these. Why give her more? Why not be content with so much? and why attribute to her also the gift of sinlessness, and believe that never for a moment was she defiled even by original stain?

I will tell you why in few and simple words. It is because the Catholic Church exalts to so much higher and so much diviner a degree than others do the holiness of her Son. We look on Him as so pure, so holy, as so repellent of sin, and even transgression of the slightest nature, that we cannot admit for a moment, or believe, that He would permit Himself to come in contact with it. We cannot believe that He, who was so jealous of purity, that He would not have His Father allow Him, although He might taste of death, and the scourge, and the buffet, to see corruption; that He would not suffer His lifeless body to repose after death in a tomb which its savour could possibly have reached,—we cannot, I say, believe He would for an instant permit to approach His animated body, filled with His Divinity, what to Him is far more hateful than the corruption of death—the defilement of sin. And because we know Him to be the new Adam, come to give fresh life to the world, we believe Him equally pure with the first, and unable to allow one drop of tainted blood to flow in His veins. Now, in no way could the attainder be cut off, save by preventing it reaching her from whom alone His blood was to be received. But further still, does it not seem natural that if He loved His mother, and must have loved her with such love as God made man alone could entertain, He must have wished to bestow on her, of all gifts, the one which she must necessarily most have coveted. He made her pure and holy, He made her detest sin above any evil in existence. But if a child had it in his power to bestow on his own mother any gift whatever, and knew there was one which she prized most highly, would it not be that which he would grant? And to a soul like her's, what would all other gifts have been to compare with this, to be able to think that never was there a moment in her life when God had turned away His face from her as from a being hateful and loathsome, as everyone must be, with the stain of original sin? And He must also have bestowed on her this very love of inexpressible purity and holiness, which would make her desire it, in order that she might be qualified to be the mother of the Holy One, the spotless Lamb.

It is not, then, unreasonable, my brethren, to honour the saints of God and to love them. It is not unreasonable, in return, to believe that they love us ; and that love is not merely an abstract or passive affection, but, like God's love for man, an active love. It is not unreasonable especially to believe, that the blessed Mother of God has privileges and prerogatives which are bestowed on none other of the saints of God, and consequently that she has greater power with her Son, and higher claims on our hearts and affections. And it is not wonderful that these thoughts, which affection engenders, should lead us by a straighter flight than the more circuitous road which theologians must tread, to arrive at once at the belief in that mystery so dear to the Catholic, of the spotlessness of the ever-blessed Mother of God, even from the beginning of her existence upon earth. One word more concerning her, and I will conclude. It is true that our blessed

Redeemer is the real Sun of justice who alone can shine on our hearts with that saving power and grace, through which alone we can attain our reward ; and it is only He, that brilliant Sun in the firmament of heaven and the Church, who can enlighten our faith, warm our hope, enkindle our charity ; for from Him alone comes grace, from Him alone is light, from Him alone is life. But tell me, is it less that same Sun, or is He less to you when, instead of being viewed directly in all His dazzling brilliancy, He comes on you mellowed, as it were, through the storied window, bearing, imprinted on His own rays, the effigies of saints and angels who would have no existence there but for His light, for all was dark, shapeless, colourless, until His rays came; and then on a sudden He gave them light and colour, and He shaped them into form, and He softened His own radiance as He shone through them; but without Him they had no existence.

And so the Church contemplates, through the saints, the glory of the Son of God. In their own nature they were sinful, frail, and helpless ; but they have been the medium through which the rays of divine grace have passed ; and as they so shone, they have had their brilliancy made endurable. For our Lord's bright virtues thus appear not only admirable, but in some respect imitable, because we can copy those of the saints as steps to conduct us to the life of Christ. And is there not one whom all should be glad to see the model especially of Christian women ? Catholic mothers, will you leave your children to pick up the type of their sex from the novel or the romance of the day ? Will you have them form their characters, either upon that stern and cold

virtue which the world admires, or upon that soft and
miserable effeminacy with which it depicts the milder
mind? Will you leave them to model themselves on
what is considered the noble form of character in their
sex, the masculine heroines of ancient or modern times,
who forgot the gentler and softer virtues belonging to
their nature, to cultivate, rather, intellect, and display
boldness even in religious speculation? Or do you wish
to find them classed with those who have passed with
cold mediocrity through the trials of life; amiable, perhaps,
but possessed of barely ordinary virtues?

Will you, I ask, leave them to follow such wretched
models, when you have before you that type of female
excellence, which, from the time of St. Ambrose, was
placed before the youthful maiden; as that on which she
must study to form herself, that in which there is found
all that is tender and yet all that is firm; and which,
from the humble virgin refusing the highest of honours,
brings before us, finally, the matron enduring anguish
and agony such as falls to the lot of no other woman on
earth? Can you, for a moment, hesitate to perceive, how
useful, how salutary, how saving it would be, if you could
make this the example that is to be imitated in every
family, and thus become at length the recognized type of
all that is great and at the same time gracious?

Then, do not listen to words that you may hear spoken
almost scornfully of her, whom it is impossible to think
on without love. Do not allow yourselves, because it may
be thought expedient to repel Catholic doctrine from you,
to hear that which is most beautiful in the whole history
of Christianity, saving Him only who has no paragon, I

x

will not merely say with contempt, but even with coldness and indifference. On the contrary, fling away with indignation such suggestions from you, and look at her character, her history, her prerogatives, with the simple feelings of nature, if not with the eyes of Catholic faith, and I am sure that there is not one of you who will not be ready to admit, that it should be a motive of virtuous pride to be able to say, that this has been her own model, and the one which she has proposed to her children for imitation. And I am sure that such a one would come at length to admit the whole of what I have said, the whole of what the Catholic Church teaches respecting the blessed and immaculate Mother of God; and that, in the end, she would find and proclaim that this copying of so sublime, yet so winning, an example, had made her path smooth and easy, nay, that it had made it the sweetest, and, at the same time, the most safe, to eternal life.

SERMON XVI.

Veneration of the Blessed Virgin.

Luke, xi. 27.

" And it came to pass, as He spoke these things, that a certain woman from the crowd, lifting up her voice, said to Him : Blessed is the womb that bore Thee, and the breasts that gave Thee suck."

The incident thus recorded in the Gospel which has just been sung,* is contained in few words, but is, nevertheless, full of consoling instruction. The woman who so fearlessly raises her voice above the crowd, had seen Jesus perform many works of mighty power ; she had heard the strong persuasiveness wherewith He delivered instructions of sublimest import; she had noted, too, the commanding grace and dignity and majesty which clothed His person, and ennobled all His actions. And yet, she exclaimed not, "blessed are those hands wherein God hath placed the staff of His power,"—nor "the lips which He hath over-spread with such sweetness,"—nor "the heart wherein He hath folded up so much counsel." But, by a transition most natural, she considered how lovely must have been the flower which produced so sweet a fruit, how hallowed and pure the body which conceived, and bore, and nourished so holy and privileged a being : herself, perhaps, a mother, she calculated the joys of *her*, to whom

* Gospel of the Votive Mass of the Blessed Virgin.

alone it had been given to nurse and caress Him in infancy, to enjoy His company and command Him in youth, and for whom alone—however the waters of His charity and graciousness might flow abroad—was reserved in His breast, that sealed fountain of man's affections— filial duty, respect, and love.   And hence, borne away by an amiable enthusiasm, and nothing fearing that by commending and blessing such a mother, she could offend such a Son, she raised her voice almost unwittingly, and exclaimed : " Blessed is the womb that bore thee, and the breasts that gave thee suck."

Nor was there any reproof of these sentiments implied in His answer.   " Yea rather," or, as it might have been, perhaps, better rendered, " Yea *likewise* blessed are they who hear the word of God and keep it."   For in like manner, when Thomas, upon touching our Saviour's wounds, proclaimed Him his Lord and God, our blessed Redeemer replied that they were blessed who had not seen, and yet believed ; (John xx. 29) and did not surely thereby signify, that we, who believe darkly, as striving against our senses, and adore at a distance, as through a thick veil, have a more blessed lot than those chosen few who were allowed to hear His voice, and touch His sacred body, and kiss His open wounds.   But He wished to teach the apostles and us that, as all could not aspire to that extraordinary happiness, it behoved us to be content with that measure which it pleases God to grant us, and thus He in part corrected Thomas for refusing to be contented with less blessed evidence of His being risen, than he himself chose to demand.   In like manner did He turn the pious woman in the Gospel, from the contemplation of a sublime and unattainable beatitude, for which none might even long, to that share which she might hope to reach, and which was proper for her condition—the blessing of being a hearer and doer of His holy word.   Thus here, as in the case of Thomas, the pointing out a happiness more within the reach of men, than that which was alluded to, does not impair, but rather enhances, the beatitude of the higher state by pronouncing it *beyond* hope.

We then, my brethren, as Venerable Bede exhorteth us, will raise our voices, with this holy woman, above the crowd, and proclaim as she did, blessed the womb that bore Jesus made man, and the breasts that gave Him suck, an infant for our sakes ; and that we may do so with greater assurance, we will consider the right she of whom we treat hath to our gratitude and veneration.   But so far from allowing those feelings to prejudice our better interests, we will, on the contrary, see how highly beneficial they may be rendered to our eternal welfare.   Thus shall we first imitate the pious example proposed to us by the Gospel, and then profit by the lessons drawn from it by our heavenly Teacher.

It is not my intention, my brethren, to enter into any controversy, for the purpose of proving to you, from sacred authority or from human reason, that it is just and proper in us to honour and venerate the saints of God, and above them all the Queen of the Saints.   For I feel that here I stand in the midst of my brethren, of those who come to the house of God, in full conviction of all the truths therein taught, and only anxious to improve in the practice of all they inculcate.   And need I tell such as you, that the contemplation of the glory of

the saints, and of their dignity and joy, so far from drawing away our thoughts and hopes from God, doth rather
raise them up more gently from the earth, to fly towards
Him ? For one who should wish to contemplate the beauty
of a glorious summer's day, would not go forth and boldly
raise his eyes, and fix them upon the burning luminary,
from which all its radiance and warmth proceed, well
knowing that he would thereby only dazzle and afflict his
sight; but rather, casting them lower, he would let them
wander over the milder diversity of Nature's face.   Or, if
possible, he would rest them upon a well-tilled garden ;
and, as he there observed the rich variety of shape, and
hue, and fragrance, and loveliness in the flowers that surrounded him, remembering that all these divers forms and
qualities are but the reflection and production of that
source of light which brings them into being, he would
thereby conceive a sweeter and livelier idea of that day's
splendour, and of that luminary's benefits, than if he had
at once gazed upon his brightness.   And in like manner
when we wish to meditate upon the glories of God's
eternal day, we will not at once dart our glance on that
Father of lights, who dwelleth in light inaccessible, but
rather will pause to meditate upon the beauties of his
heavenly Eden ; and when we contemplate assembled
together the unstained virgin, and the empurpled martyr,
and the triumphant apostle, and all the other orders of
heavenly beings, with one rising above the rest, and
uniting in herself the excellencies of them all; and when,
moreover, we remember that all these charms are but
emanations and reflections of His effulgence, we shall
assuredly form a truer and more consoling estimate of

His beauty and beneficence, and mighty power, than if we had awed and overwhelmed our minds by sternly gazing upon His splendour. Then, too, are we more easily led to reflect, that we likewise are now what these once were, seedlings, so to speak, in the nursery of the heavenly husbandman, destined, as soon as we shall reach our becoming growth, to be transplanted into that garden of His delight.

But, turning now to her, with whose higher dignity I wish principally to ennoble my discourse, it must be noted that the woman in my text was not the first that pronounced her "blessed." The first was Gabriel the archangel, who saluted her "blessed among women;" (Luke, i. 28) the second was Elizabeth, filled, as the sacred text says, with the Holy Ghost, who repeated the angel's words; (42) the third was Mary herself, who exclaimed that from thenceforth all generations should call her blessed. (48.) Now these words have the form of prophecy; and that prophecy must have been fulfilled. But by whom? Not, surely, by those who, in discourse, never bestow upon her that title; not by those who never make her the topic of their religious instruction, unless it be to reprehend and reprobate the only honour and veneration bestowed upon her on earth; not by those into the scheme of whose theology the consideration of her blessedness never enters —no, nor even her name, unless it be to denounce those as superstitious or something worse, who address her as did an archangel, and one inspired by the Holy Ghost, of whom it is said, that she walked in all the commandments of the Lord without blame. (6.)

It has, indeed, been urged by some, to excuse their

aversion to showing respect to Mary, that our Saviour
Himself, through life, treated His Mother with marked
indifference; that He answered her even harshly at the
wedding-feast of Cana, (John, ii. 4)* and that He refused
to recognize her, when told that she was asking for Him
without. (Matt. xii. 48.)   There have not been wanting
men who have seriously urged these instances, in their
writings, as a key to the feelings of our divine Redeemer
towards His blessed Mother; and have even assumed
that He thereby meant to give us a model and a rule of
our feelings and bearing towards her.   Now I will even
allow that these circumstances are usually fairly represented, and that our Lord so conducted Himself towards
our blessed lady, as to show in the strongest manner that,
when once He had entered on His sacred ministry, He
had snapped completely in sunder the bonds of the flesh,
and allowed none, however dear to Him, further to inter-
fere with His designs; and that He consequently did
appear, on some occasions, to check her eager love. Even
allow all this, and does it follow that we are to select
these instances as the rule of our conduct and speech ?

Our Redeemer often reproached His apostles as men of
little faith. (Matt. viii. 26, xiv. 31.)   Are *we*, therefore,
to forget all their labours in our behalf, and their sufferings for Christ, and the dignity of their apostleship, and
their sealing of the faith with their blood, and judge of
their Master's disposition towards them only from His
words of strong reproof?   He addressed Peter in these
harsh terms: "Get behind me, Satan; thou art a scan-

---

* On this passage see the *Dublin Review*, April, 1837, page 409.

dal to me, because thou savourest not the things that are
of God." (Matt. xvi. 23.) And will any one thence
reason, that we should overlook his warmer zeal, and
thrice-recorded love, and his confession of our Lord's
divinity, and the pastoral charge and keys of the kingdom delivered to him, only to dwell upon the sterner
moments of severe correction? And to John, too, He
said, turning round and rebuking : "Ye know not of
what spirit ye are." (Luke, ix. 55.) Must we then not
heed that he was the beloved disciple that leaned upon
his Master's bosom ; who stood alone of the twelve on
Golgotha by the cruel tree; to whom, beyond others, were
revealed the mysteries of the future ; and who closed the
inspired volume by the longing aspirations of love divine;
but feel and speak of him as one whom Jesus repri-
manded and strongly rebuked, and for whom, consequently,
He wished us never to feel or express reverence, gratitude,
or love ?

And if not, then let not a similar argument be impi-
ously or ignorantly urged with regard to Mary; and even
supposing—what God forbid I should ever allow—that
her dear Son should sometimes have seemed to act
towards her with a reserve bordering on severity, should
not we rather remember that it was she who bore for
nine months in her womb the Saviour of our souls, and
who suckled Him with her milk ; that she carried Him
in her arms through the desert to save Him from His
enemies; that she had loving care of Him for many years
at Nazareth; that she suffered three years of racking
anxiety on His account while the Jews sought His life ;
and that she endured more for Him than any other

mortal, standing to gaze on His death-hour, beneath the shadow of His bruised limbs and thorny crown? And oh! did not those last words, when, with His failing breath, He proclaimed her His Mother, and commended her to John, compensate for all past severity in His demeanour, if such *had* existed, or such had been possible, in Him who came from heaven to be our model, as in every other virtue, so in the first commandment which according to St. Paul, has a promise, (Ephes. vi. 2) that of honouring our parents?

But now that Jesus has ascended to the Father, and has dried up every tear from the eyes of His saints, can we suppose that His sentiments have changed in her regard? For, my brethren, when you think of Jesus sitting at the right hand of God, undoubtedly you love to think of Him as clothed with all that can render our human nature amiable: and as He has borne with Him our flesh, and the very wounds that pierced it, so you cannot doubt but He has raised so high with Him the gentle and sweet affections of the heart. We delight to think that whom He loved on earth, He loveth also in heaven; to whom He showed friendship here below, He denieth it not in His own kingdom; with whom He contracted obligations in the days of His flesh, He holds them good, and repays them in this season of His glory. The more we can assimilate Him in our minds to what He was here below,—the more we can divest Him of the brightness of His glorified state, the more easily and closely we can unite ourselves to Him in pure and simple affection. Shall we then see Him thus preserving every other virtuous and amiable feeling, and making charity

—that is love—the all-absorbing essence of bliss in heaven, and consequently Himself a fathomless abyss thereof, and yet bring ourselves even remotely to suspect that He has despoiled Himself of that feeling which Nature plants the first, and never again uproots— the bud at once and the firmest stem of our affections ; to suppose that He still shows Himself a generous bene- factor, a kind master, and a faithful friend, and yet wishes not to be considered as displaying the feelings of an affectionate son ?   Away from us such cruel thoughts !

Then, on the other hand, can we believe Him such, and yet imagine that He wishes not others to love and respect, and that, too, with outward demonstrations, her whom He himself loves and cherishes ? For what said king Assuerus, when he wished to express his esteem for Mardochai, who had saved his life? Why, he ordered him to be mounted on his best horse, clothed in royal robes, and wearing the diadem, and so to proceed through the public places, while the first nobleman of the land should make proclamation saying : "thus shall he be honoured whom the king wisheth to honour." (Est. vi. 7.) And I would appeal to you all, or rather to Nature speak- ing in your bosoms ; to you who are parents, whether you would esteem filial love perfect in your child, if when raised to some high dignity, he grudged you every parti- cipation in the honour he received, and sternly for- bade men to consider as his mother, or express their love and respect towards her who had borne much for him, and suffered much for him, in the days of his lowly estate ; to you who are children, if you would envy that dignity which imposed upon you the harsh condition of renouncing your natural affections, and disowning such a parent?

Nay, I will even assert, that never is our love for Jesus so feelingly excited, as when we contemplate Him in conjunction with His blessed Mother. Never has the eye of art seen Him so amiable, never do our hearts so warm to Him, and feel so familiarized with Him, as when He is represented to us a lovely infant reposing in the arms of His Virgin Mother; never do we so feel what He underwent, how He bled, and how He died for our redemption, as when we gaze upon His pale and bloodless corpse, laid upon the lap of His heart-broken Mother, and read in her countenance, a grief such as all the world else could not contain, the only measure which earth could give of the sufferings He endured for our salvation.

If, then, any one shall accuse me of wasting upon the Mother of my Saviour, feelings and affections which He hath jealously reserved for Himself, I will appeal from the charge to His judgment, and lay the cause before Him, at any stage of His blessed life. I will go into Him at the crib of Bethlehem, and acknowledge that, while, with the Kings of the East, I have presented to him all my gold and frankincense and myrrh, I have ventured, with the shepherds, to present an humbler oblation of respect to her who was enduring the winter's frost in an unsheltered stable, entirely for His sake. Or I will meet Him, as the holy fugitives repose on their desert-path to Egypt, and confess that, knowing from the example of Agar, how a mother cast forth, from her house into the wilderness, for her infant's sake, only loves it the more, and needs an angel to comfort her in her anguish, (Gen. xxi. 17) I have not restrained my eyes from her whose fatigues and pain were a hundred-fold increased by His, when I have sympathised with Him in this His early flight, endured for my sins.   Or I will approach a more awful tribunal, and step to the foot of His cross, and own to Him, that while I have adored His wounds, and stirred up in my breast my deepest feelings of grief and commiseration for what I have made Him suffer, my thoughts could not refrain from sometimes glancing towards her whom I saw resignedly standing at His feet, and sharing His sorrows ; and that, knowing how much Respha endured while sitting opposite to her children justly crucified by command of God, (2 Kings, xxi. 10) I had felt far greater compassion for her, and had not withheld the emotions, which Nature itself dictated, of love, and veneration, and devout affection towards her.   And to the judgment of such a Son I will gladly bow, and His meek mouth shall speak my sentence, and I will not fear it.   For I have already heard it from the cross, addressed to me, to you, to all, as He said : " Woman, behold thy son ;" and again : " Behold thy mother." (John xix. 26, 27.)

It is, indeed, remarkable, my brethren, how completely that motherhood of the Blessed Virgin, which the woman in my text so loudly blessed, has been delineated in the Gospel.   Almost all the other persons connected with our Saviour's history undergo extraordinary changes.   John the Baptist, from the solitary anchorite in the wilderness, becomes the herald of the Messias, the baptizer of Israel, the reprover of Pharisees and even of kings.   Magdalen first appears as the woman tenanted by evil spirits, (Mark, xvi. 9.) and is soon changed into an ardent

follower, and dauntless servant of Jesus. The apostles
begin as fishermen and publicans, to be transformed into
workers of signs and miracles, even before their Master's
passion.   But Mary never appears in any character but
that of a mother, solicitous and suffering only for her Son.
She is first seen receiving the heavenly messenger, and,
according to his promise, conceiving and bearing the
eternal Word made flesh for man's redemption ; and soon
becomes an object of persecution to His enemies, so as to
be compelled to abandon her native land.   Amidst the
flattering and glorious scenes that surround her at His
birth, we find it simply recorded of her by St. Luke, that
"Mary kept all these words, pondering in her heart."
(Luke, ii. 19.) After this did God reveal to her through
holy Simeon, the piercing grief which, as a sword, should
pass through her soul. (Luke, ii. 35.)   We meet her not
again until twelve years later, the solicitous mother
wandering about the streets of Jerusalem, seeking her lost
Son, sorrowing.   And when she has found Him, and
understands not perfectly the deep mysterious answer that
He makes her, we have the same description of her conduct,
which in one stroke sketches her mild unobtrusive character, that "His Mother kept all these things in her heart."
(Luke, ii. 51.)   After this we have total silence in her
regard, during eighteen years of a life the most blessed
which can be conceived upon earth, under the same roof
with the Son of God ; till she comes forward once more to
initiate Him into His public life, by inducing Him to work
His first miracle, at Cana.   Through the three years of
His wonderful public ministry, while all Judea rung with
His praises, while crowds pressed round Him to be healed,

while priests, and Pharisees, and doctors of the law listened with respect to His doctrines, and men would have set the royal crown upon His head—she takes no part in His triumphs and His fame : and only once approaches Him, in tender solicitude, to call Him from the house where He was surrounded by the multitude. (Matt. xii. 46.)

But so soon as we come to the last perilous trial, when disciples have fled, and apostles have denied Him ; when friends have abandoned Him, and relations are ashamed of kindred with Him ; when He is surrounded by a ruffianly mob, whose brutality seems equal to any outrage ; when He is hedged round by the cruel array of soldiers and executioners, *then* may she, the mild retired maid of Nazareth, but still the mother, be seen pressing through every obstacle to share in His sufferings, and catch His dying breath.

This, then, is the only character in which it is meant that we should know her, as the Mother of Jesus. And are not *we* the brethren of Jesus ? Did not He Himself assure us so much ; did not St. Paul, did not St. John, repeat the same consoling doctrine ? (Matt. xxviii. 10; Rom. viii. 17; 1 John, iii. 1, 2.) And to us, my brethren, who believe that every tie which connected us with Him on earth is not broken, but strengthened in heaven ; who believe that a holy union does exist between those who upon earth are fighting for their crown, and those who in heaven have received it already ; who believe that every claim which we can make to the interest and intercession of those who have reached the goal is gladly acknowledged and made good—to us who so believe, yea, and who so feel, this is not matter of vain boast or empty parade. For, if such is our faith, this title which we have received has gained a mother for us in heaven, who will often plead in our behalf. And in truth, if in life she suffered much, it may really be said that she suffered it for our sakes. By which I do not, of course, mean to say, that what she or any other mortal underwent, could, in the least measure, contribute to the mighty work of our redemption, or allay, even in small degree, the enkindled wrath of God ; but it is true, no less, that whatever she bore was from deep sympathy in the painful work of our salvation : that the blows of the hammer which drove deep the nails into her Son's feet and hands, drove deep the sword, too, which holy Simeon had placed against her bosom ; and those blows did *our* sins heavily strike ; that the drops of blood drained from His sacred head by the thorny crown, were told by her in so many bitter tears—and that it was *we* who, as with the reed of our fickle affections, beat that crown deep into His meek forehead ; that His last gasp was fearfully echoed in her mild heart, now hollowed of all that had cheered and strengthened it ; and that gasp was forced out by *our* transgressions: in fine, that through *our* iniquities she was made homeless, and friendless, and childless. And what other mother ever lost such a Son ! Thus may we say, that if we have been made her children, in much pain, and with smarting pangs, she hath borne us. While, therefore, with the devout woman in the Gospel, we pronounce her blessed, because she was the Mother of our Redeemer, it is not with prejudice to our strivings after salvation, nor to the neglect of our present

advantages; it is, on the contrary, that we may calculate
so much the more justly and nicely, the advantages which
her blessedness, as Mother of God, may bring us. And
the first of these we have now seen ; that is, the close
bond with which it knitted us to her, and the powerful
interest in our salvation which the establishment of that
bond hath given her.

Next to this, we may well ponder on the weight of
her intercession. For, if the saints in heaven have
golden vials given them, as we are told in the Apoca-
lypse, filled with our prayers, as with sweet odours,
which they pour out before the throne of God, (Apoc. v.
8) with what fragrance must those be endowed which
are shed from her's ? For inasmuch as her dignity of
Mother of God raised her, upon earth, above every order
and degree in the human race, so likewise in heaven
must she preserve the same elevation, beyond all competition. And if the word of God has told us that
Jesus, ascended into heaven, has prepared corresponding
emblems of reward for every state of holiness, golden
harps for the patriarchs, and robes of whiteness for the
virgins, and palms for the martyrs, and seats of judgment for the apostles, and crowns of glory for all that
love Him, by what emblem shall we describe the reward
which must have been bestowed upon her, who closed
the line of patriarchal holiness, forming, as it were, the
wall of separation between the two covenants, who,
though a mother, was pure so as no virgin else was ever
pure ; whose martyrdom of inward grief was deemed by
the Spirit of God fit matter of holy prophecy; who with
the apostles received the unction of the Holy Ghost at

Y

Pentecost, and who alone of all mankind could say, that she had loved Jesus with a mother's love ?

This thought, united to our former consideration, gives a powerful motive of confidence in her intercession.   Not that we believe that any created being can bestow upon us grace, or aught that can tend to our justification ; but, believing that those in heaven join their supplications with ours, and that He who so often had compassion upon His people on account of His servants Abraham, Isaac, and Jacob, will often regard their prayers, when ours are not sufficiently powerful to move Him, we have here strong and consoling grounds, much to rely on the love and influence of His blessed mother.

Lastly, I will say that the consideration of her blessedness may be rendered useful to us in the cause of our salvation, if it be a means of attracting our affections and devotion towards our heavenly country.   All that can, without diminishing our duty to God, draw upwards our feelings towards heaven, must be salutary and good. The child that should long for its bliss because, next to the enjoyment of the Divine presence, he looks forward to a reunion with a lost parent, will not surely be chid by the sternest bigotry, as indulging in an unworthy desire.   And if we, moved by the considerations I have rehearsed, feel our hearts warmed with an affectionate devotion towards one who has so many claims upon it, and find that such devotion, always subordinate, and far inferior to our love for God, is powerful in summoning up feelings of tender emotion, which on other occasions we do not experience,—believe me, it must be right and wholesome for you to indulge it.   In Catholic countries,

you might see the poor and afflicted crowding round
some altar, where their pious confidence, or experience of
past favours, leads them to hope that their prayers will
best be heard through the intercession of our dear lady;
and you would mark their countenances glowing, and their
eyes raised upwards, and perhaps streaming with tears ;
and would be struck with the heavings of their bosoms,
and the eager whisperings of their prayer, and the deep sobs
that escape them. Then, perhaps, some stranger who knew
them not, would scornfully remark to you, as Heli did
concerning Anna, (1 Kings, i. 14) that those poor creatures are intoxicated with a lying spirit of superstition,
or even idolatry. But God hath looked into their simple
hearts, and judged far otherwise. Even if that confidence
which leads them to a particular spot be unfounded, it has
drawn from them such deep-breathed sighs of devotion as
are elsewhere scarcely to be seen ; it has for a time, at least,
driven the world and its follies from their hearts, annihilated all thoughts of earth within their souls, and raised
them upon wings of love towards heaven, into the company of saints who see God, there to make interest with
her who is best by Him beloved.

Oh, that the time had come when a similar expression
of our devout feelings towards her should publicly be
made, and all should unite to show her that honour, that
reverence and love which she deserves from all Christians.
and which so long have been denied her amongst us !
There was a time when England was second to no other
country upon earth in the discharge of this duty ; and it
will be only part of the restoration of our good and
glorious days of old, to revive to the utmost this part of

ancient piety. Therefore do I feel sincere joy at witnessing the establishment of this excellent brotherhood, and its public manifestation in this town this day, both as a means of encouraging devotion and virtue, and as a return to one of the venerable institutions of our forefathers. Enter, then, fully into its spirit. Let every brother of this Holy Guild consider himself bound, by a new tie, to the practice of all that his religion enjoins, spontaneously engaged to display greater exactness in the discharge of every duty, and to go before others in observance of the Church's precepts: in frequenting the sacraments, in sobriety, honesty, industry, docility, and quiet peaceful demeanour, both at home and abroad. Remember that this day you have put yourselves and your families under the protection of the ever-blessed Mother of God and her chaste spouse, St. Joseph,—of those who were chosen by God to protect the infancy of Jesus from the dangers of a persecuting world. Entreat them to protect you and yours from the perils of a seducing and ensnaring world, to plead your interests in heaven, and secure, by their intercession, your everlasting crown. Loudly proclaim the praises of your heavenly queen, but at the same time turn her power to your everlasting advantage by your earnest supplications to her. And this you cannot more beautifully do than by that prayer which your holy mother, the Church, taught you to lisp in infancy, and to recite after the Lord's Prayer, wherein you salute Mary in the angel's and Elizabeth's words, and conclude by asking her prayers, both for your present necessities, and for the future but certain crisis which awaits us all. May *she*, who stood at the foot of the cross when her Son yielded

His meek spirit into the hands of His eternal Father,—
with him whose eyes were closed in peace by His divine
foster-child,—smooth your last bed of sorrow after having
made the road to it less burthensome and dreary ! May
they be your models, your patrons, and your encouragers
through life and its troubles, to be one day your strength-
eners and guardians under God, in death and its terrors:
that so they may bring you to Him who vouchsafed, for
our sakes, to be called their Son !

SERMON XVII.

On the Maternity of the Blessed Virgin.

St. Luke, ii. 51.

"And He was subject to them."

BENEATH the roof of a church dedicated to the glorious and ever-blessed Mother of God, where from every side shine down upon us the emblems of her dignity, on a day on which is commemorated that maternity,* which communicated to her all her sublime prerogatives; in the presence of a faithful people, who know how to love and to reverence her, it would be contrary to every sentiment that inspires me, if I spoke to you to-day upon any other subject than that which the place, the time, and the attendance so naturally suggest. It is not necessary for me to say anything to you who hear me in support of the Catholic doctrine concerning devotion to the blessed Mother of our Lord Jesus Christ; it is not requisite that I should even explain to you, as if you were an ignorant flock, the nature of this devotion, its character, its conditions; nay, it is not expedient that I should try to recommend that devotion, or endeavour to add anything to the fervour which I know animates the people of this

* The Feast of the Maternity, kept in Ireland in Autumn.

island, and this city in particular—the fervour of that
deep, most loving, most faithful affection towards her
whom they consider their patroness, their mother, their
best and truest friend, their intercessor, for ever beside
the throne of her Son. No, my brethren, it is not for
any of these purposes that I will address you, but it is
rather to give utterance to those sentiments of corresponding love and devotion which form a tie between
us, as every bond of faith and piety ever must. I will
speak to you upon the only topic which naturally comes
to one's thoughts here; and I am sure that you would
think I was wandering from what belongs to this day—
that I was withholding from you the food proper to this
festival of Mary, if I did not endeavour to place before
you such thoughts as, with my inadequate powers, may
show you how this festival of the Maternity of the Blessed
Virgin recalls to us the illustrious virtues with which she
was endowed, and the sublime privileges with which she
was invested. We will simply go through a few passages
of her life, and consider her in her various relations with
her Son; and see how we can trace these memorable
events that distinguished her in the world, that have
raised her to a place beside that throne of her Son in
heaven, to her simple but glorious title of " Mother of
Jesus."

And first, my brethren, let us begin by contemplating
her from the moment in which she verified the words of
the angel, and gave to the world the Incarnate Word. It
is certain that if we look around on earth for a type and
representation of the best and purest possible affection;
if we look for love in its utmost intensity, in its most

unselfish simplicity, in its sweetest tenderness, there at once arises to our minds that natural affection which binds the mother to her child. For that pledge of God's love she is ready to sacrifice herself, forgetting every consideration ; not only will she sacrifice health and all the pleasures of life, but life itself, if necessary ; and we cannot imagine a being more ready to give her existence for another than the mother who sees her child in danger, and resolves at once to make herself an oblation for its safety. So remarkable is this affection, that God has beautifully chosen it as the representation of His own love for man. He does not content Himself with saying to us, " I am your father," notwithstanding all the natural ties of affection the title suggests, but He compares Himself to a mother in His true love for us. He could not give us any image more complete to show the tenderness of His love for us, than by comparing Himself not to a father, but to a mother : " Can a mother forget the child of her womb ? And even if she should forget it, yet will I not forget thee." (Is. xlix. 15.)

Still, my brethren, perfect as is this love considered, as the highest and holiest of earthly affections, there must be, and there is, a love superior to it—far greater, far higher—a love divine. The mother must love God more than the infant, for which she is ready to sacrifice herself. No virtuous, no pious, no devout mother, but knows this, that rather must she lose her child than lose her God ; and it is difficult to realise the magnitude of this love that transcends the love of the mother for her child. There are times when, perhaps, in her heart she reproaches herself with not loving God, as she loves her babe. Even the

holiest mother will confess that there is more emotion and
sensitiveness, and more practical devotedness in the
mother's love for her child than in any other ; and that
willingly would she love God in the same way that she
loves the object of her maternal affections ; willingly
would she feel ready to do or to suffer as much for God
as she does for the little object of her tenderness. In
danger, therefore, is even this maternal love of being carried to excess, so intense is its nature. When the
moment of real trial comes ; when sickness strikes the
child ; when, like David, she prays and fasts for its life ;
when she offers herself in exchange that the child be
spared ; when the hour comes that she sees this little
dear one begin to pant, as its breath gradually passes
away, though she knows that the transition is only from
a life of darkness and prospective misery to one of deathless life and infinite happiness, still she regrets to part
with that child for her God, and for a short moment, perhaps, she repines and sorrows. If, after a few instants of
bursting grief, she begins to reflect well, what are the
humble words that come first to her lips ? " Oh ! I have
loved that child too deeply ; I made it too much the
idol of my affections, and God has taken it to Himself."
We see, then, my brethren, that this love of the mother,
however beautiful, however natural, however commended,
and again and again inculcated by the law of God, may
become a dangerous affection, inasmuch as it may know
no bounds, and possibly absorb all the divine love due to
the Creator and Giver of all things. This danger is
illustrative of the force and power of the mother's affection
for the child.

To only one being on earth—to only one of God's creatures has it ever been, or will ever be, granted that this love
could not be misplaced—could not become excessive.
For, by virtue of the maternity of Mary, she was constituted the Mother of God ; and there was no possible danger of her ever carrying the maternal affections, I will
not say into excess, but even to the nearest approach of
anything that was not pure and perfect, holy and most
acceptable.   The caresses she lavished upon her child she
lavished upon God.   Exercising the right of the mother,
she embraced her child, and it was God she embraced.
Every time she administered to Him the nourishment
which His infancy was pleased to require, she was giving
to the incarnate God a part of herself, bestowing upon
God a gift which no other being was entitled or permitted
to confer.   This union of the maternal love with the
divine love was indissoluble.   The two branches of
charity growing in her were so completely intertwined,
that no power on earth or in heaven could separate the
one from the other, or even for an instant disunite them ;
giving her, consequently, this singular prerogative, that,
taking the highest, the most pure and perfect standard
of human love, she was privileged to exercise it towards
her God, so that it was impossible by any effort of her
virginal heart to love too much, for she was loving God
with all the power of a mother's affection for her child,
and was at the same time, rendering the love which others
could only direct to the creature, to her Creator.

Surely, then, my brethren, we have here, referable to
the maternity of our dear and blessed lady, all that constitutes at once, in this earthly love of the mother for her

child, and divine love of the creature for her God, saintliness in its highest possible perfection.   What is the
standard of holiness ?   The love of God, the observance
of the first commandment: "love God above all things";
for those who thus love God, fulfil the law.   If, therefore, the love of God constitutes the very form and
substance of holiness, if to Mary was given the privilege
of loving with a fervour of love that could belong to no
other creature, if she could love her God with all that
intensity of affection the highest that earth can furnish
as the representation of the most complete and perfect
love, that of the mother for her child, which was her
relation to God ; she had consequently communicated to
her a character of love incommunicable even to blessed
spirits.   And it was this love of her God which raised
Mary to the height of holiness, and made her become the
most precious and the most beautiful of His saints.

Let us now dwell for a few moments upon the second
stage of the relations between the Blessed Virgin and her
Son, and see what character it bestows at once upon her,
different from that which belongs to any other person.
The gospel of this day, the words which I have chosen
from it for my text, give us at once a clue to this.   Our
Lord has grown into that period of life when a youth has
a will of his own which he may follow, and when he knows
full well his prerogatives.   But He lived in Nazareth, subject to His parents ; " He was subject to them."   You
understand, of course, what that must mean.   It follows
that from that time He obeyed any order given Him, in
that relation of parent and child.   It does not mean that
in greater or more important things He conformed to the

will of His mother and of Joseph, His reputed father.
The word "subject" signifies, as every one well knows, that
submission which is due from the child to the parent, from
the subject to his prince ; which characterizes the servant
in his bearing to him who rules over him.   It means the
habit of constant obedience, the observance of every behest,
the readiness in every time and every place at once to do
what is bidden ; it means the disposition of mind, and of
will, and of heart, to sacrifice a personal wish to the will of
another, to substitute another's will for one's own.   Such
is what we understand by these words ; and now let us see
what is the depth of their meaning.   Our Lord is living
familiarly at home, as other children might live with their
parents ; He works at a menial trade ; He is in that poor
household the attendant upon His mother.   He is not
called Rabbi, or Master, or Lord, as afterwards He was.
He is still known by the name of His infancy—by the
dear name which the angel communicated to Mary—by
that sweet name of Jesus,which was always upon the lips
of His mother and of Joseph. He is called, He is sent, He
is commanded, or, command being unnecessary, He is
desired to do whatever is needful for that little household.
As His reputed father advances in years, and is approaching to his end, the obligations assumed by the blessed
Youth, His industry, His submission, His labors only
increase.

I have asked already, what does this imply ?   Our
blessed Lord is God as well as man.   As God, His holy
will is none other than that of His eternal Father, with
whom His union is so complete, that it is impossible for
Him, in any way, to have any will in contradiction to

that of the Father. He cannot, however slightly or im-perceptibly, decline from the will of His Father; for it is His own. No authority, no jurisdiction, no command can possibly induce Him to depart in the smallest degree from that eternal will in which He is Himself partaker, and which is His own divine will, and in which there can never be otherwise than full and perfect identity, not con-formity, with the will of God. Now, my dear brethren, when our Lord obeys man, when He puts His will at the disposal of a creature, it cannot be except on the con-dition of complete certainty, that there will be in every command and in every desire that may be expressed to Him, a perfect uniformity with the will of God. It must be the same to Him to obey the will of Mary as to obey His divine Father ; for, if the two are at variance, He must disobey the creature. Not only must this fact of conformity between the commands of the one and the will of the other be such ; but it must have been to the knowledge of God a certainty, that it would be always such. The fact of declaring that Jesus was subject for eighteen years to that blessed mother, at once implies that He knew, during the eighteen years, as during the years that preceded, that there would be no discrepancy between the will of her and the will of His Father, with whom every act, every thought, every breath of His must be in necessary unison. Now, my brethren, we may desire to love God to the extent of our power. Man may seek to the utmost to do what pleases the Almighty ; and yet we know it is impossible for him, in this world of imperfec-tions and temptations, always to be sure that his will and his acts are in accordance with the will of God. On the

contrary, it is only after he has discovered the will of God
that he can truly say he has endeavoured to follow it. It
is a perpetual study, a constant care and anxiety with him,
that whatever he does be conformable to God's will. We
must endeavour, as it were, to move in the same line or
the same orbit, following exactly, step by step, Him from
whom alone we can learn and derive that power of conformity to His will in all things. The privilege and the
blessing of knowing that they thus conform to Him is
reserved for those blessed spirits, the souls of the just made
perfect, who live in God and in the eternal enjoyment of
His presence, who cannot for a moment change in their
devotion to Him, or in their state of perfect uniformity
with His will. This will be the happy lot of man
redeemed and saved, when the time of trial is gone by, and
when he can no longer follow his own earthly desires.
But to Mary, upon earth, was granted this high prerogative
of being in perfect conformity in her own actions to the
will of God. So complete was this identity of sentiment,
that the Son of God Himself was able to obey her with
the full certainty that every command of her's, that every
request of her's, would be in perfect and entire concord
with the will of His heavenly Father. And so every look
of Mary was but the reflection of the eye of God ; every
word that passed from her mouth was the echo of the
voice of God coming from His throne ; every command or
wish she expressed, every impulse and every suggestion
harmonized with His. Beloved brethren, what is the
condition necessary for love ? The desire of being in
perfect unity and harmony with the object of affection ;
and Mary can truly be said to have possessed entire union

of heart and soul with God, and not alone in love but in action and in word.

Is there yet a higher step which it is possible for a human creature to aspire to, for bringing himself or herself nearer still to God? There remains but one, and it is that higher love and uniformity with God's will, which naturally inspires the creature with a desire, if possible, to co-operate with the Creator; to be not merely a material instrument, but truly a sharer in His own work; to be chosen to act in His name, and to exercise power which, emanating from Him, is still so entrusted, that it may be used with the freedom that gives merit to its application. Do you not think that the angels in heaven who see the face of the Father, passing a blissful eternity in contemplation of Him, esteem it a distinction to be still further deputed to perform the will of God? Do you not believe that the guardian-angel, who is sent in charge of the least castaway amongst the children of men, the poor foundling that is left to perish, considers himself invested with a mission full of dignity, full of glory, because he is thereby doing the will of God, carrying out His purpose, the salvation of mankind; or that when an illustrious angel like Gabriel, Raphael, or Michael, receives a commission to bear some glad tidings to the world, or perform some great work of divine dispensation, he unfurls his wings with delight, leaves the immediate presence of God, which we imagine him locally to contemplate, but which never departs from him, and proceeds gladly, whether it be to Daniel to expound prophecy, or to Mary to bring the message of eternal love, considering it the highest honour to be thus enabled to assist in

carrying out the glorious, the magnificent designs of
God?   And what was the position of those great men of
the Old Law, commencing with Moses and proceeding
down to the Machabees, who were ordained to become the
chiefs of God's people, to whose guidance and care was
committed the carrying out of His great mercies, who
bore in their hands the rod of His omnipotence, who
carried in their breasts the secrets of His wisdom?   Were
they not honoured beyond all other men?   Did they not
consider it a glory to be thus entrusted with any great
mission of providential action?   There was too, my brethren, in all this some reward of honourable distinction
for those so engaged.   The angels thus employed are distinguished amongst the heavenly hosts, and have specific
names, recorded that we may single them out for devotion;
and those who were so honoured amongst the men of the
Old Law, were thereby raised above the rank of ordinary
prophets, and became the heroes, the great ones of the
earlier dispensation.

But to take part in the work of God silently, unknown,
without reward from mankind, at least during life, without those incentives which make men equal to a great and
high mission in the world, that was a merit reserved for
her, without whose co-operation it is hard to say in what
state mankind would have been.   God was pleased that
it should depend on her that the greatest of mysteries
should be accomplished.   He gives her time to deliberate;
He accords her permission to suggest difficulties, to make
her own terms, that she shall not have to surrender the
precious gift, which she values higher than the highest
imaginable of honours, so that it requires the assurance

that to God's omnipotence even the union of the two prerogatives is possible, and that attribute is to be exerted
for her. And so it was not until she had said "Behold the
handmaid of the Lord, be it done unto me according to
Thy word," that the great mystery was accomplished.

And now pause for a moment. Here is the greatest
of God's works, not since the creation of the world, but
during the countless ages of His own existence, the Word
incarnate, the Word made flesh. Yet how singular is
the part of Mary in'this mystery ! She utters the words;
they scarcely fall from her lips, and she alone remains
entrusted, not only with the precious gift itself, but with
the knowledge of it. No one else can have known it.
Joseph himself was not aware of it, till an angel revealed
it to him. Allow me now for an instant to deviate from
the line which I was pursuing. I have addressed you as
good and faithful Catholics, believing what the Church
teaches you, and also as servants of Mary, feeling true
devotion towards her ; but I beg here to make a remark
which may, perhaps, be useful in conversing with others.
Look at those men who, unhappily for themselves, know
not, and understand not, the prerogatives of Mary; look,
I will not say, at those more wretched men who have the
hardihood, the unfeelingness, the brutality, to decry her,
but to those who, in more respectful terms, profess simply
to overlook her. Just see the position in which such
persons are placed, as to their belief. They say, "we
cannot worship," as they call it, "the Virgin Mary ; we
cannot honour her, because in doing so we should be de-
rogating from the honour due to her Son, to the Word
incarnate, to Jesus Christ." I would say to these men:

z

How do you know that He was incarnate? How do you know that the Son of God became man? You say in your creed that He was conceived of the Holy Ghost. Who gave you evidence of that conception? Gabriel did not manifest it. He vanished as soon as he had delivered his message. You do not believe, no Protestant believes, that the Bible is a simple *revelation;* that is, a series of truths not known, and which could not be known by human means. The Evangelists themselves—the one from whom I have quoted—tells us that " Mary laid up all these words in her heart," and that he sought information from those who knew everything from the beginning. Mary was the only, the sole witness in the world, to the mystery of the incarnation. There was only her word that she conceived thus miraculously of the Holy Ghost. She told it to the Apostles, and they believed it, and recorded it with the sanction of the Holy Spirit. The real source of the historical and inspired testimony of the accomplishment of the great mystery of the incarnation is Mary; and those who reject her could not have come to believe, except through her testimony, that God took upon Him our nature. It is through her that they know it; yet they pretend that honour to her is at His expense. But as it was with her co-operation that this great mystery was wrought, so was it right that through her it should be communicated.

The time at length came for the awful completion of that eternal mystery of our redemption, which was to astonish angels and men. There was one heart in which all that was to come was faithfully treasured—her's who had listened to the wonderful and mysterious words of the venerable old man that told her, in the days of her motherly happiness, that the sword of affliction would pierce her heart. Oh ! she had often, no doubt, conversed on the painful topic with her Divine Son. She knew too well what was the course He had to run. She knew wherefore He had come into the world, and how every breath of His was an act of obedience to the will of God. She knew well that He had bitter food, indeed, to take, which was not prepared for Him by her hands. She had lived, by anticipation, in the suffering which naturally resulted from this knowledge communicated to her; and she well knew the time was come when, at the last passover with His disciples, He was about to cast aside this world, and enter into the kingdom of His Father. Then did she know that another cup, besides that of His paschal feast, was to be placed in His hands, to be drained by Him to the dregs. She knew that well—so well that it is hardly necessary even to have recourse to the pious tradition, that she saw in a vision what passed in the garden of Gethsemani. But certain it is, that the morning dawn saw her hasten to her Son, in order to carry out that conformity which she had preserved with the will of God during the whole of her life ; that conformity which had been so great, that her Son, in obedience to her will, anticipated the time for the performance of His first miracle. It was right that this conformity should at length be transmuted into a perfect unity, incapable of the slightest separation ; and that could only be done, as it was accomplished, on Calvary at the foot of the cross.

My dear brethren, why was Mary there ? That simple question in its answer solves a great problem. Why was

Mary there? It was no part of the sentence on Jesus, as
if to increase or to enhance the bitterness of His death,
that His Mother should stand by; and it never was commanded in any nation, however barbarous, that the mother
should be at the scaffold when her son expiated what was,
rightly or wrongly, imputed to him as his guilt. It was
not compulsory on Mary to be at Calvary ; she was not
driven there, nor was it usual in her to seek publicity.
She had followed Him, indeed, through all His mission in
Judea ; but she used to stand without, and the people
who surrounded Him would say, " Your mother and
brethren are outside." She did not claim the privileges
of her rank to be close to Him when he was disputing
with the Pharisees, or instructing multitudes. When He
went into a house to perform His miracles, or to a mountain to be transfigured, He took Peter, James, and John.
We read not that Mary presumed to follow Him, and
exult in the magnificent exercise of His divine power, or
the manifestation of His heavenly glory. No, she followed
at a distance ; she kept near Jesus, watching over Him.
But she knew that it was not her hour ; that it was not
yet the time when her parental duty was to be associated
with her parental rights. She had lived the whole of her
life in retirement, first in the Temple, then in the
cottage at Nazareth. And she, who naturally shrunk
from the assemblies of men, came forth at the time most
trying to her feelings, to be present at the execution, the
brutal execution of her Son, in that form of suffering
which was most revolting, and most fiercely rending of
her tender heart. Mary came forth to witness the death
—of whom ? Of her only beloved Son, of her only child,

whom she remembered once an infant in her arms. She will draw nigh to see those hands cruelly pierced, which she had so often pressed to her lips ; she will stand by to see that noble, that divine countenance—the first look from whose eyes beamed upon her, the first smile of whose lips shone upon her heart—bedewed with blood, streaming from the thorny crown ; to see Him still bearing the marks of having been beaten, and buffetted, and defiled by spittle, and mocked by His persecutors. She came to seek Him at the hour of this suffering. And why ? Because the heart of the Mother must be near that of the Son, in order that they may be both struck together, and so endure most perfect union of suffering, that she may be said truly to co-operate, in sympathy, with the divine work of salvation.

Suppose, my brethren, you have two masses of un-alloyed gold. Let the one be heavier than the other, of incomparably greater value, more beautiful in its colour, more pure in its substance, and in every way more precious from a thousand associations. Let the other be also indeed of great price, though very inferior to it. What will you do that they may become only one ? Cast them into the same crucible, heat them in the same furnace, and they will melt into one, so that you may not separate them again. What a furnace of affliction, what a crucible of torture and of anguish was that, in which the two hearts of Jesus and Mary were fused in that hour on Calvary ! and could it have been possible that there should arise a difference of thought, of feeling, even of desire between the two ? could it have been possible to unravel them, having lost every other thought, every other idea, in the predominant one of accomplishing the great sacrifice which God had appointed for the salvation of man ?

As musical chords, when in perfect harmony, will so sympathise, that if the one is struck its vibrations will be communicated to the other, and agitate it in strict accord, so did the fibres of those two most blessed hearts, agreeing so justly in tone, utter the same sweet strain of patient love ; and every pang and throb of one was faithfully repeated in the other.

Then this conformity went further still. In that most solemn hour Jesus formally recognized Mary as His Mother, as He proclaimed God to be His Father. What could she aspire to but imitation, however imperfect, of what the Heavenly Father was accomplishing in His well-beloved Son ? Then, as she knew that the Eternal Father was surrendering Him to sacrifice and to death out of love for man, could she do less than surrender Him too ? And she is come hither for this very purpose. Therefore does she stand at the foot of the cross, that for lost man she may make a public and willing sacrifice of all that is dear to her on earth. Only she, His Mother, can thus put herself into strict uniformity with His Almighty Father. As she accepted Him at His incarnation, she yielded Him at His death, saying : "The Lord giveth and the Lord taketh away ; blessed and fully accomplished ever be the will of God." Yes, although it may wring her maternal bosom, and drive the sword of affliction deep into her loving heart, even to its inmost core. Thus it is she became a co-operator, as far as possible, with God in His great work ; she became the priestess on the part of all mankind, who was allowed to accomplish the holocaust, which was considered too difficult and painful for Father Abraham, the sacrifice of a beloved child. While we know that Jesus Christ is alone the high-priest and the victim to His Father, we do not derogate from the infinite majesty, efficacy, and sublimity of the oblation of the Lamb upon our altars, by believing that He permits us, His unworthy priests, to be in a certain degree, His coadjutors in the work, not in any way increasing its efficacy by aught that we can do, but still, standing as it were at His side, His ministers, soliciting and producing the divine action, without which nothing that we can do would take effect. In some such manner it may be said that Mary, loving God as no other creature over loved Him, loving in uniformity with His divine will, in a way never granted to any other being on earth, at length reached that which must be the very consummation of the desire of love, that of acting, working, and suffering with God ; taking part, so far as human infirmity can do, in the accomplishment of His sublime and glorious work of redemption.

My brethren, I am sure that many of your hearts have been suggesting, that this maternity of Mary extends beyond one dear Son ; and you ask, are not we her children ? Do we not commemorate this day her kind, affectionate, and efficacious relationship with us of a mother to her children ? I need not tell you that, when the two sacred hearts of Jesus and Mary were so melted together in affliction as that they could not be separated, that was the hour in which the fully-recognised brotherhood between Jesus and us was established. The relationship which

commenced with the incarnation, caused us to become **His**
brothers truly, and Mary consequently to become **our**
mother ; but His parched and quivering lips, just before
He uttered His last cry upon the cross, proclaimed this
kindred, and bade her receive from John his love as from
a child, and John to receive her's as of a mother. We accept these words in their fullest sense. We take our place
willingly with the beloved disciple without fear of being
rejected, and gladly send up our prayers to Mary for intercession, as our mother sitting on her throne in heaven.
We cannot place her in the ranks of other saints who are
partaking of bliss with Him.   There are amongst them,
no doubt, those to whom we owe special devotion, those
who are the patrons of our country, those who planted and
defended its faith, who were celebrated for having
honoured it, and, still more, blessed it.   There are also
there our guardian angels, with the mighty host of blessed
spirits that we know to be ministering before the throne
of God.   Yet, not with the honour that we pay, or the
prayers which we address, to any of this glorious array of
saints and angels, can we classify the deeper devotion, the
more fervent supplications, still less the filial duty which
we owe the Mother of God.   We speak to them as saints,
as faithful servants of the Lord, as our friends who have
preceded us to glory, and can assist us there ; but to none
can we use the words which we can apply to Mary ; to
none can we speak as a child to its mother; with none
other can we establish our claim to the patronage, care,
and love, which, as children of a common mother, every
day and every night, we are at liberty to demand from
Mary. Even as Solomon, when his mother was announced,

rose and bowed to her, and placed her at his right hand
on a throne before all others, so is Mary placed between
the heavenly host and her Son. And so when we think of
her, we may lift our minds and thoughts to her as to one
adorning heaven, its second brilliant luminary, shining
next to its Sun and above the highest rank of the blessed
hosts. And why ? Because she is the Mother of God.
Her maternity has bestowed upon her that which, after all,
is the completion of her love. Her love is perfect, her
conformity is rendered eternal, and her co-operation with
Jesus perennial, in the constant flow of her kindness to
us, in her perpetual representing of our wants to her
Divine Son, in her faithful intercession for us all, con-
sistently with her singular prerogative as the Mother of
God. Then, beloved brethren, relax not in your affection
to her.

Mind not more than you do the winds that fly
past you, words which you may hear in disparagement of
this most beautiful devotion, as if the worship of our
Divine Lord suffered from devotion to her. Pray frequently to her in your necessities, in your wants, in your
trials, personal or domestic, and feel sure that she will
attend to your petitions. Be assured that the link which
bound Him to her on earth, and continues to unite Him
to her in heaven, also binds us to her ; so that in Jesus
and Mary we may place our confidence, and our hope, in
the end, of eternal bliss.

PASTORALS ON DEVOTION

TO

The Sacred Heart of Jesus Christ,

IN CONNECTION WITH EDUCATION:

No. I.

On the Sacred Heart.

AN established usage requires us to solicit your charity, for the education of our poor; and we hardly know how we could more effectually appeal to it, than through those motives which the festival whereon we address you, especially presents us, in the inexhaustible charity that is centred in the Sacred Heart of Jesus.

This festival forms the close of that series which, commencing with Christmas, has crowded into less than half the year, the commemoration of our dear Lord's life, death, and glory. And how appropriately! We saw Him born into the world of sin, which He came to redeem, and in every circumstance which preceded, accompanied, or followed that wonderful advent, we read additional proofs of the love which caused it. Then

shortly, almost suddenly, we found ourselves hurried into
the midst of sorrowful scenes, where agony instead of
smiles, blows in place of maternal caresses, a cross for a
cradle, gall and vinegar instead of virginal milk, eyes
closed in death instead of their first radiant opening to
life, gave evidence of the same love, to the same man,
from the same Incarnate God.   And even death changed
into life once more, and ignominy into honour, and earth
exchanged for heaven, with man's welfare for sole motive,
were only additional demonstrations of the same divine
charity for us.   After passing through this course of
festivals, which followed our blessed Saviour to heaven,
and thence received from Him His holy Spirit, we
gathered together once more to feast upon the inheritance
which He had left behind.   It was a banquet spread with
every deliciousness, filled to overflowing with every grace;
there was the Bread of Life, the Manna of Angels' Lord :
there was the Cup of salvation; the Wine which cheereth
the heart of man ; there was the concealed Divinity of
Bethlehem, there the real sacrifice of Calvary, there the
same glorified Flesh which rose, ascended, and sits at the
right hand of God.   All the mysteries by which we were
ransomed, saved, and brought to Him, were there united
in wonderful truth and living reality.

What love for man ! What tenderness of charity !
what unselfish devotion to his interests !   May we not
seek out its source ?   Shall we not drink there to the
full, drawing water with joy, from the fountains of our
Saviour? (Isai. xiii. 3.)   How inexhaustible must be its
supply of mercy and grace !   Where, then, dearly beloved in Christ, is it to be found ?   It is the Heart of

Jesus, that contains, and sends forth perenially, this rich abundance ; filling the pure vessel itself with sweetness, and thence flowing in an unfailing stream, stronger than the torrent of Cedron, (2 Chron. xxx. 14) brighter than the rivers of Damascus ; (4 Reg. v. 12) more cleansing than the waters of Siloe, (Jo. ix. 7) and holier than the stream of Jordan. (Mar. i. 9.) To come not only to see, but to taste also, how sweet is the Lord, we are invited by Himself: (Ps. xxxiii. 9) and we will draw nigh with Thomas, not unbelieving, nor doubting, but full of faith, of confidence, and of love, and, instead of touching with our hands the open floodgate whence flowed this inundation of tenderness, we will reverently drink of it, till our souls are filled.

For, what tongue can describe the treasures which issue thence, to enrich our poverty, as well as to slake our thirst ? One only, dearly beloved children ; His, who has given us the measure whereby the depths of His own Heart can be fathomed, and its various gifts duly valued. When He said to us, that, " out of the abundance of the Heart the mouth speaketh," (Mat. xii. 34) He at once suggested to us, how we may judge of the emotions and impulses of His own blessed Heart. In Him there was no deceit, no double heart ; (Ps. xi. 3, in corde et corde locuti sunt. Eccli. i. 36, duplici corde) but all was sincere and plain, and just in Him. Then out of His Heart He uttered His words ; (Job viii. 10, loquuntur de corde) and they are but the overflow of the abundance treasured there. From His sacred lips you descend to His blessed Heart : and you cannot be deceived.

Then, when He first appears on earth, He speaks those few but pregnant words, "Behold, I come." (Ps. xxxix. 7 ; Heb. x. 7, 9.) They were the utterance, not of the lips, but of the heart: they were expressed by the first breath that passed inarticulate from His humanity, un- heard even by the attentive ear of Mary, which conveyed thus early to her immaculate heart whatever proceeded from His. (Luc. ii. 19, 51.) To the world which hates me, those words say, to a people that knows me not, to a generation obstinate and hardhearted ; to earth reeking with sin detestable to me, to creation perverted from all its beautiful ends and enslaved to the devil ; to a barren desert compared with my Paradise above ; to a dismal land overspread with the darkness of sin and the shadow of death ; to direst poverty, distress, cold, hunger, and toil ; to contradiction, ingratitude, scorn, and calumny ; to disappointment, abandonment, treachery, and denial ; to ignominy, pain, anguish, and agony ; to buffets, scourges, to the cross, and death—O man ! for *thy* sake, "behold I come." Willingly, deliberately, lovingly, the words are breathed from that infant Heart, the first incense rising from that living temple of divinest charity. And must not that Heart have needs been full of mercy, full of pity, and full of kindness, to have given them utterance ? Good measure, indeed, and well pressed down, shaken together, and running over, was that cha- rity which, in His very incarnation, was poured into His bosom. (Luc. vi. 38.) Those words began that overflow, which ceased no more ; but, like the waters of Jerusalem, which, issuing from the upper fountain, gathered to them- selves, as they passed, those of the lower one, and so ran

on, still increasing, till they became almost a torrent; so
do these thoughts of charity take up in their course so
many others, spoken at every step of our dear Redeemer's
life on earth, till we are overpowered by their strength.

Whence proceeded those words of compassion, in which
we all have such a part; "I have come to call not the
just, but sinners to repentance ; I am sent to the sheep
that have perished of the house of Israel ; there is more
joy in heaven for one sinner that doth penance, than for
ninety-nine just that need not penance"? (Mat. ix. 13 ;
x. 6 ; Luc. xv. 7.) From what source came forth the
words which He spoke to Zaccheus or to Matthew, the
publicans, to the sinful woman brought before Him for
judgment, to the paralytic sinner laid at His feet, to
Magdalene of her own accord prostrate there : words of
gracious self-invitation, or of a generous call to apostleship ; words of kind forgiveness of past sin, and encouragement to persevere in grace ; words of most tender
and soothing pardon, full of charity, that filled even a
Pharisee's house with a sweeter savour of that unknown
virtue, than did the broken alabaster-box of spikenard ?
(Luc. xix. 5 ; Mat. ix. 9 ; Jo. viii. 11 ; Mat. ix. 2 :
Luc. vii. 48.) Whence ? do you ask ? It was from that
same gentle and loving Heart, which, pure and holy
itself, had ample space enough in it to hold and embrace
there, even sinners, and the whole world of sin ?

From what source came out those wonderful words of
pleading, " Father, forgive them, for they know not what
they do ;" or that sweetest of forgiving reproofs, " Dost
thou betray the Son of man with a kiss ;" or that mildest
of just expostulations, " Many good works I have done ;

for which of these works do you stone me?" or that
sweetest of rebukes, "if [I have spoken] well, why dost
thou strike me?" or that almost maternal consolation,
"weep not over me, ye daughters of Jerusalem, but over
yourselves and over your children;" or in fine, the eloquence of that silence, which went to the heart more than
words, as He stood before the priests or Pilate; and the
mute power of that look which spoke to the heart of
Peter and made it overflow in tears? (Luc. xxiii. 24;
xxii. 48; Jo. x. 32; xviii. 32; Luc. xxiii. 28; Mat.
xxvi. 23; xxvii. 14; Luc. xxii. 61.)   Whence? do you
ask again?   Oh no!   Your own hearts tell you, better
than our words can do; that all these and many other
such words came surging forth from, not a well-spring,
but an ocean, of love for man; for man the worthless, for
man the reprobate, that lies deep and wide, and ever
heaving in that most amiable Heart of Jesus.   What an
abundance, indeed, and a superabundance of charity was
required, to give truth and reality of feeling to such
words, so spoken as they were!

And whence, again, dearly beloved children in Christ,
come such words as are constantly escaping those gentle
lips, for the encouragement and consolation of loving
souls: "Come to me, all you that labour and are heavy
laden, and I will refresh you;" as though His own tra-
vails and burthens, the cross being one, were not enough
for Him: or "Learn of me, because I am meek and
humble of heart, and you shall find rest in your souls;"
as if persecution and humiliation gave Him joy, because
they procured us peace: or "I am the good shepherd, I
know my sheep and my sheep know me;" (Mat. xi. 28,

29 ; Jo. x. 14) as if forgetting that we have "all wandered as sheep," (Isa. liii. 6 ; Ps. cxviii. 176) and have forgotten to follow Him our Shepherd ; or "Cannot you drink of the cup whereof I shall drink," (Mar. x. 38) making our little sorrows comparable, and associated, to His own ? Oh! what unselfish tenderness, what mild considerateness for our weakness, our discouragements, our continual imperfection! And whence come these kindly feelings, this unpretending love, that asks no return but our own souls' salvation and happiness? From nothing ever created on earth, save Thy benign Heart, O Saviour of man, glowing furnace of charity, sending forth not sparks merely to enkindle ours, so cold beside Thine, but a calm stream of heat and light, to warm them throughout, and make them beam with celestial joy. Who will repine, should bitterness fill his heart, if only some drops of the balm, into which gall itself is changed in Thine, overflow to mingle with it ? Who will care for calumny, reproach, or persecution, so long as within hearing of the Master, who will not have His scholars, in this respect, better than Himself, but cheers their hearts, if they follow Him in meekness, with the sounds of joy that break forth from His ?

But listen now to other words which come from that divine breast, on which reposes a witness that will not let one of them escape. Time will not permit us to quote them ; for they compose the whole of that unrivalled address, and that sublime prayer, which closed our Lord's ministry on earth, before His passion. What pure and unalloyed love, soft and tender enough to move a heart of stone, comes flowing forth from that blessed mouth !

2 A

Not an allusion to an enemy, but in accents of unresent-
ing kindness ; not a thought for self, in the anxious care
for those whom His Father has given Him. What a wide
and distant aim of love, beyond His Apostles, to us, and
all who should in future ages, and remote regions, come to
know Him!   What close and eternal, and mysterious
compacts of love are established between the believing soul
and Himself;   and through Him what privileges of
familiarity bestowed even with the unseen, but no longer
the unknown, Father! What riches of light and guidance
secured from the all-wise Spirit, for erring, ignorant man !
What omnipotence of prayer bestowed upon the feeblest of
creatures, with the very key of God's treasures put into
his hands !   And then the new commandment, the very
charter of His new covenant with man, delivered, and
what is it ?   Love ; " that you love one another, as I have
loved you." (John xiii. 34.) And with these first words
begins that divine discourse, throughout which burns an
ardour of love for man, the more intense, that it is the
more calm, and the more serene.   Peace to the heart of
man, amidst the storms that shake it ; peace to his soul in
spite of the passions that assail it ; peace to the Church,
upon the ocean-world that tries its utmost to wreck it ;
peace to His people in the midst of the war which Satan
wages perpetually against it : such is the great gift which
this love bequeaths. And whence alone can it come?
Throughout every sentence of that heavenly discourse, to
which angels must have listened with wondering love,
there are diffused a charity and a peace, such as nowhere
else ever existed, so combined, except in the adorable Heart
of the Incarnate Word.   It was, indeed, the purest over-

flow of that Heart, which ever yet had found its way to earth. Gushing forth its streams had ever been ; incessant its supply of refreshment to the soul; but it would seem as though, now that the end was approaching, He found it still so full of its rich and sweet abundance, that He must needs open its very floodgates, and pour it out, in one unchecked volume of burning words over our hearts, our souls, our lives ; over the Church, and over the entire world itself. Charity and peace, the union of God with man, and of man with His God, the brotherhood of Jesus with us, the bond of love between God and His Spouse on earth ; these are the gifts which the lips of our divine Master drew forth unsparingly from the treasury of His Heart on that memorable night, and embodied in that matchless discourse, sealed by a prayer such as only God could utter to God, which has done more to raise man's dignity, and ennoble his being and his thoughts, than all the treatises of ancient philosophy, or the efforts of modern civilization.

And yet what was all this sublime teaching of love, but merely the adornment of something more admirable still, and more sublime ; of something done as well as spoken ? It was at the same time, and at the same table, that Jesus took bread, and broke it, saying : " This is my Body ;" took the cup and blessed it, saying " This is my Blood." The Heart of Jesus has given us love, has given us peace: and in these words It gives us Itself. It was that Heart's delight to be with the children of men ; (Prov. viii. 21) and thus it gained its object, to our infinite gain. What abundance of divine attributes were not required there, to prompt, and to pronounce efficaciously these words !

Unbounded wisdom to devise such a mode of uniting man
to God, his Saviour ; unfailing foresight to know that such
an Institution, if made, would form the very life of the
spiritual world, in the midst of man's corruption ; unerring
prudence, to temper in it so perfectly the seen with the
unseen, as to fill the soul with the reality, and save to
faith its merit ; unlimited knowledge of man, his nature,
his wants, his feelings, his frailties, his dangers, his
powers, his wishes, such as only belongs to the Creator,
and the Searcher of the reins and heart, to adapt it exactly
to every possible desire of his spirit, and every imaginable
craving of his weakness ; almighty power to put nature in
perpetual bondage to grace, so that to the end of time a
marvellous combination of supernatural effects should take
place, in obedience to a continuous law, without disturbing
or ruffling the visible current of natural things ; supreme
dominion to communicate and delegate to man the exercise
of this very act of omnipotence ; and above all, consummate and incomprehensible goodness and love, to set all
the rest of these divine attributes in motion, and bind
them in one harmonious action :—such was the abundance
of the Heart from which alone the mouth of Jesus could
have spoken those words of life.

To them we owe the best and sweetest privilege of love,
that of being able to draw grace and life from their very
source, by receiving Him within us, who contains it in
Himself. There the heart of man reposes upon the Heart
of his Redeemer, not outwardly as John's did, but in closer
and even holier union, when his frail and perishable body
becomes the Temple of God, the Tabernacle of his Lord,
the abode, however humble, of his Saviour. Thence his

very body sucks in immortality, from that imperishable
Body which could not see corruption; there his soul feasts
spiritually upon the virtues and excellences which adorn
the Soul of God made man ; and there, more wonderful
still, his whole being becomes invested with the dignity
and glory of the Divinity, which dwells within him, and
bestows on him rights and privileges, that have their final
fulfilment and possession in heaven. How truly, indeed,
may it be said of man, that " God entertaineth his heart
with delight "!

O rich abundance of the Heart of Jesus, whence all
these good things issue, through His unfailing words !
Who will refuse to love Thee, and to adore Thee, O blessed
Saviour ! Who will not own that in that blessed Heart
of Thine, are centred all the manifold forms of Thy love
for man, from Thy cradle to Thy cross ? And if in Thy
sacred Word, even the heart of man receives praise from
God, for good qualities amidst its shocking corruption, how
much more must all these be found in Thine, sinless, and
untainted by the contact of evil ! Thy heart, then, is
perfect, (Jos. xxiv. 14 ; 4 Reg. xx. 3 ; Is. xxxviii. 3) one
and undivided, (1 Reg. xii. 20; Ps. cxviii. 2; Jer. xxix. 30)
simple, (2 Reg. xv. 11 ; Job, xxxiii. 3) right before God,
(Ps. xxxv. 11 ; lxxii. 1 ; Prov. xxvii. 21) strong ;
(Ps. cxi. 8) it is wise, (Eccles. viii. 5 ; Eccli. iii. 32)
prudent, (Prov. xviii. 15) intelligent, (Deut. xxix. 4)
watchful, (Cant. v. 2 ; Eccli. xxxix. 6) profound; (Prov.
xx. 5 ; Ps. lxiii. 7), it is great (2 Mac. ix. 14) and wide
as the sands of the sea ; (Ps. cxviii. 52 ; Eccli. iv. 29;
Cordis latitudinem quasi arenam) it is clean, (Ps. xxiii.
4 ; Mat. v. 8) innocent, (Ps. lxxvii. 72 ; c. 2) pure,

(1 Tim. i. 5) spotless, (Ps. cxviii. 80) splendid, good, (Eccli. xxxix. 6, Cor splendidum et bonum) holy, (Dan. iii. 87) burning, (Jer. xx. 9 ; Luc. xxiv. 32) inflamed ; (Ps. lxxii. 21) it is humble, contrite, (Ps. 1. 19 ; cviii. 17) ready, (Ps. lvi. 8 ; cxi. 7) joyful, (Prov. xv. 13) mourning, (Lam. i. 22) constant, (1 Mac. ix. 14) mild ! (Mat. xi. 29.)

But enough, dearly beloved, of this inexhaustible theme : let us come to ourselves. If the Heart of Jesus has been thus good to us, if we have tasted its sweetness in so many ways, in compassion, in forgiveness, in liberality, in kindness, in forbearance, in patience with us, shall we refuse to requite It, by some mercifulness, generosity and charity on our side? Let our hearts be tender, too, and loving, and full of affection to others. And to whom more than to those whom the Heart of Jesus particularly loved on earth, and recommended to our care ?   His little ones, He will tell you, are starving, are naked, are pining with distress, of the spirit more than of the body ; and in honour of His adorable Heart, He claims from you relief and succour for them.   Honour Him thus, and you will honour Him worthily, for you will honour Him by imitation.

No. II.

On the Mysteries of the Sacred Heart.

IT has been most becomingly appointed that the general collection, on behalf of the Poor School Committee, should be made on the Feast of the most Sacred Heart of Jesus. And this selection has been confirmed by the authoritative and paternal sanction of our Sovereign Pontiff, who has granted for that day the Indulgences announced to you on Sunday last.

And in truth, dearly beloved in Christ, what could be a more appropriate day for a general, a combined, a Catholic act of spiritual mercy and charity, than that on which the Church sums up and symbolizes in the Heart of Jesus, all that He has done and suffered for the salvation of souls ? This, indeed, is the purpose and the feeling of this festival, lately conceded to us in this country.

Whatever the teaching of science may be, it will never divest mankind of the idea, or the instinct, that the heart is connected with our inward affections ; that it is warm in the kind and loving, and cold in the selfish and un-generous ; that it is hard in the oppressor, fluttering in the anxious, faint in the cowardly, calm in the virtuous. To speak of the heart is to speak of the passions, the emotions, the sympathies of man : it embodies our ideas of tenderness, of compassion, of gentleness, of forgiveness, of long-suffering, and of every sweet variety of love. For there the child, the parent, the spouse, the friend finds his specific kind of holy affection. It is the well-spring whence they all gush out, and manifest themselves in action and in word : " for out of the abundance of the heart the mouth speaketh." (Matt. xii. 24.)   And if that abundance is to be measured by that which flows abroad, what shall we find of treasured bounty, mercy, grace, and love in the Sacred Heart of Him, whose love redeemed us, and continues to enrich us with gifts of eternal value ? Who shall presume to fathom or to measure this abyss of love ?   Who shall "be able to comprehend, what is the breadth, and length, and height and depth" of this " charity of Christ, which surpasseth all knowledge?" (Ephes. iii. 18, 19.)   So soon as the Word Incarnate appeared on earth, that blessed Heart began to beat in love, and gave at every pulse a homage to God, more valuable and more acceptable than that of the celestial spheres, moving in their order and beauty.   And all this was given up at once to man.   To whatever manifestation of Godlike and Divine excellence It impelled Him, whether to mighty works, or to lowly disguises, whether to glorious triumphs, or to abject suffering, all, all was for us ; ever varying, ever inexhaustible, ever unthought of, workings of that one principle of love : fruit of every sweetness springing from one Tree of Life.

Through the now closing cycle of our annual festivals, we have contemplated the love of Jesus for man, step by step, and form by form.   First it was shrouded in the charms, and almost the blandishments, of infancy; it was winning, it was enticing; it was softening ; but seemed almost inactive.   We contemplated Him as fair, gentle, amiable ; His infant glance, His speechless lips, His

helpless frame appealed with a natural eloquence to our
hearts, when we remembered that, inert as they appeared
in our regard, they were in Him, but a disguise that
covered a boundless love for man.

Then we approached Him, as He trod the path of
labour, pain, and sorrow : we saw hands hardened with
toil, and brow bedewed with the sweat of Adam's curse ;
a frame attenuated with long fasting in a desert, feet
wearied with rough travel, a head unrested by a pillow,
unsheltered by a roof. Then came before us a scene of
suffering more systematic, more universal, more intense :
when pain and torture were not consequences of actions
and journeyings and privations, undertaken or borne for
love : but were direct inflictions coveted and loved on its
account. Here we saw anguish and agony, and the
rending of every tie of life, strong or tender, of that
which breaks only with excruciating violence, as of that
which easily snaps, but with exquisite torture ; filial love,
brotherly affection, fatherly tenderness all rudely torn in
His bosom; and the bonds of gratitude, reverence, almost
adoration of a fickle people sundered from His still loving
Heart. And in His body we contemplated the head
crowned with thorns, the hands and feet transfixed, the
body gashed and livid with lashes, every limb quivering
with convulsion.

At length we came to see Him burst through His
rocky sepulchre, radiant with splendour; dart like a heavenly meteor from place to place, penetrate the closed
doors, cheer and console His disciples : and then ascend
to His Father's Right Hand, amidst angelic greetings.
And last of all we meet Him, now as then, in the won-

derful Mystery of Love, in which all the marvels of love
displayed in His Life are concentrated; from the lowliness of the Infant, to the immolation of the Victim, and
the glorification of Humanity—in the Eucharist, ever
blessed, ever adorable.

And while we follow Him thus, as a giant, exultant
through His career of love, all that is external and
visible, changing, and shifting forms; what gives to the
whole unity, and identity; what brings Him before us as
the same yesterday and to-day; where resides the un-
changing principle of all these phases of His existence in
our lower firmament? One Heart, unchangeable within
that kingly abode, continued from its first beat, to throb
with unvarying charity, sweet yet strong, gentle yet irresistible. It gave equal life, vigour and intensity to every
stage and state of His being. It beat as steadily in the
Child as in the Man; in the Manger as on the Cross,
when Mary felt It gently knock against her own Heart,
as when John leaning on His bosom felt Its throes of life,
at His last feast. It is this that binds together the
various aspects of His human form; the infant's radiant
eye, the youth's toiling hand, the Master's winning lips,
the Holocaust's wreathed head. To each in its turn the
Heart sent forth its streams of life, with Him but streams
of Love. And to each function of charity It administered
its fitting agent: from that Heart were furnished those
tears wherewith He wept over the unrepenting; that
mysterious dew which started from His pores as He lay
prostrate in Gethsemani; that full flow of sacred Blood,
which poured out from the four great wounds on Calvary;
that mystical stream of regeneration which issued from

His blessed side, pierced by the lance. And His death even, what was it, but the very breaking and bursting of the sacred vessel itself, that not one drop of its divine treasure might be withheld from man ?

Then, assuredly, in that Heart we may see collected, and presented, as in one holy symbol, the immensity of the love of Jesus for us ; and sum up in this one festival —the epilogue of our fuller commemorations—all that He hath suffered and done for us poor sinners, that we might be saved. For here, as in·a mirror which concentrates the rays from every side, we look upon all united in a smaller space, though not for that less clear and bright. Or we may consider it as a deep and fathomless gulf of pure and stillest water, which, while it is in its depths unsearchable, yet reflects for that more accurately all that has grown, from its fertilizing power, around it. And in either, he who gazes shall not fail there to see himself, as the first and clearest object. Yes, there he truly is, in the very Heart of Jesus ! From whatever side any of us looks into it, in the midst of its sweetnesses, its mercies, its pangs, its agonies,—he beholds himself present ; ever there, thought of, cared for, loved so tenderly and so prominently as to be the first seen ! Then, who will not love and adore that Sacred Heart, so full of us, so rich for us ! Fountain of redemption, source of salvation, spring of life, abyss of love ! Heart so pure, so sinless, so holy ; so gentle, so meek, and so benign ; so sparing, so merciful, so gracious ; so tender, so loving, so en-dearing; so noble, so generous, so magnificent; so royal, so heavenly, so divine ! Seat and throne of every virtue, of every excellent quality, of every sublimest

attribute!　All hail! in this our festival of charity, be
to us and to our little ones, a shield, a shelter and a
home!

For, dearly beloved in Christ Jesus, where could we
have found a truer model, or a higher principle, on which to
frame and conduct the education of our children, than this
all-holy and most innocent Heart, which, from childhood
upwards, ever throbbed in love to God and man? Who
would not rejoice to see these little ones grow up, each to
be "a man according to God's own Heart"? And what is
Catholic education, but a striving after this moulding of
the yet tender and pliant heart to this heavenly form?
What surer pledge of future virtue could you desire, than
to see the pupils of your schools trained in that higher
school of love, whereof the Sacred Heart of Jesus is the
type; in the docility and meekness, the obedience and
industry, the piety and innocence which it represents?

Take heart then, this day, and give as you wish God to
requite you. How powerful, how efficacious, will the
prayers of so many thousands of Christ's favourites be,
warmly sent up for you! How sweet the offering of their
holy communion! How, if we may so speak, the Lamb
of God will love to see Himself led by the innocent and
guileless, with the garlands of simple affection which they
throw about Him, to the very foot of the Throne, round
which the martyred children of Bethlehem play; (Hymn
for H. Innocents) and there with unspotted hands, beg
acceptance of Him, for you their benefactors! The
Church, too, unlocks the treasury which she keeps in that
ever inexhaustible Heart, and offers you her spiritual gifts,
as your future pledge and present reward. Make then

this day doubly holy, doubly consecrated.   Honour with devotion the Sacred Heart of Jesus; imitate in charity the love which It bore you.   Charity for man is the special characteristic virtue of the feast, spiritual charity ; love for man, but love for his soul.   And, be assured, that as you cannot better practise this, than by exerting yourselves, and making sacrifices, to procure the blessings of a sound religious education for your poorer brethren, so your alms will be cast this day into a better treasury than that of the temple built with hands ; into the Temple of the heavenly Jerusalem, which is " the Lamb," (Apoc. xxi. 22) whose treasury of grace is His adorable Heart.   You will not merely be " shutting up your alms in the heart of the poor," (Ecclus. xxix. 15) as the Old Testament exhorts you ; but, you will at the same time be placing them in the Heart of the Most-rich, and the Most bountiful, though He, too, became poor for love. Yes, you will be casting them into that glowing furnace of love, where all is purified, and comes forth again, no longer dross, but that refined and sterling gold, from which alone crowns of bliss and glory are made for the heads, phials of sweet odour for the hands of Charity's Saints in heaven.

No. III.

On the Fire of the Sacred Heart.

DEARLY beloved children in Christ,—There is hardly
any topic more constantly kept before your mind, or more
frequently pressed on your attention, than the education
of the poor. In one form or another, we may say that
"the poor ye have always with you." (Mat. xxvi. 11.)
Whether it be the orphan, or the youthful transgressor, or
the inmate of the poor-house, or simply the child that lives
exposed to the seduction of a false religious training, or to
the temptations of idleness and ignorance, scarcely a day
passes, but some institution for the averting or mitigating
of these evils and perils is brought before your notice, as
requiring your charitable aid.

But the day on which this our pastoral address will be
read to you, merges in its wider and deeper claims all
other specific demands. It is the feast of charity itself,
of unrestricted charity for our poor children.

It is the feast of charity, not corporal but spiritual,
directed to feed, to refresh, to clothe, to free, and to
elevate the soul, by the bread of God's word, (Mat. iv. 4)
the waters of saving wisdom (Ecclus. xv. 3), the raiment
of heavenly grace, (Gal. iv. 3) the liberty which Christ
has purchased for us, from the slavery of sin and
corruption. (Luke, xv. 22.)

It is the feast of charity, universal and thoroughly
Catholic ; not confined by the limits of our respective

dioceses, nor administered by local commissions, nor distributed on a narrow scale of comparison. Like the springs, which, rising in many different and distant spots, unite their waters into streams, that converge and flow into one common reservoir, whence those waters are again subdivided and beneficently redistributed, so do the many sources of charity through our island this day contribute their shares to one general and united treasury, from which an impartial division is made, without regard of place, according to the urgency of particular claims.   And this distribution, as you know, is under the care of our excellent Poor School Committee, whose long, patient, and consciencious administration of the fund thus collected and confided to its management, is beyond all praise.

And finally, this is the special feast of charity, in the symbol and patronage under which this general subscription is raised, those of the Sacred and Adorable Heart of our divine Redeemer. For this is the seat of that sublime charity which brought Him from heaven, to become man for our salvation ; this is the link of brotherly love which made Him prefer kindred with us, to alliance with angelic spirits ; this is the fountain whence flowed the stream of life, outpoured for the cleansing of sin and the propitiation of the divine wrath; this is the wine-press which furnishes with inexhaustible abundance, the wine to the chalice of salvation, on the Table of His house, the Church.

Every form of love, of benignity, of kindness, of meekness, of long suffering, and of generosity ; in giving, in pardoning, in rewarding ; whensoever, wheresoever, and towards whomsoever displayed, is found naturally in that

Heart, which, as in other men, so in the best and holiest
of men, is the very abode of every good and perfect
emotion.   And what shall we, or what will the world gain,
from this commemoration of so sweet and so sublime a
symbol, if it remain no more than such to us, not a living,
warm and throbbing reality in which we take our share,
not only for ourselves, but for many others.

"*Nonne cor nostrum ardens erat in nobis* ?"—" Was not
our heart burning within us, whilst He spoke on the way ?"
(Luke, xxiv. 32) said the disciples, whom Jesus overtook,
on the day of His resurrection.

To be with Him, to hear Him speak, to drink in His
wisdom and imbibe His sentiments; to bring, or have
brought, their hearts into consonance and harmony with
His Heart, set theirs on fire, inflamed them with similar
affection ; so that they immediately returned home, to
communicate their burning thoughts to their brethren.

For, what else was it that set their hearts a-burning,
but that fire of which Our Lord had long before spoken,
when He said : " I have come to cast fire upon earth, and
what will I but that it be kindled ?"   (Ib. xii. 49.) And
what was this fire ?

Not that flame of insurrection and disloyalty, which
made all pretenders of the Messiahship firebrands, men to
be pursued with the sword, into the wilderness. (Mat.
xxiv. 26.)   For even His enemies, when they sought for
proof of His rivalry to Cæsar, did not think of referring
to this expression.

Not the heartburnings and jealousies which characterised
the religious and political parties in the Jewish people, at
that period.   He had naught to do with Pharisee or

Sadducee, Essenian or Herodian, who hated one another "with perfect hatred." (Ps. cxxxviii. 22.)

Not the fiery zeal of Scribes and priests, who scorned the Gentile, as the Greek did the barbarian, and scrupled not to shed the innocent blood of their holiest Lord, from fear that the prerogatives of their class and nation should be injured through Him. (Jo. xi. 48.)

Not even that more specious but mistaken ardour of His own disciples, which would have brought down fire from heaven, to destroy His enemies and persecutors. (Luke, ix. 54.) For He said to them : "Ye know not of what Spirit ye are."

Now, by this rebuke, He seemed to warn and remind them, that as yet they were not of that Spirit who was to descend, indeed, in flakes of fire, but soft and lambent as the soothing and healing tongue; separate, so as to be carried away by each Apostle of faith and love, to his own allotted province ; parted and cloven, like the root from which have to spring many plants, each fertile and pregnant with further, and endless, and inexhaustible life.

And well He added to His reproof : "The Son of man came not to destroy souls, but to save." (v. 56.) Yes, this fire of love, this burning, bright, inextinguishable, and unconsuming flame of Pentecost, was the fire which Jesus scattered over the earth, from the wings of the dove-like Paraclete, and which He so earnestly desired should everywhere be kindled. It was a fire that would save, not destroy, souls.

And what was the first and natural impulse of this new motive power to the hearts on which it seized? To go forth instantly and communicate it to others. As the two dis-

2 B

ciples whose hearts felt burning at Emmaus, could not
remain quiet at their journey's end, but must needs return
back, impelled irresistibly by the flame kindled within
them, to set others on fire with their own joy and love,
so rushed the apostles amidst the crowd, to kindle in
thousands the fire which the Holy Spirit had just cast
upon themselves. And as fire, sometimes creeping silently
along, sometimes bounding from fuel to fuel that it meets,
like a quick and active thing, makes it burn and blaze,
till it create a wide-spread conflagration, so did the sparks
fly from heart to heart that day in Jerusalem, till the few
tongues of fire which had descended in the morning, had
multiplied before evening, or had been divided into three
thousand separate flames.   For such was the number
added to the Church that day.   (Acts, ii. 41.)

And how, dearly beloved children, was the wonderful
propagation and enkindling, of the fire thus cast on earth,
accomplished?   Ah! by how simple, how homely a
process! Not by a miracle, as later, at the Beautiful
Gate of the Temple, when the lame man was healed;
(Ib. iii.) not by an exercise of majestic and judicial
authority, such as punished Ananias and his wife. (Ib. v.)
For though the gift of tongues attracted, amazed, and
overawed the multitude, it did not convert them, but
rather provoked jeers and scoffs.

No! it was by simple instruction; we almost said, by
education.   It was not till Peter had spoken, that the
assembly was moved to compunction, to the profession
of the truth, and to virtuous life, in communion with the
almost unknown and calumniated Church of Christ.

And now let us trace the course of this most wonderful

and mysterious fire, which has descended as an inheritance even to us. It came from heaven ; it had existed there from all eternity, its symbol the Holy Spirit, its reality the bond of unity in the Godhead ; for this is charity. Rays or reflections of it had reached earth; its substance never. The " lamp of fire" which passed between Abraham's victims ; (Gen. xv. 17. the flame which, breaking out from the rock, consumed Gideon's holocaust ; (Jud. vi. 21) the " fire of the Lord" which, falling, swallowed up not only the victim, but the altar, of Elias's offering ; (3 Reg. xviii. 38) in fine, that miraculous fire which was obtained from the sediment of the well in which the perpetual fire of the temple had been hidden, and kindled itself anew upon the whole-burnt sacrifice of God's people, redeemed from captivity ; (2 Mac. i. 22) these, and other symbolical interpositions of a celestial fire in ancient sacrifices, were a foreshadowing of that divine flame which was to be steadily and actively in operation, after the figurative sacrifices of the older dispensation should have given way to the real and clean oblation of the New Law.

For, in fact, to bring down to earth that really heavenly love, it required, not an angel or a burning seraph, but One in whom it lived, and from whom it could not depart, even if He seemed to quit the eternal throne to which it bound Him in indissoluble union. And hence the only-begotten and co-equal Son of the Father declared, " Sacrifice and oblation Thou didst not desire ; then, said I, behold *I come.*" (Ps. xxxix. 8.) And to this declaration seems naturally to attach itself the expression on which we have been commenting : " I *have* come."

First, He promised, or offered to come, to supersede those oblations which the typical fire consumed. Then He proclaims to us that He has come, the living, loving, enduring Victim, to bring down the real warmth, light, and flame of heaven, that CHARITY, unknown before, which, as it has been from all eternity the very bond of divine Unity, was now to become the principal motive and cause of the new alliance of the divine with the human nature. For, not dissolving His essential and necessary community of being, in the adorable Trinity, Jesus Christ associated His divinity to our humanity, through that unspeakable love wherewith God loved us. "In this has the charity of God appeared towards us, because God hath sent down His only-begotten Son into the world," (1 Jo. vi. 9) whereby we have "fellowship with the Father, and with His Son Jesus Christ." (Ib. i. 3.)

The charity or love, therefore, which reigned eternally in heaven, was the fire which our Lord and Saviour first brought down on earth at His incarnation, to be the link of union between God and man, and to be the consuming fire of His voluntary and priceless immolation.

And where was this fire treasured up, which Jesus Christ brought to scatter over the earth, except in His most adorable Heart, whence John drew his stores of love, and which, from the moment that it was formed, beat and throbbed only with love for God and man. And therefore would He have it opened on His cross, that its unreserved richness of charity might be all poured out to earth.

From that fervent and ardent Heart of Jesus, then,

came that fire, to kindle which He sent His Comforter after Himself. (John, xv. 26 ; xvi. 7.)   For, John foretold that He whom he announced should "baptize in the Holy Ghost and in fire." (Mat. iii. 11.)   And this fire was communicated first to the hearts of the apostles, and from theirs to those of the faithful ; as St. Paul assures us, that "the charity of God is poured forth in our hearts by the Holy Ghost who is given us." (Rom. v. 5.) Thus are this fire, and this charity but one and the same.

And this inpouring of the divine fire of love is made, first, by the sacraments, in which the grace of the divine Spirit is directly communicated, and then, as we have seen, by the teaching of the Church, or by Peter's speaking to the multitude of the faithful in the person, and on behalf, of the entire apostleship.

What follows, dearly beloved, but this : that if we desire to have share in this blessed office, that of transfusing the riches of the sweet Heart of Jesus into yet innocent hearts, more worthy of them than our own sinful ones, we must generously attempt it by instructing, in the knowledge and love of Him, those in whom, more than in any others, He wishes this double flame of light and fire, of wisdom and charity, to be enkindled.   But what have we said ?   Will not that act on your parts, by which you communicate to Christ's children this fire of love, through a religious education, be itself a bright and shining evidence, before God and His Church, that the fire of charity has been already kindled in your own hearts ?

Then draw nigh to-day to this furnace of brilliant flame, to this burning Heart of Jesus, and there renew your spirit of charity, by imitating its peculiar love for His favourite poor and little ones.   Give abundantly and generously, that so the interests of the Sacred Heart may be fully carried out by our zealous and devoted Poor School Committee.

Make up, therefore, this year for the deficiencies of the last, and kindle far and wide, by your greater liberality, that divine fire, which our Lord and Saviour came to cast upon the earth.

And to Him earnestly and warmly we commit the care of your reward.   " For He is faithful that hath promised; and let us consider one another, to provoke unto charity and good works." (Heb. x. 23.)   The grace of God be with you.   Amen.

No. IV.

On the Most Precious Blood of the Heart of our Lord Jesus Christ.

BY a liturgical combination, which cannot happen again within the lives of most of us, this Sunday, instead of being dedicated to the celebration of a feast in honour of the Sacred Heart of our Divine Redeemer, will commemorate instead His most precious Blood.   It can, indeed, scarcely be said that the two festivals are different.   The primary object is the same in both.   They are expressive of the same worship, the same adoration, the same gratitude, and the same love, directed to Him whose heart poured out its life-blood for our redemption. Whether in its deep cistern, or in its unfailing out-flow, we honour and venerate alike the price of our freedom and our life.

And what else is the blessed Heart of Jesus but the wonderful alembic which transmuted the food of earth, not merely into the nourishment of one body, and the life-stream of one person, but into the quickening support of millions, into the circulation of unity through the entire Church of ages, into the ransom beyond price of all mankind, into the golden flood, which flowing ever from the foot of the Lamb, waters and fertilizes heaven and earth, becomes the river of life to one, the stream of grace to the other.

For what, again, is the adorable Heart of Jesus but the fountain of Paradise, whence springs the river that is divided into four branches, carrying refreshment, healing, and life to every region, and to every race ? One is a laver of cleansing and regenerating water, washing away all sin and stain ; another is a bath that restores or increases tone and vigour to those who have to wrestle and fight for God ; a third is a rich flow of consecrating unction such as streamed from the head of Aaron ; while the last and best is the refreshing torrent of delights, at which saints drink with renewed rapture, and forgiven sinners with strengthening relish.

All these streams of salvation, however different their immediate action, are but one in source and in substance. For what is it that washes away our stains but " the blood of Jesus Christ, which cleanseth us from every sin ?" How did the oil of unction acquire its power to strengthen and to consecrate, but from those first instalments of our ransom, which flowed upon the root of the olive, trickling from the pores of our prostrate Lord, like an enriching dew that pervades their fruit. But direct from the divine Heart, in full warm surge, wells forth the tide of a spiritual abundance, water for our purification, unction for our consecration, and the chalice of salvation. Hence the eucharistic "wine springing forth virgins," (Zach. ix. 17) the juice of the true vine, whereof we are the branches, the balm of soothing and healing virtue which issued, from His body, to the very hem of our Lord's outer garment, but now rushes out through the open gash, that reaches to the very core of that celestial plant.

Yes, dearly beloved in Christ, whatever is good, whatever is holy, whatever is perfect upon earth has come to us from, and through, and by the most precious Blood of our divine Lord and Saviour Jesus Christ. This, from the beginning, was more variously, and more abundantly symbolized to us than anything else in the New Testament; though its excellence is manifested by the contrast in which it stands with its types. It was to be innocently shed like Abel's, that it might be shown to plead better and more efficaciously than it for mercy, not for vengeance. It was poured out in sacrifice, that it might be proved infinitely superior to the blood of oxen and of goats, which had no power to cleanse the soul. (Heb. ix. 13.) Finally, the paschal lamb, the noblest type of our redemption, by the anointing with its blood of the doorposts of the Israelites, scared away the destroying angel, and made Pharaoh relax his grasp on God's captive

people, and so freed them ; only to prefigure how the
Lamb that taketh away the sins of the world would baffle
and overcome the prince of darkness and of eternal
death, and force the tyrant of earth and hell to let His
own people go free, to offer sacrifice even in this wilderness.

And how was this ? The posts of the gate which alone
leads to life immortal, the cross under which all must
stoop who desire to enter into Paradise, are richly
streaked, nay, thickly painted with the Blood of " our
immolated Pasch," more terrible to His enemies than the
brightest flash of Heaven's lightning. And so, when we
partake of the Divine Mysteries, the threshold of our
mouths, our lips are dyed with the same rich drops that
fell so copiously on Calvary.

With what devotion, then, should we not commemorate
this shedding of our Saviour's precious Blood, at the very
mention of which the Church makes her ministers bend
their knees, in awe and adoration of a mystery so profound and yet so sweet, so fearful and yet so tender. As
the more deep and terrible is the gulf that opens beneath
us, the more we feel drawn towards it, and tempted to
plunge into it, so is this abyss of wonderful and unfathomable goodness, awful to contemplate, yet inviting
our love to dive into it fearlessly, and taste unsated of its
delights.

To think that God should have taken flesh, the very
body of man, with all its lowliness of nature but wonders
of construction, merely that He might die, and that He
should have blood to shed, for man's ransom, salvation,
and nourishment ; to contemplate by what harrowing

and afflicting ways this outpouring should have to be
made, by what stripes, buffets, wounds, gashes, piercing
and transfixing of every part of that thrice-holy Body, to
the very rending of its divine Heart; to meditate on the
overwhelming truth that God, the Father who loved Him
with an infinite affection, should have been pleased, propi-
tiated, soothed and turned to love from just anger by this
tremendous atonement, baffles and sets at naught all our
estimates, and all our reasonings on the eternal and infinite ways of a divine dispensation.   Yet how bright this
depth, how richly lighted by every tender hue of love!
How meekness and gentleness, mercy and forgivingness,
disinterestedness and self-sacrifice, bounty and liberality,
affectionateness and familiarity, parental fondness and
brotherly caress play through the abyss, as profound and
as measureless, and as incomprehensible as itself!   How
unsearchable are the ways of God's love, as much as those
of His might!   Who hath been His counsellor but Himself—the infinite goodness urging on the infinite energy
of the Divine in all things.

   But what multiplies beyond the bounds of a limited
conception the immensity of this love is, that it is individual and singular.   " Sic totum omnibus quod totum
singulis."   Every drop of blood, so unreservedly poured
out on Golgotha, was gathered into one cup, the whole
contents of which every soul may drink and make its own.
The entire price was paid for each : the value of each
soul is the equivalent of the whole ransom.   The treasure is not divided and paid out in single coins, but the
entire sum is lavishly given to each prodigal.   Who can
penetrate to the depths of this almighty mercy ; yet

who can forbear to love it and do his utmost to be worthy of it !

Hence, dearly beloved children in Christ, when we put before you the claims of little ones—little by age or by worldly insignificance—we are accustomed to lay our principal stress on this one motive, that their souls have been thought worth His precious life-blood, by Jesus Christ, their and our Redeemer.   When especially we call on you to exercise the highest act of spiritual charity, to save their souls rather than sustain their bodies, the plea comes home with tenfold urgency.   Will you not concur and assist to the utmost in saving the souls which He so dearly bought, and loved beyond His own precious life ?

To this appeal you cannot answer, no: it is impossible. Such, then, especially, is our pleading the day that you hear these words.   It is only by multiplying the means of religious education that thousands of your poor children can be ensured that salvation which Jesus Christ purchased for them.   The society to which you are asked to contribute has this for its sole and universal object.   It seeks, like the charity of our Lord and Saviour, to embrace all and each, to extend its salutary effects throughout the whole country, and to reach the smallest and most neglected child with individual assistance.

So may God requite you, and give you of His abundance, through the redemption which is by Christ Jesus. Amen.

On the Education of the Heart of Jesus.

WHEN, lately, our Holy Father condescended to manifest his sympathy for our poor children, he sent, as the symbolical expression of that feeling, a representation of the Sacred Heart of our Divine Saviour, with a loving message to assure us how sincerely he had their welfare at heart. And, in this selection, he only approved and confirmed that choice which the Catholic Church, over which he rules, had long made of that same sacred emblem, to represent the charity of our Lord Jesus Christ, towards all mankind, and consequently more especially towards those objects of His tenderest affection.

Yes, dearly beloved in Christ, the education of poor children, under the auspices of the adorable Heart of Jesus, possesses large, and ample claims upon your charity. This beautiful symbol, in fact, holds and comprehends in itself the whole design and purposes of the education which we aim at giving.

When our blessed Lord Himself instructed, or rather educated, (for He had to deliver the very first rudiments of religious wisdom, to men more ignorant of them than a child is now,) we may imagine His audience to have been very like that which now surrounds His priests in this metropolis, when they catechise, or when, without reputation for eloquence that attracts, they labour to instil simple doctrine into the minds of crowds. Very like, even the many who gather as yet round Him in His tabernacle, in less central churches, about which none live but the poor, must have been the congregations which first heard the sublime elements of Christian doctrine. They are simply described, again and again by the word which characterises such a body :—" the crowd." In the singular or in the plural—*turba* or *turbæ*, "the *crowd*," or "*crowds*," they are so mentioned upwards of forty times, in each of the gospels according to St. Matthew and to St. Luke. It is not thus that the rich are spoken of.

It is not thus that a select congregation at the feet of a fashionable preacher would be denominated. They would be sorry to be so designated. Yet it is of this congregation that we read, that " the crowds wondered at, or admired His doctrine," (Mat. vii. 28 ; xxii. 33) and His miracles; (Mat. ix. 33 ; xv. 31 ; Luke, xi. 14) that they recognised His rank and title saying, " Is not this the son of David ?" (Mat. xii. 23) that they spread their garments on His path, and gave Him His triumphal entry into Jerusalem, (Mat. xxi. 9.) Nay, it was this *crowd, mob*—as no doubt the priests and Pharisees loved to call it, which these proud men feared in their plots against Him. (Mat. xxi. 26 ; Luke, xxii. 6.) Indeed, we are told, that " of the people," (*turba* in the Vulgate,) " many believed in Him," (John vii. 31) so that the Pharisees said, " Hath any one of the rulers believed in Him, or of the Pharisees ? But this multitude (*turba*) that knoweth not the law are accursed." (49.) Bitter words these, and how like words often spoke now-a-days ! Rulers and Pharisees—the leading men, and the learned men of the nation, not one had publicly acknowledged or followed Jesus : the common people, the poor " who know not the" Bible, are accursed —degraded, outcast, for their faith.   The one exception, Nicodemus, who rises to impugn this abominable declaration, is described as "he that came to Him by night," and is so secretly a believer, that his companions ask in surprise, "Art thou also a Galilean?" (50, 52.)

The powerful men occasionally come on the stage, to tempt, or entrap, or impugn His words, (Mat. xvi. 1; xix. 3 ; xx. 17; Luke, x. 25) or even to calumniate and vilify Him to His face. (Mark iii. 22 ; Jo. vii. 20; viii. 42 ; x. 20.)   Or they invite Him to their houses, and scorn His humility and charity towards penitents, (Luke, vii. 39) or captiously watch His exercise of loving power on the Sabbath, (xiv. 1) or ask Him to work a miracle and be jeered for attempting it. (v. 38.)

It is not a crowd of noble or dainty people who would go for three days into a wilderness, without provisions, or servants to procure them, and sit down in ranks upon the grass to be fed like children, or beadsmen at a gate.   He has told us, " What went you out in the desert to see ? A man clad in soft garments ?   Behold they who are clad in soft garments are in the houses of kings," (Mat. xi. 8) not in deserts.   No, the crowd which surrounded Him was a rude jostling crowd, which so pressed Him on all sides, that His disciples said it was impossible to ascertain who touched Him ; (Luke, viii. 45) which almost drove Him into the sea, and compelled Him to teach from a boat, (v. 1) which let down its sick through the roof of a house, to reach Him. (v. 19.)

Such were the men and women to whom Jesus Christ taught the first Christian catechism; the same class as He

selected His disciples and apostles from, the poor, the unlettered, the weak and the despised. It was "to the poor
that His gospel was preached." (Mat. xi. 5.)

Now it was of such a crowd as this that we are told
that "they brought Him young children that He might
touch them;" (Mark, x. 13) and of the children of such
parents when the disciples rebuked them, He said :
"Suffer the little children to come unto Me." But He
was not content with doing what those poor good people
asked.   St. Mark tells us that He went far beyond this :
" and *embracing* them, and laying His hands upon them,
He blessed them." (16.)   More pointedly still, when He
wished to place before His apostles and disciples—His
fishermen, His sailors, His publicans, a type of perfection,
and representative of those who were fit to enter into His
Church, He Himself "*calls* unto Him a little child." (Mat.
xviii. 2.)   What sort of a child ?   He did not send for
him, He calls him, one at hand, one of the poor, a child
from the crowd, the rude vulgar crowd.

Intending to show them what they must *become* to enter
the kingdom of heaven, would it not have been almost
harsh and ungentle, to put in the midst of them one
whose entrance into it was likely to be as difficult as
the passage of a camel through the needle's eye, a child
bright with beautiful health, sleek and clothed in soft
garments, a type of earthly prosperity, training and happiness ?   "Alas !" would they not say, " nothing can ever
make us like that child."   But let us rather imagine a
little child called there and then from amidst those who
habitually followed and admired Jesus,—a wan, emaciated,
sickly child, neglected, and uncared for, poorly attired,

perhaps in tattered raiment, with bare limbs, and uncovered head : one in whom the poor would see little
unlike themselves outwardly, little to mortify them or
humble them, nothing in fact different from themselves,
except in the innocence and simplicity of its age : and we
shall understand the full beauty of this passage in our
Lord's life, and the sublimity of its lesson.

Now what doth Jesus with this poor little thing, picked
up in the street or the lane ?　Does He merely, perhaps
authoritatively, call it, and set it in the middle of His
followers, scared or insolent to be lectured on, like a model
or a machine ? Surely not : listen once more to St. Mark.
" And taking a child,"—*taking* it, mind, not ashamed of
handling or caressing it,—" and taking a child, He set
him in the midst of them, whom when He had embraced,
He saith to them : whoever receiveth *one* such child as this
in my name, receiveth Me." (Mark, ix. 35.)　It is with
this little poor, and perhaps outcast, child in His arms,
that He spoke those words of grace, the motto inscribed on
the charity of to-day.　But this is not the whole mystery
of the act.　For it comprises the entire scheme, and principle of Catholic education.

Jesus *embraced* that little child, His representative on
earth : that is He pressed it to His own living, warm, and
palpitating Heart ; to that Heart which, by every pulsa-
tion, sends salvation and eternal life through the frame of
the whole Church, which darts, with irresistible thrill, the
price of redemption to the utter bounds of earth.　It was
a dearly-bought distinction to holy Simeon, earned by a
long life of hope and prayer, to hold in his arms, his
infant Saviour, to whom he could nothing give.　What an

honour for *this* child to be taken up into His arms, who could give him all things. But no, this is not enough : that poor little creature has forestalled the place of John, the place of honour and of love ; that place far beyond what John's mother had dared in her maternal presumption to ask, which was only that he might sit on the right or left hand of Jesus. When He rejected her petition, He reserved for him much more, that he should recline upon His glorious bosom, the tabernacle of His self-immolating Heart. But the child had climbed up there, had nestled there before even the beloved one, and had come down again educated as the contact with that adorable Heart alone can educate—the very God-child of Jesus. So necessary a consequence was this, that in the ancient Church it used to be thought that this chosen child grew up to be the holy Martyr and Bishop Ignatius, the most like to John, in burning love, of the early saints.

But as we said just now, in this sweetest incident of our Redeemer's life, we have the whole theory of Catholic education.

First listen to His words and learn : " He who receiveth *one* such child as this, in my name, receiveth Me." How easy a thing it is, then, to receive Jesus ! How easy, especially in this metropolis ! Come ! two need not receive the same. Our Lord asks you to receive one a-piece, to enjoy the stupendous privilege of receiving Him. We have them ready. Come ten thousand strong, ye rich ! come twenty thousand in ranks, ye who are not in want ! We have one at least for each of you, in the streets, and lanes, in the courts and corners, in the garrets and cellars of luxurious London. And how will you receive these

2 c

tender ambassadors from your Lord, these delicate and frail little images of God Incarnate? Will you.be harsh and ungracious to them ; or haughty and imposing ; will you be repulsed by their rags, their uncleanliness, their rudeness, or their stolidity? Or rather will you be kind and gentle, generous and handsome, in your dealing with them; will you warm them at *your* hearts, give them rest on *your* bosoms? It was thus, at least, that Jesus treated them, when He received them, and asked you to receive them.

And now, dearly beloved, in our love for Him, you will ask us how is this to be done? Simply and easily. Every child whom you will provide with a Catholic education, you bring to the very Heart of our Lord, and educate there. Science and letters, if taught in His spirit, may indeed be as His two arms, which raise the child from the earth, and its grovelling thoughts ; but religious and moral truth alone puts His seal upon all other teaching; and that seal is the pressure of His sacred Heart, of its diamond strength and brilliancy, on the yet soft wax of the childish heart. By this holy impulse is the one clasped close upon the other, and the infinite graces of the one are inhaled, as was man's first breath of life, by the awakening intelligence and expanding feelings, from the living fountain of all-redeeming love !

For, what is there in the divine Heart of Jesus, which you would not gladly transfuse into the child's, even though it may seem to be a pouring from a golden vessel into one of clay? Would you not gladly enrich that little heart with some drops of His mildness, gentleness, patience ; of His humility, meekness and sweetness ; of His charity, affectionateness, tenderness ; of His purity, innocence, holiness ? And where are all these virtues to be found ? He has told us, " Learn of Me, because I am meek, and humble *of heart.*" (Mat. xi. 12.) If the treasure-house of His humility is His heart, if the school of His meekness is in His breast, there also reside those other virtues which you wish to infuse into the child's heart, there is the school at which you would have it trained. For " where its *treasure* is, there its *heart* should also be." (Luke, xxi. 34.) And long before, the proclaimer of the eternal wisdom had said : " Incline thy heart to know prudence. . . . . If wisdom shall enter into thy heart, ... counsel shall please thee, that thou mayest be delivered from the evil way, keeping the paths of justice, and guarding the way of the saints." (Prov. ii. 1–12.) If, then, the treasure of virtue is in the sacred Heart of Jesus, thither speedily take the young heart to be filled ; if the training in the way from which the youth and the old man ought not to depart, (xx. 6) is by the whisperings of the Wisdom uncreate into the heart of the child, surely the perfection of its education is the bringing it into closest contact with the sacred Heart of Jesus, which our charity desires and strives to do.

Yes, dearly beloved, if we have spoken to you of fearing not to bring the children of the poorest into your bosoms, as Jesus taught you to do, we now tell you a still better thing, to bring them to His. Teach them there, train them there, warm them there, fill their heads, their hearts there ; and you will indeed have done more than receive them in His name, you will have taken them up in your arms, only to place them in His ; you will have obtained for them His embrace, besides your own.

And now, dear children in Christ, does it not sound strange that we should propose to you to barter perishable riches against immortal souls ? Does it not seem profane, that this embrace of which we have spoken should be purchasable by vile dross ? Yet so it is. It is literally a matter of computation, how much suffices, to give to each single child in London, now spiritually destitute, and morally abandoned, the full privilege of this holy education. A small sum, a very small sum—less than a day's excursion for pleasure, less than a journey to see a race, less than a very simple attire—than a small ornament, less than at times a modest nosegay, perhaps a single flower, would cost, given once a-year to this charity,* will rescue one child from the defilements of the street, or the idleness of home ; will purchase the one child who may represent Jesus to one of you, and place it to be nursed at His Heart.

For, dear disciples of this loving Heart, once there it departs no more. Whence in course of time will flow the waters of eternal life, but from their source in that blessed Heart, which, at every pulse·during thirty-three years, distilled new drops, every one of which was a world's ransom? When for the first time that child shall quaff that cleansing blood from the cup of salvation, when Jesus returns its early mystical embrace, by bringing the entire well of

---

* It has been calculated that the education of a child costs £1 10s. for a year.

His mercies into nearest contact with that panting heart, which has longed for the hour of that sacramental embrace; is it possible that you can purchase this sublime felicity for that child—nay, that you can purchase it for its Lord? Oh! give the price cheerfully, ungrudgingly! say, when this is read to you—say generously, "I will have my own poor child this year: though it may cost me a slight sacrifice, I will give my dear Saviour one, especially mine, to embrace."

And so, if one day it stray away from its Good Shepherd, whither will it return, whither will it be allured? To His Heart first, and then on to His shoulders. For first it will be forgiven, and then it will be sustained. And where is the mercy that pardons, where the kindness that encourages, save in His loving and mighty Heart? No: once place the child where a Catholic education alone can, in the adorable Heart of Jesus, and nothing but hardened sin can fully separate him from it. It will be his refuge, his fortress, his home, his pharmacy, his fragrant garden, his fruitful field, his sure path, his paradise, his gate of salvation. There he will find his gold, his balm, his fragrance, his light, his food, his refreshment, his comfort, his joy in life, his hope in death.

Ever holy and adorable symbol of love immense and undying, yet compressed and death-stricken, Heart not of Jesus alone in the flesh, but Heart of the entire Church, Heart of the Universe, beating still, in blissful throbs, the hours and the minutes, nay the instants, of forgiveness, of grace, of salvation to earth, of joy, and beatitude, and ecstacy to heaven! we salute Thee in homage, we worship

Thee in adoration, we entreat Thee suppliant! Take to Thyself, in tender embrace, the children of Thy poor in this city, where light is the most brilliant, and darkness the most deep ; where strength and weakness, life and death, all excesses of good and evil, virtue and vice, wrestle as no where else, for the mastery of Thy loved ones, and the destruction of Thy Church's hopes. Shield and harbour them, feed and strengthen them ; for power and abundance are laid up in Thee, O great and admirable Heart! If not, how would the world have been redeemed ? But be it our honour and our merit, that Thou receive them from us. We will snatch them up from their dereliction, we will break their snares, we will rescue them from the wicked fowlers who are spreading nets on every side ; and we will consign them to that happy embrace, which joins heart to heart, the weak, fluttering, trembling heart, to the noble, the impregnable, and yet most sweet and tender of hearts :—to Thine, O Jesus !

No. VI.

Institution of the Forty Hours' Adoration of our Lord in the Blessed Eucharist, 1849.

If the rule of the Christian fast is that prescribed by our Blessed Lord, not to be "as the hypocrites, sad," (Mat. vi. 16) the Church will not fail to provide you, during this holy season of fasting, the means and motives of spiritual joy. She will associate with the hard, but consoling, task of imitating our Divine Redeemer, in the practice of His virtues, that devotion towards Him in His adorable humanity, which more than any other pours the unction of gladness (Ps. xliv. 8) over the soul, and makes the spirit to exult in God its Saviour. (Luke i. 47.) Yes, beloved in the Lord, on her behalf, and through the Divine mercy, we have thought it our duty to provide for you, during this season of mourning, an unfailing source of consolation, of grace, of devotion, and of love. We have therefore so disposed, as that throughout the whole of Lent, the Most Blessed Sacrament shall remain exposed in one or other of the public churches or chapels of this metropolis, so that every day it may be in each one's power, not only to assist at a solemn service of the Church, but, at whatever time he chooses, to pour out his affections at the feet of his Saviour. And we doubt not that every one will gladly seize any moment of leisure, to pay his tribute of homage to Him, at that particular place, where on each day He shall be more especially honoured.

And as this devotion, called the Forty Hours' Exposition of the Blessed Sacrament, is as yet but little known in this country, we will proceed, in a few words to explain it : premising no more of its history than to say, that it was first instituted at Milan in 1534, that it was thence introduced into Rome, through the instrumentality of its great modern Apostle the holy St. Philip Neri, and was formally sanctioned by Pope Clement VIII. in 1592, in consequence, as he says, of the troubled state of Christendom, and the sufferings of the Church. (Raccolta di Orazioni, &c. Rome, 1841, p. 181.)

As a condition of the Incarnation of the Word, an

exchange was made, not unequal, between earth and heaven. We gave to it, not only the spirits of the just made perfect, in the glorious choir of saints who fill the seats of fallen angels, but, in anticipation of the resurrection, one precious instalment of humanity glorified, in Her the spotless, who rules, in the very body, over the hosts of angels, as their queen. But even higher this our flesh has penetrated, yea into the very sanctuary of God's light inaccessible. For in the very midst and centre of that dazzling radiance, towards which blissful spirits bend gazing and adoring, is to be seen the gentle "likeness of the Son of Man," (Apoc. i. 13) in all things resembling us. And in return, heaven has bestowed on earth, not merely communion between us, and its happy citizens, but the permanent dwelling of God among us, who, under the name of the Emanuel, or, "God with us," lives ever in the midst of His Church, to be the direct object of our adoration and love.

And so it comes, dearly beloved, that Heaven worships now the nature of man indivisibly united with the Godhead, and Earth adores the Deity, joined inseparably to our humanity, in the Person of the incarnate Word. Hence is our worship and theirs but one ; one in object, one in value, one in sentiment, one, if possible, in form. For so identical, throughout this communion of saints, is the essence of divine worship, that the very mode of its performance necessarily becomes similar, not to say one. So that in reading the glorious visions of heaven's sanctuary, thrown open to St. John, it becomes difficult to determine, whether he there beheld counterparts to what the Church had already instituted upon earth, or types which served her, under apostolic guidance, for the framing of her ritual. But rather would we say that the same divine instinct guided both : and taught angels in heaven, and saints on earth, to adore and to love with the same outward expression. And so the whole forms but one Church, and one worship. There is one altar in both, beneath which the slain for Christ rest, and on which the same Victim-Lamb reposes ; one censor from which prayer rises fragrant, from minister's to angel's hand; one bench of venerable elders, that sit or fall prostrate in rich array around ; one choir, one song, one voice, one heart, one life.

In one only respect would these services appear to differ : that theirs is perpetual, uninterrupted, unceasing; that the thrice-repeated " Holy" echoes ever through those golden vaults, while we, only at brief and distant periods, can unite in formal worship. But even here the Spouse of Christ on earth would not be outdone ; and wishful to rival the very deathless and sleepless watchfulness of those eyes, that sparkle all over the Cherubim round the Throne of God, (Apoc. iv. 6) she has instituted at different periods modes of imitating the unfailing worship of heaven. In early ages she taught her religious in desert and in monastery, to divide themselves into choirs, that day and night kept up the praises of God in uninterrupted psalmody ; and in our days (O happy and heavenly thought !) she has instituted this perpetual adoration of the Blessed Eucharist, of Him whom in heaven they so worship, with us present as truly as with them. This it is, dearly beloved, that we are going to introduce among you.

But it is not your Saviour, "as the hidden Manna" (Apoc. ii. 17) of which you partake, that you have here to reverence and love; it is your Lord, your God, triumphant over death for you, yet shrouding from you His overpowering glory, to whom you have to pay your open and solemn homage;—not enshrined in His poor tabernacle, where, because unseen, He is often unhonoured, but enthroned, as in heaven, above His own altar, Lord of His own Sanctuary, centre of all surrounding splendour, challenging, with love, deep adoration. Around Him shall flame the hallowed tapers, by whose pure ray the Church symbolizes, however feebly, the bright spirits that shine around His heavenly throne. At His feet earth shall scatter its choicest flowers, as its graceful tribute to Him that bloomed so fair from Jesse's root. (Isai. xi. 1.) On all sides shall be arrayed whatever of richness and splendour our poverty can collect, to adorn the chosen abode of Him, who hath said: "the silver is mine and the gold is mine," (Aggeus, ii. 9) and does not disdain any manifestation of our reverence. Hasten then, dearly beloved, to bring whatever may be necessary to enrich the solemnity of that happy day, when your Lord, in His kingly progress, shall visit your own temple, saying, " I will fill *this* house with glory," (Ib. 8) and, whether it be splendid or lowly, shall there abide in special state. Give proof to all that come there to visit Him, that you prize, you cherish, you love this privilege which He bestows; and that, like Solomon and the people of Israel, you have "gladly offered all those things" (1 Paral. xxxix. 17) which are requisite to its becoming, and even splendid, enjoyment. And "presently the Lord whom you seek, and the angel of the testament whom you desire, shall come to His temple." (Malachi, iii. 1.)

Oh! then go forth with joyful hearts, to meet and welcome Him ; and leave Him not alone, so long as He shall condescend to dwell in the midst of you. From that lofty mercy-seat whereon He hath been placed, from that bright radiance in the midst of which, as a peerless and priceless gem, He hath been set—beauty Himself, essential Light, and matchless Splendour—there go forth on every side, not scorching rays of glory, not burning shafts of might, but a mild and constant flow of holiness and grace, which fills the entire space from roof to pavement, with the very breath and air of heaven. Silent and soft, as wave impelling wave of fragrance, goes forth, and diffuses itself around, that savour of sweetness, that balm of life, that virtue which, emanating from the sacred humanity of Jesus upon earth, healed all diseases. (Luke, viii. 46.) And from the threshold of this, His palace now no less than, His temple, it will pass abroad, and spread itself on all sides, till it reach your dwellings ; and, more powerful than that blessing which the Ark of the Covenant (type, whereof you now possess the reality,) shed over the house of Obededom, (2 Reg. vi. 12) it will impart to them peace and grace, and welfare spiritual and temporal. " I will fill this house with glory, saith the Lord of Hosts . . . . and in this place I will give peace, saith the Lord of Hosts. (Ag. ii. 10.)

But now it is that you will practise that angelic worship, lost and unknown out of the Catholic Church, the worship of pure adoration. For, beyond her pale, men may praise God, or address Him, or perform other religious acts, but they cannot know nor make that special homage which His presence, as we possess it, inspires ; when, without word spoken, or sound uttered, or act performed, the soul sinks prostrate, and annihilates itself, before Him, casts all its powers, and gifts, and brightest ornaments, as worthless oblations before His altar, and subjects its entire being, as a victim, to His sole adorable will. When first, then, you approach the place where He is solemnly worshipped, as you humbly bend your knees, and bow your heads, let this deep and silent adoration be your first act. Speak not in words, forget all selfish thoughts, repress even all eager longings of your hearts ; and receive the benediction of your mighty Lord in solemn stillness ; while you, reputing yourselves but dust and ashes at His feet, a nothingness before Him, tender Him the homage of loyal vassals, humbled as the clay before the potter, (Isai. xxix. 16) as the creature before its God. Then raise up your eyes, those keen eyes of Faith, which, through the veil of sacramental elements, see, as John did, " in the midst of the seven golden candlesticks, one like to the Son of Man ;" (Apoc. i. 13) yea, the adorable Jesus, the king of your souls, and there feast long your sight upon that sacred Humanity, which love hath given Him, and with it kindred and brotherhood, and ties of tenderest affection with you. And now speak to Him, but with outpoured souls, with the unrestrained familiarity of warmest friendship, face to face—no longer with the awful Lord, like Moses or Elias, on Horeb, (Exod. xxxiii. 11 ; 3 Reg. xix. 11) but with them, and Peter, and John, on Thabor,

(Ps, cxxxi. 7) where you see Him radiant with His own light, but mild, and inviting love.

Pray to Him now for your own salvation and for that of all mankind. Pray for the exaltation of His holy Church, for the happiness and prosperity of the supreme pastor, our holy and afflicted Pontiff. Pray for the propagation of the true faith, and the conversion of all in error, and especially of our own dear country. Pray that God will mercifully remove from us the scourges and judgments which we have deserved by our sins, and remember no longer our offences, nor those of our parents, but rather show us mercy, and give to us His good gifts, but principally, His grace, holiness of life, and perseverance in His divine service.

And then, oh ! never think of rising from before Him, without thanking Him, from your hearts, for this miraculous institution of His power and goodness, this sweetest pledge of His love. Adore Him now again, as the Treasure of your souls, the Food of life, the living Bread that cometh down from heaven, your Consoler, your Strengthener, your surest Hope in life and death. Speak to Him of the kindness, of the self-abasement, of the immense condescension which He here exhibits ; of the untiring affection for poor man which He displays, in bearing with so much coldness, ingratitude, and even sacrilege, as this blessed memorial of His death exposes Him to ; of the still more incomprehensible excess of love, which makes Him communicate Himself daily to us, frail and sinful creatures, as our food, and thus brings our very hearts and souls into contact with His ! And offer Him your humble tribute of reverence and love, in reparation and atonement for those scoffs, contradictions, and blasphemies to which He has long been, and is daily, subject in his adorable Sacrament, and nowhere so much as in this unbelieving land.

But, dearly beloved in Christ, confine not your devotion to the time when the opportunity for this heavenly act of worship shall come to your very doors. Say rather, "we will go into His tabernacle, we will adore in the place where His feet have stood." (Ps. cxxxi. 7.) Make this, if possible, a daily devotion throughout the Lent—this daily worship of your divine Saviour, in His Blessed Eucharist. Fear not to penetrate where His humbler temples stand in the midst of His poor ; let your faith guide you beyond the range of your ordinary occupations, and the beat of worldly recreations, holding that spot to be the most noble, the most sacred, and the most highly privileged for the time, in which He is manifested, to be publicly adored.

THE END.